Teaching as a Design Science

Building Pedagogical Patterns for Learning and Technology

Diana Laurillard

Routledge
Taylor & Francis Group

NEW YORK AND LONDON

First published 2012
by Routledge
711 Third Avenue, New York, NY 10017

Simultaneously published in the UK
by Routledge
2 Park Square, Milton Park, Abingdon, Oxon OX14 4RN

*Routledge is an imprint of the Taylor & Francis Group,
an informa business*

© 2012 Taylor & Francis

Library of Congress Cataloging-in-Publication Data
Laurillard, Diana, 1948-
Teaching as a design science : building pedagogical patterns for leaning
and technology / Diana Laurillard.
    p. cm.
Includes bibliographical references and index.
1. Teaching—Philosophy. 2. Professional learning communities.
3. Educational technology. I. Title.
LB1025.3.L375 2012
371.102–dc23   2011037142

ISBN: 978-0-415-80385-4 (hbk)
ISBN: 978-0-415-80387-8 (pbk)
ISBN: 978-0-203-12508-3 (ebk)

Typeset in Minion
by Cenveo Publisher Services
Printed and bound in Great Britain by
CPI Group (UK) Ltd, Croydon, CR0 4YY

"Schools and colleges have invested billions in technology with the promise of radically improving learning. It hasn't. Why not? Diana Laurillard's penetrating new book provides an important part of the answer. Affirming that teaching is both art and science, she argues that faculty have been left out of the development equation. Only when teachers are directly involved in designing educational technologies can we create the tools necessary to improve learning. This book is a 'must read' for those wrestling with the complex questions about how to improve teaching effectiveness in a world of diverse learners and messy realities."

—**Gail O. Mellow**, President, LaGuardia Community College, City University of New York

"As researchers, we can no longer close our eyes to what is NOT happening in schools. For those who want to improve teaching, this book will inspire the design of powerful pedagogical patterns."

—**Pierre Dillenbourg**, Professor, CRAFT, École Polytechnique Fédérale de Lausanne

"Professor Laurillard's book argues forcefully and persuasively that teachers remain the lifeblood of education in a digital age, while also underlining the necessity for pedagogical practice to be transformed if we are to really seize the opportunities technology presents for significantly improved learning outcomes—to the broader benefit of society as a whole."

—**Lord Puttnam**, CBE

"*Teaching as a Design Science* presents the case for the next generation of scholarly research and implementation of technology in education. It brings together the rigor of existing research with the promise of teacher-led collaboration for the sharing of good practice with technology. If the ideas of Web 2.0 and user-generated content have the potential to transform teaching practice—we can call this Teaching 2.0—then this book provides an outstanding foundation for this new field."

—**James Dalziel**, Macquarie University and Inventor of LAMS

"Teachers increasingly understand that the only way to enjoy their chosen profession is to work collaboratively, sharing their expertise in learning design and incorporating the best use of available learning technologies in their day-to-day work. What exactly is meant by learning design and how you arrive at best use of the available learning technologies is thoroughly explored in Diana Laurillard's book, which will make a significant contribution to the thinking and practice of teachers who have an interest in the effective use of learning technologies in teaching and learning. An invaluable book to have if you want to be an innovative and more effective teacher."

—**Chris Morecroft**, Association of Colleges President, 2010–2011

"This book is born out of a vision: a science of the art of teaching, from the point of view of the rapid development of information and communication technology. Instead of marginalizing the teacher, this development will be catalytic to teachers regaining the production of their shared professional knowledge. I believe this is the best and most beautiful educational idea of the millennium so far."

—**Ference Marton**, Professor of Education,
University of Gothenburg, Sweden

"In *Teaching as a Design Science*, Diana Laurillard provides a roadmap for how teachers can become collaborative, active designers of ways to use emerging technologies that deeply enhance learning. Laurillard opens our eyes as to how technology is a resource for educational change, not a ready-made solution, and uncovers the critical role of teachers in describing and sharing ways to use this resource to meet today's educational aims. As a comprehensive primer for teacher activism in advancing learning technology, this book explains why teachers *must* become designers, what they need to know to design effectively, how they can test and improve their designs, and, most critically, how they can codify and share their designs as reusable pedagogical patterns.

Building not only on solid scholarship, but also her on own state of the art projects, Diana Laurillard gives us a much needed path forward that respects teachers as professionals and addresses the real challenges of adapting technology for use in teaching and learning. Every twenty-first century teacher needs to know what a pedagogical design pattern is and that they can use pedagogical design patterns to easily create, share, and improve uses of technology to advance classroom learning."

—**Jeremy Roschelle**, Center for Technology in Learning, SRI International

"The idea of teaching as design has come of age: Laurillard offers sharp concepts and powerful strategies for improving the use of technology in education"

—**Peter Goodyear**, Professor of Education,
University of Sydney, Editor-in-Chief, *Instructional Science*

To Brian, Amy, and Anna, my constant teachers

Contents

Figures

Tables

Preface

There is something extraordinary happening in education. Teachers and learners are embracing technologies that will change the way we develop and share human knowledge and skills. But it is a very gradual change.

The digital technologies available to education have already expanded dramatically in recent years, but it takes more than technology infrastructure to transform a profession. How can teachers do this at the same time as fulfilling their current teaching duties?

People are fond of pointing out that the nineteenth-century time traveller would be astonished by our banks, factories, and operating theatres – all transformed by new technology – while the classroom has hardly changed. However, bankers, industrialists, and surgeons have had huge resources devoted to developing the specialised systems they need for transformation. Teachers have not. Yet it is a much more tractable problem to model the activity that moves a credit from one account to another than to model the activity that moves a mind from confusion to understanding. Governments provide education with the tools developed for industry and commerce, but who is there to help teachers and lecturers work out how to use them to transform teaching and learning?

This is only feasible if we harness the work of individual teachers who, every day, in all sectors, discover and test new ways of using digital technologies for teaching and learning.

It will take a while to work out how best to use the extraordinary collection of technologies now available but, with a new perspective on the profession of teaching, education could be discovering a fundamentally different way of developing and sharing human knowledge and skills.

This book explores what it would mean for teachers to take on this complex design project themselves.

1   Teaching as a Design Science

Teaching has always been recognized as an art, because it demands creativity and imagination. Teachers perform and respond to their audience to inspire and enthuse their learners. They discover how to make a productive connection between themselves, their learners, and their subject. Teaching is certainly an art. But in the arts anything goes; the imperative is to create a powerful experience for the audience. That is not true for teaching; it must do more than that. It also has a formally defined goal. The imperative for teaching is that learners develop their personal knowledge and capabilities.

So is teaching also a science? Educational researchers do science when they investigate teaching, but do teachers do it themselves? They do not, after all, develop and share theories and explanations based on experimental evidence. Teaching is not a theoretical science that describes and explains some aspect of the natural or social world. It is closer to the kind of science, like engineering, computer science, or architecture, whose imperative it is to make the world a better place: a design science. Herbert Simon made this distinction in his classic book on *The Sciences of the Artificial,* contrasting them with the sciences of the natural world, including the social sciences, which aim to understand and explain: "the natural sciences are concerned with how things are ... Design on the other hand is concerned with how things ought to be" (Simon 1969: 132–133).

A design science uses and contributes to theoretical science, but it builds design principles rather than theories, and the heuristics of practice rather than explanations, although like both the sciences and the arts, it uses what has gone before as a platform or inspiration for what it creates. Teaching is more like a design science because it uses what is known about teaching to attain the goal of student learning, and uses the implementation of its designs to keep improving them.

The story of this book is to explore what it means to treat teaching as a design science, and how the teaching community could collaborate, as design professionals do, to make things work better – in this case the institutions of formal learning. The hero of the story is technology – not a knight in shining armor, or a saintly savior. This hero is the flawed and misunderstood anti-hero who ought to come good in the end. At least, that's my intention.

The Role of Technology

There has always been a strong relationship between education and technology. Tools and technologies, in their broadest sense, are important drivers of education, though their development is rarely *driven by* education. Writing, one of the most important tools in the development of human civilization, was not invented for education but for commerce. Books were used initially to spread the word of religion, not to educate (Manguel 1997). Education adopted both, but had little effect on driving the development of either. Blackboard and chalk was one of the very few tools ever invented specifically to serve education, and its modern counterpart, after all the years of digital technologies, is the virtual learning environment or VLE. That's all. Even slide presentation tools were invented for the business community. We have to acknowledge that, typically, education does not drive technological invention. Instead we appropriate the useful inventions of the business and leisure industries. In an age of rampant technological invention, this becomes a critical issue.

The arrival of digital technology over the past three decades, increasingly impacting on work, leisure, and learning, has been a shock to the educational system that it has yet to absorb. In fact, the variety and power of digital technologies probably means they cannot be easily assimilated – the system will probably have to adapt to embrace them fully.

Precisely because of their potential to change education unbidden, it is imperative that teachers and lecturers place themselves in a position where they are able to master the use of digital technologies, to harness their power, and put them to the proper service of education. This is a theme that will repeat throughout the following chapters – education must now begin to drive its use of technology.

To do that, we have to be clear about where education is driving itself – what is its role and purpose in twenty-first century society? And we cannot leave consideration of technology development far behind in our thinking, because even though education must lead, it must do that in the knowledge of what technology has to offer, and the changes it is making to student life. We may not have decided that what education really needed was an online folk-generated encyclopedia, such as a wiki, but neither should we ignore its existence, and the fact that many students use it more often than their university library. If we are confident in our use of technology then we can go beyond mere awareness to full exploitation of these new opportunities. It is a rational response to interrogate every new technology for its potential to serve educational aims. But being beholden to the inventiveness of other fields, education could easily be sidetracked into inappropriate uses of technology if we are not clear what we want from it.

Harnessing Technology for Educational Ends

The academic community should challenge digital technologies, and we have to do that from a position of strength, with a clear and continually renewed understanding of what education requires of them. These are "knowledge technologies" in the sense that they change our relationship to what is known and how it can be known. That strikes deeply at the heart of the educational process.

Knowledge technologies shape *what* is learned by changing *how* it is learned. Let's think about three different ways of learning in a business studies course:

- one learner reads and writes about a new business as a case study;
- a second role-plays the same case in a small-group business simulation; and
- a third experiments with a spreadsheet model of the same case.

Their respective learning outcomes will share a lot in common about the factual details of the case, but their very different experiences will yield very different ways of knowing. Reading and writing enables an inquiring analytical approach into what has been done and what lessons might be learned, to generate knowledge in the form of propositions and principles. Role-play elicits thinking about the relationship between actions and goals mediated by human relations, which develops a more experiential understanding of the case. The spreadsheet model offers a way of engaging with the flow of supply–demand and income–outgoings in a developing business in an experimental way. This is the kind of learning that can only be done through digital technology. It enables the learner to experiment with different decisions about, for example, how much to invest given different rates of interest and different trajectories of sales. The model shows them the results of their different decisions in terms of cash flow – giving intrinsic feedback on their actions, very different from the extrinsic feedback of the teacher's comment on their essay, and from the social rules operating in the role-play feedback. The learner is building knowledge of the behavior of the business as a system.

All of these forms of knowledge – analytical, experiential, and experimental – are valuable. It means that as the teacher thinks through the curriculum topics to be covered, and how they are to be taught, the range of learning outcomes it is possible for their learners to achieve is being determined to a great extent by the range of teaching methods they employ. If they have no access to technology, for example, the spreadsheet experience is impossible. If the learning outcome "awareness of the parameters involved in building a viable cash flow" is sufficient, then reading and writing about a case study will be sufficient as a teaching method, but it could not in itself achieve an outcome such as "understanding how the context of investment decisions can affect short-term profits." Similarly, working with a cash flow model will not engage learners in thinking about the human relations that affect the case they are studying. That may or may not matter, depending on the teacher's aims. The point here is that the curriculum being covered – *what* is learned – is significantly affected by the range of teaching methods used – *how* it is learned.

There is a danger that technology could undermine formal education. The notion of a formal education system was challenged originally by radical thinkers such as Illich, who wanted to free the learning mind from the constraints imposed by the transmission model of teaching practiced in the formal system (Illich 1973). Arguments against formal education are now current again but, uninformed by any understanding of the theory of teaching and learning, they plunge us back into traditional approaches. Technology opportunists who challenge formal education argue that, with wide access to information and ideas on the web, the learner can pick and choose their education – thereby demonstrating their faith in the transmission model of teaching. An academic education is not equivalent to a trip to the public library, digital or otherwise. The educationist has to attack this kind of nonsense, but not by rejecting technology. It is a stronger attack when we argue that first we must ask what learners need from education and therefore from technology.

Educationists must resist the idea that because of new technologies students can do it for themselves – instead they create an even more critical role for the teacher, who is not simply mediating the knowledge already articulated, but is more deeply involved in scaffolding the way students think and how they develop the new kinds of skills they will need for the digital literacies. Roger Säljö puts the challenge like this:

> To deal with these issues, we should try to be even more explicit about issues such as epistemological beliefs, learning styles, and the problem of what counts as valid knowledge and valid arguments in various disciplines and areas of study. The critical and productive learning — and meta-learning — of how to use technologies is itself one of the most important socialising practices of modern education, and that will have to be high on the agenda.
>
> (Säljö 2004: 493)

The following chapters attempt to demonstrate that we need much more from technology than access to information and ideas. Technology has much more to offer than that, and it is up to the academic teaching community to define and defend the role it should play.

We cannot challenge the technology to serve the needs of education until we know what we want from it. We have to articulate what it means to teach well, what the principles of designing good teaching are, and how these will enable learners to learn. Until then, we risk continuing to be technology-led.

Learning about Teaching

For some years now, educators have insisted on a greater focus on learning than on teaching. The point of teaching is to enable students to learn. But how do we learn about teaching? The education system has an absence of feedback loops – we define the outputs of the system (intended learning outcomes), we design the means by which they are achieved (teaching methods, teaching schemes, lesson plans), we specify and judge the criteria for the success of the outputs (exams and grades), and we use that information to judge the student and the institution, but not – why not? – the teaching design. In a research project, it would be equivalent to framing the hypothesis (that these teaching methods will lead to these learning outcomes), measuring the result (through exams and grades), and concluding that, in the event of the hypothesis being not proven, the experimental subjects were deficient and the hypothesis remains intact. Teaching is clearly not a science.

Nor could it be. Teaching is not rocket science: it is much, much harder than that. Rocket science is about moving atoms from a to b; teaching is about moving minds. And the whole point is to change those minds into independent thinkers who will not necessarily bend to the will of the teacher. The independence of the student makes it unfair to judge the quality of the teaching wholly by what the student learns. So we don't, but without using that feedback loop, we cannot learn how to improve the design of teaching. Every individual teacher has the opportunity in their interaction with students to discover which methods or techniques work best, and in that sense the feedback loop between teaching design and learning outcome may be completed. But the knowledge they develop is not articulated and shared – this is the big difference from science. Developing the knowledge base in a discipline is done by building on the work of others, innovating, testing, improving, sharing, and the cycle continues. In education it is the research community that does this, not the teaching community.

If teaching, like engineering and architecture, were treated as a design science, then the practitioners themselves would be building the knowledge base.

Education as a Design Science

There is a history to this idea. The appropriate methodology for a design science for professional practice has been a matter of debate between positivist and constructivist approaches – whether good practice can be formalized, or most depend on the practitioner (Cross 2001). In the unstructured, unformalizable world of much professional practice, do we need design principles or might it be more appropriate to develop an "epistemology of practice" (Schön 1987)?

The idea that education can be treated as a design science originated in the 1990s, with the ambition to take educational research out of the laboratory into practice. To do that researchers had to confront "the complexity of real-world situations and their resistance to experimental control" (Collins, Joseph, and Bielaczyc 2004). When educational researchers take an innovative teach-ing method, or educational intervention, into the field, the messy business of the normal teaching process takes over, and the actual implementation can turn out to be very different from the intended design. The solution was to develop a methodology of "design research" that is not classically experimen-tal, but iterative, progressively refining the initial theory-based design as it is actually implemented. Then it can refine both theory and practice. Allan Collins clarified the contrasting features of laboratory studies and design experiments, characterizing the latter as dealing with messy situations, flexible design revision, social interaction, developing a profile rather than testing hypotheses, and most importantly, using co-participant design and analysis rather than experimenter design (Collins 1999). By bringing researchers and teachers together this way, the design experiment steered a careful pathway between the two ends of the earlier design science debate, and reconfigured it as a form of principled reflective practice.

This approach produced a set of design research guidelines for researchers and teachers to work together to design, test, analyze, redesign, re-test, and report on an educational intervention. These are the competences of *principled reflective practice* in education, keeping close to the rigor of testing, and also adjusting to the requirements of the local context. But the guidelines are not quite complete: although researchers emphasize that the theoretical principles of an intervention are the key elements of its design (Cobb *et al.*, 2003; Collins, Joseph, and Bielaczyc 2004; diSessa and Cobb 2004), and the intervention must be evaluated in those terms, there is nothing in the guidelines to ensure this. They are offered as guidance for people to do design experiments, but they expect to involve specialist researchers rather than empower the teachers. The outcome that emerges from this process takes the form of a report on the goals and elements of the design, the settings where it has been used, and the lessons learned. This is how the practitioners would build their knowledge base, although a discursive report may not be the best way to build knowledge in the teaching community.

In fact, the authors see their approach as requiring "much more effort than any one human can carry out" (ibid.: 33); it is not a methodology meant for teaching practitioners.

Design science research has been developed especially in the information sciences – one of the "sciences of the artificial" – and defined as a rigorous set of methodological principles to underpin the academic research (Hevner 2007). Practicing teachers cannot match the methodological rigor of a research team, but there are nonetheless several parallels with what a teaching profes-sional actually does. The following extract defining the nature of design science research includes my interpretation (in italics in square brackets) to show how the practicing teacher comes very close to this kind of professional activity:

> Design science research [*teaching by a reflective practitioner*] is grounded on existing ideas drawn from the domain knowledge base [*theories of*

teaching and learning]. Inspiration for creative design activity [*new lesson designs*] can be drawn from many different sources to include rich opportunities/problems from the application environment [*the classroom, seminar, lab, etc*], existing artifacts [*other teachers' lesson designs and resources*], analogies/metaphors [*for good pedagogy*], and theories [*of teaching and learning*]. Additions to the knowledge base [*new teaching methods, pedagogic ideas*] as results of design research [*reflective teaching*] will include any additions or extensions to the original theories and methods made during the research, the new artifacts (design products and processes [*lesson designs and teaching resources*]), and all experiences gained from performing the iterative design cycles [*design and re-design of lesson plans*] and field testing the artifact [*the implementation of the lesson plan and resulting student assignments*] in the application environment [*the classroom, etc.*].

(Hevner 2009: 127)

Ideally, teachers should be able to enact design science as part of their normal professional practice, and have the means to act like design researchers themselves, i.e. documenting and sharing their designs. Without this they remain the recipients of research findings, rather than being the drivers of new knowledge about teaching and learning, able to critique and challenge the technology that is changing their profession.

Design Patterns for Learning

In the same tradition, of looking to design science for inspiration, there has been a recent resurgence of interest in the idea of "design patterns," often explicitly to address the problem of design technologies for learning. A review of the literature in this area defines this particular type of design approach:

a design pattern is a semi-structured description of an expert's method for solving a recurrent problem, which includes a description of the problem itself and the context in which the method is applicable ... Design patterns have the explicit aim of externalizing knowledge to allow accumulation and generalization of solutions and to allow all members of a community or design group to participate in discussions relating to the design.

(Mor and Winters 2007)

As a methodology, this approach is immediately relevant to teachers because it presents design patterns as the means by which the teaching community can participate in design. The key elements of a design pattern are the "problem," the "context," the semi-structured description of the "solution," and the fact that this is "externalised knowledge" (Goodyear 2005). Being able to externalize the knowledge is what makes it a shared object in a community that can therefore critique and build its knowledge:

> design patterns are usually drafted, shared, critiqued and refined through an extended process of collaboration. Thus patterns have the potential to make a major contribution to the sharing of techniques between developers of learning activities.
>
> (McAndrew, Goodyear, and Dalziel 2006)

Here, the knowledge developed by the teacher is externalized in the form of a design pattern, rather than a "report." If it properly represents the teacher's pedagogic design, then it can act as the means by which the knowledge base builds.

But what does it take to represent the teacher's pedagogic design? The exact form of a learning design pattern is still in contention. This is partly because of the multiple origins of interest in design approaches (McAndrew, Goodyear, and Dalziel 2006). A textual description sacrifices the technological advantages of a machine-readable version, but makes the pedagogic points more simply, in terms of context, problem, solution, and illustrative diagram. The disadvantage of the machine-readable version is that although it can reproduce the author's design and run it online, the teacher may find it difficult to adapt. A human-readable version means that the teacher can be inspired by the design, and apply their own expertise to it (McAndrew and Goodyear 2007). This type of pattern format is semi-structured, where the headings are used to elicit text and diagrams from the teacher-designer to represent their pedagogy for others. However, unless it can be expressed computationally it cannot exploit technology to assist the design and collaboration process. Some kind of structured and formalizable design pattern is needed for expressing pedagogic ideas, as the basis for the teaching community to collaborate in building its own knowledge of what learners need, how to teach, and what to demand of the technology.

To summarize the argument so far:

- Teaching is a design science in the sense that its aim is to keep improving its practice, in a principled way, building on the work of others.
- The continual challenge from digital technologies has forced education into the position of following rather than leading innovation, and the academic teaching community needs to gain better control of our use of technology.
- Because technology is changing both what and how students learn we can only lead educational innovation by being clear about the principles of designing good teaching and learning, and therefore what education needs from technology.
- The teaching community itself has to contribute to building the knowledge base because it has to develop fast, in response to the rapid changes wrought by the technology.

- This has to be done collaboratively, in order to achieve the aim of improving practice through building the knowledge base for the academic teaching community.
- Teachers must be able to enact design science as part of their professional practice; therefore they need the means to do it – to be able to articulate and share their pedagogic practice, the outcomes they achieved, and how these outcomes related to the elements of their design.

This is how we arrived at the need for a structured and formalizable pattern for learning designs as the means by which teachers build the design knowledge of teaching practice. But what form should it take? Working out how best to represent a teacher's pedagogic design and the principles that underpin it, is the task of the remaining chapters.

The Foundations for Teaching as Design

A design task begins with a requirements analysis. The next chapter does this by going to the heart of the formal education system, to examine the nature of academic learning, the knowledge and skills that constitute the contribution that education makes to society. It is a contested issue, so Chapter 2 sets out to understand it from the perspective of the various stakeholders who take the trouble to define it. As students confront this provider-defined offer they come with their own ambitions, expectations and ideas, to provide a rich mix of contrasts and common purpose. Chapter 3 surveys and summarizes the research studies on what students bring to learning, and how this affects the quality of their learning. Teachers do not always begin their courses with detailed data on their student population, and yet learner characteristics are an important influence on how well the teaching is likely to work. Are there ways we can build on these studies to be better prepared to help the students we find ourselves teaching?

Thinking through what it takes to teach means understanding what it takes to learn, so Chapter 4 works through what some of the major studies and theories tell us about this. They come from a variety of contexts, educational sectors, and subject disciplines. The type of learning that takes place in formal education is distinct from, but still builds on the processes of learning that occur as a natural part of human development, which have no curriculum, and no formal teaching. Chapter 5 uses this analysis to understand what it takes to teach, working through alternative approaches in the literature to make the bridge between what learners need and what, therefore, teachers must do. There is no clear deterministic link between the two, so there can be no certainty that even the best designed teaching will necessarily facilitate the intended learning. That is why teaching has to be an iterative design process.

Clearly we need an educational system with a different structure from the one we currently have – with a more iterative dialogic structure that enables students to learn, but also enables the teachers and the system to learn as well. Chapter 6 develops the broad design principles that acknowledge this iterative character of the teaching-learning process in a way that can both guide and challenge the pedagogies we develop, and in particular, the way they use digital technologies. The chapter argues that we need to be able to represent those principles in learning design patterns.

The following chapters work through the main types of learning, to marshal the lessons learned from the research literature. The studies are chosen for what they tell us about good ways of teaching, and may or may not involve the use of digital technology. The aim is to explore what we know about the different ways of learning and identify what education needs from technology. Then we can test how well technology is serving those needs. The final chapter consolidates the principles as design patterns for teaching, and ends with a plea for changing to a professional culture in which teachers play their proper role in meeting our local and global aims for education.

2 What is Formal Learning?

Introduction

This chapter is about what is being learned within a formal educational environment, school, college, or university. What contribution does formal education make to the development of the individual student that is different from their everyday "informal" learning?

Until quite recently, it was the prevailing view, especially in universities, that teaching is about imparting knowledge. Sadly, "imparting knowledge" has usually been only a partially successful teaching activity, as every essay and examination paper testifies. While higher education was an elitist enterprise, and exams were designed to select the best minds, it was possible to make this failure the responsibility of the student. This has changed. Higher education has become less elitist, and has taken on the task of educating a much larger proportion of the population to degree level, and we have articulated an approach to teaching that has a higher ambition: "The aim of teaching is simple: it is to make student learning possible" (Ramsden 2003: 5). "Making student learning possible," where the learning is the kind that helps them "expand and test knowledge," places much more responsibility with the teacher. It implies that the teachers in all education sectors must know more than what it takes simply to impart subject knowledge, and must understand something about what it takes to learn and reconceptualize that knowledge.

The nature of formal learning is clearly more than passing on information, or imparting subject knowledge, but how do we define it now? We need a clear definition because this is the foundation on which we then build an approach to designing teaching.

The following sections select the principal sources of influence on how the education system defines itself – the educational establishment of policymakers and curriculum developers, the workplace that will employ our formally educated students, the educational researchers who investigate and theorize the formal curriculum, and the teachers themselves. The analysis begins with the definitions for post-16 education, since that has a strong influence on the school curriculum. The point was clearly stated, for example, by former

US Secretary for Education, Margaret Spellings: "States must adopt high school curricula that prepare all students for participation in postsecondary education and should facilitate seamless integration between high school and college" (Spellings 2006).

The View from the Educational Establishment

In most countries, education is a political issue because it is organized and funded primarily by the state. There are some impressive ambitions to be found in educational policy documents, the most ambitious being the United Nations' millennium goal for education, which every nation inherits: to achieve universal primary education by 2015. This is the ultimate challenge for education, and as I write in 2011, we are only halfway towards it.

National policies for education have to recognize competing pressures on the formal curriculum, and because participation in higher education is increasing across the world the school curriculum is harnessed closely to the needs of the post-16 curriculum. Governments are therefore keen to influence the formal curriculum at all levels, to be sure it meets all needs.

In the UK the most recent review of higher education identified four roles for a university education as knowledge-oriented, personal, economic, and social, with main pressures on the curriculum deriving from the aims to:

> inspire and enable individuals to develop their capabilities to the highest potential levels throughout life so that they grow intellectually, are well-equipped for work, can contribute effectively to society and achieve personal fulfilment...

> increase knowledge and understanding for their own sake and to foster their application to the benefit of the economy and society...

and

> serve the needs of an adaptable, sustainable, knowledge-based economy at local, regional and national levels.

> (NCIHE 1997)

The academy and economy will always be sources of influence on the formal curriculum, while the fourth aim, the social role, is more political, recognizing the importance of the graduate's role as citizen, "to play a major role in shaping a democratic, civilised and inclusive society" (ibid.: 72).

Citizenship and human rights education is now part of what is becoming a global curriculum for formal education across all sectors for all countries, advocated by bodies such as OECD and UNESCO (Robertson *et al.* 2007; UNESCO 2005).

These are ambitious aims. They impose on the teacher a much tougher task than telling students what they know, and one that cannot be achieved simply by being knowledgeable in their field. The challenge is compounded by the twenty-first century ambition to increase the proportion of people educated beyond school. Educational policy documents demand not only higher quality but broader reach as well.

At European level the Lisbon agreement of 2000 was "to make the EU the world's most competitive and dynamic knowledge-based economy by 2010," and led to a succession of follow-up documents placing on universities the responsibility to change their approach to teaching and learning in order to achieve this ambition:

> In order to overcome persistent mismatches between graduate qualifications and the needs of the labour market, university programmes should be structured to **enhance directly the employability of graduates** and to offer broad support to the workforce more generally.
>
> (CEC 2006: 6) (original bold)

Recent UK government policy was equally concerned to foster employment skills and emphasized basic skills, such as literacy and numeracy, and generic skills, such as team working and communication, as being applicable in most jobs (Leitch 2006; UKCES 2009). The importance of the broader generic skills is enshrined in the OECD approach to its Programme for International Student Assessment (PISA), which defines the benchmark for schools across all its member states:

> PISA defines each assessment area (science, reading and mathematics) not mainly in terms of mastery of the school curriculum, but in terms of the knowledge and skills needed for full participation in society.
>
> (OECD-CERI 2003)

The EU policy also wants to enable new disciplines and cross-disciplinary research and teaching to emerge, which will require "focusing less on scientific disciplines and more on research domains" (CEC 2006: 8), so that students can move between disciplines through new approaches to teaching and curricula. It is not just the professional workplace that needs graduates who can work across the disciplines: those who go into university research must be able to acquire the skills and habits of interdisciplinary thinking, and not be constrained by departments "at a time when innovation occurs increasingly at the intersection of multiple disciplines (including business and social sciences), curricula and research funding remain largely contained in individual departments" (Spellings 2006).

All graduates should have the chance to develop the high-level cognitive skills that can be applied within any discipline because it will not be possible to predict which other subjects they may have to engage with.

For the educational establishment, therefore, the foundational knowledge in the formal curriculum is not just the detailed understanding of systems of ideas and explanations of the natural and social world that a traditional curriculum offers. It embraces equally the high-level cognitive skills that the knowledge society requires of its professional workforce and its citizens.

The View from the Workplace

The increasing attention to high-level skills in the workplace, the idea of life-long learning, and the rapid production and communication of knowledge made possible by the internet during the 1990s, led to a rethink of the role of education. Higher and further education need to recognize the importance of the emerging knowledge society, where a greater proportion of the workforce are graduates capable of contributing to the production of knowledge, and ready to learn and hence innovate:

> Among the most significant effects of mass higher education ... is the great increase in the market for continuing education, and thus of the learning society, one in which life-long study, as well as training and retraining are possible ... This readiness to learn greatly increases the capacity of a labour force to respond to rapid technological change.
>
> (Gibbons *et al.* 1994: 74)

The pull from the workplace that requires an adaptable workforce is also reflected in the demands of students and the wider community. Local conditions determine the degree to which a university carries out market research to discover which courses have most appeal to potential students or where the public and private sector find there are gaps in graduates' skills and knowledge. Market research on curriculum requirements has not been a strong feature of higher education in general, and at school level government is the dominant influence. However, because so many universities are now excluded from access to the highly competitive sources of major research funding, their only source of growth is student numbers. If the curriculum is to be an attractor, the courses must either provide a ticket to a good job, or address the student's personal interests. For these universities, academics find they have to shift the boundaries of their own discipline interests in order to build an attractive curriculum: engineering re-badges itself as design studies, and sociologists turn their expertise towards media studies.

The problems of interfacing successfully with the requirements of the workplace run deeper, however, because they cannot always be overcome by shifting disciplinary boundaries. The workplace requires capability in a different kind of knowledge than that generated through research and scholarship, which remain at the heart of the university curriculum. This continuing schism between academic and workplace knowledge led to the rise of an interest in "work-based learning" during the 1990s in the UK, Europe, and Australia (Boud and Solomon 2001; Osborne 2003). It generated a greater interest in articulating high-level skills, such as interpersonal, communication, goal-setting, self-management, and team work skills, that the formal curriculum could be seen as facilitating (Brennan and Little 1996). However, although there was an impact on the rhetoric, the HE curriculum did not significantly adjust to the nature of knowledge in the workplace; instead the cognitive skills identified were mapped to the nature of learning already evident in discipline-based courses. The problem remained:

> Learning in educational settings presents a stark contrast to learning in work and life ... Learning in educational institutions tends to be decontextualised. Courses are often constructed as islands apart from the bodies of knowledge and practices from which they are generated and on which they focus.
>
> (Boud and Falchikov 2006: 406)

The schism remains because it is not possible to derive workplace knowledge from discipline knowledge: it is produced in a very different way. Workplace knowledge

> is created through the implementation of a new work system, through solving problems which arise in the rapidly shifting context of work or from the employees' need to understand a complex situation.
>
> (Reeve and Gallacher 2005: 228)

A work-based learning curriculum could potentially embrace this form of knowledge (Solomon and McIntyre 2000), but it does not mix easily with disciplinary knowledge:

> There are substantial challenges in making existing course units available within a work-based learning framework as [disciplinary and workplace] knowledge may be qualitatively different and unable to be translated from one to another. It is easier to imagine a dialogue between disciplinary and professional frameworks within a conventional course, than in a work setting.
>
> (Boud and Solomon 2000: 10)

An analysis of several workplace learning projects developed a typology of learning outcomes that embrace more than the disciplinary forms of knowledge, to include: task performance, awareness and understanding, personal development, teamwork, role performance, academic knowledge and skills, decision-making and problem-solving, and judgment (Eraut 2004: 265). The typology helps to clarify why there is a problem because as Eraut points out, "few of them comprise only skill or only codified knowledge because ... these categories do not match attributes of performance at work" (ibid.: 265). The workplace puts the highest value on generic cognitive skills such as willingness to learn, teamwork, and collaborative learning (Coll and Zegwaard 2006;

Crebert *et al.* 2004), but places little emphasis on discipline knowledge except in technical roles in the specialized professions.

The knowledge industry is negotiating and generating new knowledge in the workplace by applying high-level cognitive skills, which it therefore values more highly than specialized formal knowledge. On the other hand, academic teaching practice tends to follow academic research interests, which must focus on specialized knowledge in order to compete. The higher education curriculum is still in the process of resolving the tension between developing specialized codified knowledge and the broader workplace demand for generic cognitive skills.

Meanwhile, the school system is required to orient its curriculum directly to twenty-first century needs "to consider the integration of 21st century competencies and expertise, such as critical thinking, complex problem solving, collaboration, multimedia communication, and technological competencies demonstrated by professionals in various disciplines" (USDoE 2010: xvi).

The View from Educational Theorists

The concept of "the curriculum" in formal education is largely absent from the discourse of the educational establishment, except when it addresses the topics and skills necessary for employment and the world of work (Barnett and Coate 2005). As government policy began to focus more on the role of universities, they had to move beyond the knowledge-oriented curriculum, to describe also the high-level skills it is developing in a graduate. In the UK this led to a benchmarking process by the Quality Assurance Agency (QAA), the first attempt to identify standards across the curriculum. The subject benchmarking was conducted by academics working in separate subject groups, rather than through a cross-disciplinary approach. They were asked to give an account of the nature of their discipline in terms of its skills orientation: the knowledge, generic intellectual, and personal transferable skills it inculcates. It is an interesting case, because although the benchmarking process succeeded in providing a comparable set of standards across subject areas, educational theorists saw the exercise as "reducing" academic aims to "mere" outcomes.

The argument against the "curriculum as outcomes" approach is that it fails to address "what is required for capability in the disciplines" (Barnett and Coate 2005: 25), i.e. what would go beyond knowledge and skills to embrace also personal dispositions such as critical thinking and personal autonomy. While the curriculum must include both "knowing and acting," i.e. what is known, and how that knowledge is used in practice, it must also embrace "being" as one of the building blocks of the curriculum. This would be a way of responding to a world in which an individual finds that their hard-won knowledge and skills have become irrelevant, or outdated by changes in science, technology, politics, and culture. For the curriculum to prepare students for such a world, it must go beyond the current horizons of knowledge and skills in a discipline, to help them develop a sense of "self," which may be interpreted as a personal relationship with their subject that enables them to go beyond the happenstance of current expertise and adapt to new conditions. The curriculum must be "future-proof," as it were. The student should not emerge as a slave to the current state of the discipline knowledge they studied.

There has occasionally been reference to the idea of a "use-by" date for qualifications in certain rapidly developing subjects. But if education is serious about developing deep knowledge and high-level skills, this idea should be an absurdity – theories and world conditions may come and go, but the well-educated scientist or historian, or graduate in any field, should be equipped intellectually to cope with such changes. That is what Barnett and Coate seem to mean by "being" as an aspect of curriculum. It is similar to the outcomes of a college education that William Perry discerned in some Harvard students as a commitment to a generalized relativism and to personal values (Perry 1970).

A further critique of the subject benchmarking approach is that it has been too narrow in its ambitions. As we have seen, the workplace wants the curriculum to embrace the high-level skills of new knowledge production in the knowledge society, but this is not reflected in the learning outcomes generated by subject-oriented academics: there is no mention of broader personal attributes, such as *developing multiple identities* and the *competence to work across disciplines*. Because they have been grounded within discipline boundaries in the way the QAA set them up, there has been no attempt to take a generic viewpoint on the curriculum (Barnett and Coate 2005). It would take a different, deliberately cross-disciplinary methodology to address the requirements of the educational establishment and the workplace.

The problem of knowledge and the curriculum is tackled from a different perspective in the sociology of education, where the aim is to transcend the division between the "traditional" curriculum, which transmits received knowledge to the next generation, and the "instrumental" curriculum, which is oriented towards building a particular form of society (Young 2008). The "social realist" approach recognizes both the power relations that drive the curriculum towards relevance and vocational practice, and the specialist communities that maintain and develop the cognitive interests that are critical for the development of the discipline:

> the extent to which the capacity of any curriculum to be the basis for acquiring new knowledge in any field depends on *cognitive* interests, which will be expressed in the social networks, trust and codes of practice among specialists that give it an objectivity and sense of standards.
>
> (Young 2008: 33) (original italics)

From this point of view the formal curriculum should be understood not only as the means to develop society, but also as having a role in the development of knowledge itself. Young argues for "reorienting the debate about curriculum standards from attempts to specify learning outcomes ... to identifying cognitive interests and building the necessary specialist communities, networks and codes of practice to support them" (ibid.: 34). This discipline orientation wants to reclaim the special nature of history, physics, or music as having distinctive and mutually exclusive elements in their curricula. From this point of view the current focus on generic skills and learning outcomes swings the pendulum too far from the traditional separation of the disciplines. Like Barnett and Coate, who also attack the "curriculum as outcome" approach, this is a plea for redressing the balance between discipline knowledge and generic skills that would be lost by focusing higher education too much on the skills needs of employment.

These two major forces influencing the curriculum, academic knowledge and stakeholder requirements, are reflected in the way educational change is conducted, where theory is always in conflict with government policy – necessarily so in the view of sociologists such as Foucault, who argue that the role of the intellectual is to remain critical of those in power, not assist them (Foucault, Kritzman, and Sheridan 1990). As a social realist Young preferred to resolve the conflict between theory and policy through a "collaborative model" in which educational researchers work alongside policymakers to influence educational change. After some lengthy experience of the collaborative model in practice, however, he is led to the conclusion that "neither conflict nor collaboration adequately characterizes the relationship between research and policy" (Young 2008), because the objective of the researcher is different from that of the policymaker: the former must preserve an autonomy in the development of concepts and theories, whereas the latter must implement change.

So although discipline-based academics have been working with policymakers and educational researchers to generate changes in the way the curriculum is articulated, implemented, and then quality-assured, and have been engaged in what Young would call a "collaborative model," what they have produced is seen by the educational theorists as going too far in yielding to the requirements of government, and neglecting the needs of the disciplines.

Certainly, there is a danger that if learning outcomes are made too generic then we lose the articulation of the specific capabilities needed for a discipline. The right balance is important. We need both specific knowledge and generic skills because knowledge and skills have an internal relationship: the skills enable the learner to engage with knowledge at the right level of complexity, and the knowledge acts as a vehicle for rehearsing and developing the skills. Each is an aspect of the other.

A balanced curriculum will include some learning outcomes focusing on high-level cognitive skills and some focusing on the specifics of a discipline that will not translate easily across disciplines. Specific knowledge will be peculiar to the discipline, but the generic skills needed for twenty-first century employment and citizenship are widely applicable across the disciplines. It is this latter part of the curriculum, in particular, which should be common to teaching in all subject areas, and will be an equally important aspect of formal learning.

Teachers' Views of Formal Learning

Academics have ambitious definitions of formal learning and, in the UK at least, subject benchmarks provided a good indicator of how the teaching community defines the nature of formal learning, and what the school curriculum has to feed into. At an international level, the European Union "Tuning Project" has taken on the task of standardizing such definitions across all the participating countries (Gonzalez and Wagenaar 2005), and there are similar mechanisms in other countries, such as accreditation agencies that set and assure common standards in universities and colleges. The process is collective, drawing on the experience and expertise of leading academics, working on behalf of their peers, consulting widely, and updating the standards progressively over the years to take account of changes in the developing disciplines. It is reasonable, therefore, to expect these agencies to be a valuable resource of collective understanding about the nature of formal learning.

These exercises have effectively established a common core of achievement that a graduate can expect from a qualification in, say, history, or computer science, no matter where they study. It must be a complex and difficult process to agree on the common core of skills and knowledge for a subject discipline. The problem is an unfamiliar one at school level, except at national or state level as there is little reason to achieve consensus between countries. But for the movement of students across Europe it is important to achieve "tuning."

So for the purpose of understanding the nature of formal learning, it is useful to have these documents. We can compare the outputs of different agencies to see how closely they agree on the nature of formal learning in a discipline. History is a highly contested discipline, for example, but if we compare the QAA "summary of learning outcomes" with the Tuning "subject specific competencies," it is possible to discern nine broad areas of agreement between them, such as:

- Awareness of and respect for points of view deriving from other national or cultural backgrounds (Gonzalez and Wagenaar 2005).
- A command of comparative perspectives, which may include the ability to compare the histories of different countries, societies, or cultures (QAA 2007).

Sometimes the expression may be different, being more or less specific, but the intention is similar, and points to a similar kind of academic knowledge and competence:

- Knowledge of and ability to use the specific tools necessary to study documents of particular periods, e.g. palaeography, epigraphy (Gonzalez and Wagenaar 2005).
- Competence in specialist skills which are necessary for some areas of historical analysis and understanding cultures (QAA 2007).

They do not always agree: although both agencies set out to define supersets from which courses may select, each also has items that have no counterpart in the other. Nonetheless, the degree of broad agreement, albeit with varying degrees of specificity, does help to validate the idea that there can be a common core of achievement at degree level for graduates of a subject discipline.

More interestingly, to what extent can a common core of achievement be defined *across* subject disciplines? Are the disciplines really distinct in the type of knowledge and cognitive skill they foster?

A recent research project, "Enhancing teaching-learning environments" (ETL), worked with 28 diverse university courses to analyze their aims and learning outcomes, and how best to align these with their teaching methods. The emphasis was on the particular requirements of each discipline, so this is a valuable account of how formal learning is defined within each area. A key outcome of the project was to reconceptualize the nature of formal learning as going beyond subject matter knowledge to "ways of thinking and practicing" within the discipline (Entwistle 2005). The methodology used here contrasted with the quality assurance agencies' approach to developing clear statements of learning outcomes:

> While clarity about outcomes is essential, formal statements of intended learning outcomes may fail to communicate the essence of the individual disciplines and professional areas, which depends on a holistic view of the knowledge and values involved.
>
> (Entwistle 2005: 72)

Instead, the ETL project interviewed academics, many of whom criticized the "restrictive nature" of the formal learning outcomes they had to use, to find out what was important to them as teachers. An initial analysis of six disciplines – Biology, Economics, Electronic Engineering, History, Media Studies, and Music – documented the "fundamental differences that exist between subject areas in the nature of learning outcomes" (ibid.: 67). The argument is, therefore, that the disciplines are indeed distinctive and we cannot expect to find commonality. This is a problem for my attempt to discern a generic account of the nature of formal learning, so I want to look closely at the nature of the distinctiveness.

The first step is to compare, within subject area, the outputs of the quality assurance agencies with those of the teachers in the ETL case studies, to discern where they want to go beyond the restrictive definitions of the formal outcomes. In the case of History, for example, all the statements summarized by Entwistle are as follows, that it requires students to:

- interpret texts and write essays in which personal viewpoints are encouraged, as long as they are well supported;
- achieve a greater awareness of the contested nature of knowledge;

- achieve a greater awareness of how evidence was used in argument;
- *break away from previous, more restricted, ways of thinking about the subject;*
- see history in a wider social and temporal context;
- develop a perspective of the past that avoids ... interpreting past events in terms of current understandings of authority and society;
- view matters from alternative perspectives;
- *build up a more sophisticated, differentiated picture of a particular area;*
- gain a greater maturity of judgment which would encompass the [ability to take different perspectives];
- *[undertake] a cumulative process of refining skills and developing capacities and understanding;*
- express their own views in discussion and feel part of a joint enterprise that allow[s] them to believe that their views and interpretations [have] value;
- communicate ideas in academically acceptable forms of expression and argument (Entwistle 2005: 75–79) (my italics).

Interestingly, although these twelve statements were from what the teachers saw as their local idiosyncratic outcomes, only the three in italics appear to have no clear counterpart in the outputs of the quality assurance agencies. They are not incompatible, but are expressed in a way that does not fit very well with the greater specificity the agencies prefer. This perhaps accounts for the perception of them as "restrictive". In fact, Table 2.1 shows a reasonable degree of agreement between several aspects of the overall aims derived from these different sources.

The restrictions imposed by the agencies do not look too onerous from these comparisons. It seems to be possible, therefore, to achieve agreement about the nature of formal learning in the discipline of History. Most of these statements, despite their complexity, are expressed at quite a high level of abstraction, and do not appear to be particularly "constraining," especially as both QAA and Tuning documents emphasize that courses should select from the complete list, and not necessarily attempt to cover all the items.

Even within the relatively contentious discipline of History there is a sufficient degree of abstraction in the main learning outcome statements to allow a broad consensus on what graduates should achieve. The other disciplines achieved a similar consensus in their own sets of outcomes and competencies for these agencies. However, looking at the statements for History, apart from the specifically history-oriented ones (such as the interpretation of past events), most appear to be sufficiently abstract to be applicable in other subject areas as well, which is intriguing. Statements such as "the ability to take different perspectives" are hardly unique to History. How far could the consensus go across discipline areas?

To test this, we ran a survey at the Institute of Education, using the 43 statements collected from the six discipline areas studied in the ETL project, to ask

Table 2.1   Comparison of Selected Learning Outcomes for History Defined by Individual Academics, the Tuning Process, and the QAA Benchmarking Exercise

ETL project: History requires students to	*Tuning: History enables learners to achieve*	*QAA: History enables learners to achieve*
achieve a greater awareness of the contested nature of knowledge;	awareness of and ability to use tools of other human sciences (e.g., literary criticism, and history of language, art history, archaeology, anthropology, … etc.);	an understanding of the varieties of approaches to understanding, constructing, and interpreting; and, where relevant, a knowledge of concepts and theories derived from other disciplines;
achieve a greater awareness of how evidence is used in argument;	ability to comment, annotate or edit texts and documents correctly according to the critical canons of the discipline;	the ability to develop and sustain arguments in a variety of literary forms, formulating appropriate questions and utilizing evidence;
develop a perspective of the past that avoids interpreting past events in terms of current understandings;	a critical awareness of the relationship between current events and processes and the past;	an appreciation of the complexity of reconstructing the past, the problematic and varied nature of evidence;
gain a greater maturity of judgment which would encompass the ability to take different perspectives.	awareness of and respect for points of view deriving from other national or cultural backgrounds.	a command of comparative perspectives, which may include the ability to compare the different countries, societies, or cultures.

13 teachers from a different range of disciplines to say for each statement whether it was "relevant", "possible", or "irrelevant" for their undergraduates. In some cases specific content words were substituted with more generic words. All the Engineering statements were about "circuits", for example, but by substituting "circuit" with "system/case" all these ways of thinking and practicing could be rendered applicable to other areas. For example, the outcome:

- develop analytic skills, as complex systems/cases [circuits] have to be analyzed to understand how different parts operate in contributing to the whole was identified as relevant by teachers in math, philosophy, social science, and cognitive psychology. In some cases, this was not possible. For example the History statement:

- develop a perspective of the past that avoids interpreting past events in terms of current understandings

does not lend itself to a generic form, and all other teachers identified this one as irrelevant for their undergraduates.

Across subjects as diverse as math, sociology, philosophy, cognitive science, and computer science, four of the 43 ETL items were identified by the majority of teachers as "irrelevant", while 17 (40%) were seen as "relevant" by more than 75% of them. These were statements such as "the student should be able to":

- bring appropriate concepts and research findings to bear in developing solutions;
- build up a more sophisticated, differentiated picture of a particular area;
- communicate ideas in academically acceptable forms of expression and argument;
- develop thinking that is logical and analytic in abstracting the key elements of a problem;
- focus on the way in which theories and models help to make sense of the real world;
- master the types of critical thinking about evidence which will be expected of them in professional work in the field.

The commonality across disciplines of the relevance of these general statements of learning outcome is quite high, and suggests that although some learning outcomes are clearly unique to a subject discipline, there can be broad agreement on many of the aspirations for formal learning in terms of the cognitive competencies being developed. This is significant because it means there are high-level generic cognitive skills for formal learning that are common to all areas. Formal learning consists in more than "content" or "subject knowledge," as has been argued from the other viewpoints in this chapter. It also concerns the way that knowledge is developed and used by the individual, and this is a capability that transcends content and context.

We can certainly, as the ETL project suggests, reconceptualize the nature of formal learning as going beyond subject matter knowledge to "ways of thinking and practicing" within the discipline (Entwistle 2005). But we can go further, and use some of these statements to define the nature of formal learning in general. Of course there will be statements that are unique to a discipline, such as those in History that refer to the "diachronic framework of the past," but in general, teachers are not treating formal learning as being merely the acquisition of specialized subject knowledge. Every discipline is aiming for the same kinds of high-level cognitive skills, or "ways of thinking and practicing."

This is an important conclusion. We have to focus on how to help learners develop these ways of thinking and practicing, and this means a collaborative effort is possible: teachers can learn from other disciplines and share experiences and results. History teachers are not alone in the difficult challenge of enabling learners to "understand how evidence is used in argument." Most teachers find that relevant. In Engineering, students have to "grasp the function and mode of operation of a wide variety of different circuits," but by generalizing this to "a wide variety of different systems/cases" it becomes so generally applicable that teachers in math, computer science, and HCI also find it relevant. A collaborative approach to discovering what it takes to help learners achieve these high-level cognitive learning outcomes is feasible.

Summary

This chapter set out to clarify the nature of formal learning as a basis from which to improve the way we design teaching. There are clear stakeholder views on the aims of formal education and the nature of the learning to be done. We have explored a range of views to define the scope of what the following chapters must cover. To summarize, over the past decade or so, there has been a developing consensus about the nature of formal learning:

- For the educational establishment: formal learning is not just about the detailed understanding of systems of ideas and explanations of the natural and social world that a traditional curriculum offers. It embraces equally the high-level cognitive skills that the knowledge society requires of its professional workforce.
- From the point of view of the workplace: fostering high-level generic cognitive skills is more important than the specific knowledge base for many professional areas. There is a tension to be resolved between the specialized development of codified knowledge in a discipline and the broader workplace demand for generic cognitive skills.
- From the educational theorists' point of view: we need a careful balance of both specific discipline knowledge and generic cognitive skills. Specific knowledge will be peculiar to the discipline, but generic skills are widely applicable across the disciplines.
- From the teachers' point of view: a large part of the formal curriculum, as expressed in learning outcomes, is common across subject disciplines, so it is feasible for teachers across different discipline areas to collaborate on discovering what it takes to help learners achieve high-level cognitive learning outcomes.

This book is taking a generic view of teaching, so a degree of common interest across the disciplines is important. It means that we can use learning theories and practices in a common academic enterprise to help educational institutions enhance and develop their teaching and learning performance. In thinking about the design of teaching we have to contend with the educational goal, determined by our rapidly developing knowledge environment, of equipping students with the cognitive skills they will always need:

> More than ever, the sheer magnitude of human knowledge renders its coverage by education an impossibility; rather, the goal of education is better conceived as helping students develop the intellectual tools and learning strategies needed to acquire the knowledge that allows people to think productively about history, science and technology, social phenomena, mathematics, and the arts.
>
> (Bransford, Brown, and Cocking 2003: 5)

This chapter has covered a broad scope across the contending expectations of formal education, but in practice it is the relationship between teacher and learner that does most to achieve the demanding goals now set for education. Chapters 3 and 4 look at this from the learners' point of view – what students bring to learning, and how the demands of formal education impact on what it takes to learn. From this, Chapter 5 then analyzes what it takes to teach.

3 What Students Bring to Learning

Introduction

Having begun with a review of the wider context of expectations of what formal teaching must achieve, we now look at the wider context that students themselves bring to learning. This chapter surveys and summarizes the outcomes of studies of how this affects the quality of their learning.

Knowing our students will be a difficult problem as our mass education systems continue to require large class sizes, and that in a world where we are still so far from universal access even to primary education. Expansion of student numbers and an increase in educational access to all sectors is the aim in every country, although this is not commensurate with the expansion of teaching.

There are particular challenges for university teachers, who have to find a way of providing the teaching needed by a hugely diverse cohort of students, as class sizes can rise to hundreds and their cultural origins span the world. There is no foreseeable end to the dilemma of how to manage student-focused teaching in a mass higher education system. The expansion of student numbers includes a necessarily wider range of academic attainment as well as an internationalization of the student body. The Western university system has stuck resolutely to Western-oriented curricula, and has not really taken advantage of the multicultural opportunities these changes could have provided. So far this has been tolerated by the many different cultures represented in its student body, perhaps because they bring with them a respect for and an orientation towards academic achievement that outweighs the cultural divide they will undoubtedly experience (Otten 2003). The HE curriculum has had to become much broader in other ways, by responding to the diversity of professional jobs and the demands of globalization (Marginson and van der Wende 2007; Teichler 2004), and this is another trend likely to continue.

In all education sectors, knowing who our students are, and what they need from our teaching, has become so challenging that the hard-pressed teacher, busy with the task of continually renewing and updating the curriculum, tends to trust to the intelligence and motivation of the students themselves to construct the bridge between what they bring to their studies and where those studies are taking them.

Research on the influences on student learning in HE has investigated many different factors that contribute to the way students approach their studies. The literature refers to these as *presage* variables, (or *input* variables in the US) that will affect the *process* or *environment* variables of what happens during study, and in turn the *product* or *output* variables they lead to (Biggs 1993; Gibbs 2010). The relationships between them are complex, because "student characteristics" interact with the learning environment that the institution and the teachers provide (Entwistle and Peterson 2004). The characteristics identified as most salient are: (i) previous knowledge, self-confidence, abilities and motives; (ii) conceptions of knowledge and learning; (iii) approaches to learning and studying; and (iv) expectations. All these have in turn been influenced by the students' previous experiences of teaching and learning (Biggs 1993). This is not a uni-directional causal relation, as the interaction between the individual and their learning environment is inevitably an internal relation, where each helps to shape the other, for any learning context. A clear expression of this is in Bandura's account of why it is difficult to interpret the role of human agency:

> in an interpersonal transaction, in which people are each other's environments, a given action can be an agentic influence, a response, or an environmental outcome, depending arbitrarily on different entry points in the ongoing exchange between the people involved. In human transactions, one cannot speak of "environment," "behavior," and "outcomes" as though they were fundamentally different events with distinct features inherent in them.
>
> (Bandura 2006: 165)

The term "environment" is especially problematic, because while studies of students learning certainly attend to the learning environment, and are aware of the interrelationships between environment, behavior and outcomes, even the locations of the different kinds of "environment" inhabited by a student are not distinct. Students now move comfortably between the real and virtual worlds, and the virtual world does not separate work and leisure as clearly as the real world does. It raises the question of what counts as "the learning environment," and how much of it does the teacher take responsibility for?

This chapter reviews some of the key studies that offer insights into these issues, and considers what they mean for the teacher who is aiming to facilitate the progress of diverse learners towards a common learning outcome, and how the teacher might prepare for responding to what students bring. We will look at studies of the emotional characteristics of self-confidence and motivation, the intellectual characteristics of prior knowledge, conceptions, intellectual skills, and approaches to learning, and finally the contrasting informal contexts for learning that students experience alongside the formal context of education.

Student Engagement

The emotional engagement that students bring to their studies is the most elusive characteristic, because it is probably the least stable. We will not find in the studies here any clear guidance on how to manage such diverse experiences among students, but some of these insights will help to place the more academic considerations in context.

Self-Efficacy and Motivation

This section is entitled "student engagement" because the term focuses attention on why the emotional aspects of study are important. It is a useful term for embracing the motivation to study, students' sense of self-efficacy, and the role that emotional experiences play in learning. The work in psychology on the concept of "self-efficacy" makes a strong claim about its interrelationship with independent "self-regulated" learning in a digital culture:

> Students ... can use [internet] resources for educating themselves ... This shift in the locus of initiative requires a major reorientation in students' conception of education. They are agents of their own learning, not just recipients of information. Education for self-directedness is now vital for a productive and innovative society. Proficient self-regulators gain knowledge, skills, and intrinsic interest in academic areas; deficient self-regulators achieve limited self-development ... At the student, teacher, and school levels, a sense of efficacy contributes to academic development ... We are entering a new era in which the construction of knowledge will rely increasingly on electronic inquiry. Students with high perceived efficacy for self-regulated learning are the ones who make the best use of Internet-based instruction.
>
> (Bandura 2006)

Students may have a strong sense of self-efficacy born of their internet capabilities, and may bring this to bear on their approach to study. But a sense of self-efficacy is context-dependent, influencing and influenced by their experiences within an environment, and does not necessarily carry over from general internet activities to education. A student's "perceived efficacy for self-regulated learning" has to be developed through their successive encounters with a formal learning environment in which they are encouraged to be an agent of their own learning, and able to develop their capacity for self-regulation. The implication for teachers is to be aware of the importance of self-efficacy for the student's academic experience and to foster a context in which they can develop it, using the basic principles to:

- help students maintain relatively high but accurate self-efficacy beliefs;
- provide students with challenging academic tasks that most students can reach with effort;

- foster the belief that competence or ability is a changeable, controllable aspect of development;
- promote students' domain specific self-efficacy beliefs rather than global self-esteem (Linnenbrink and Pintrich 2003).

What we can take from Bandura, and the work that follows his approach, is the importance of enabling students to become "proficient self-regulators" with respect to their academic learning; they may become proficient in using the internet independently of their education, but they are still likely to need help in applying those skills to the context of formal learning. In education, they are indeed not "just recipients of information," but the internet does not educate, nor does it actively support learning. Mostly, it provides information. So to be able to use academic resources, internet-based or otherwise, students have to become highly proficient self-regulators, using the kind of high-level cognitive skill the knowledge society requires, discussed in Chapter 2. It is part of the job of formal education to enable that.

Motivation to Study

Chapter 2 established the different purposes of a formal education, so it is inevitable that students will have different reasons for continuing post-compulsory education. In broad terms the forms of "motivation" or "orientation" to study are classified as:

- *intrinsic* – focusing on the content or process of learning itself to develop a deep understanding of the subject, and a sense of self efficacy in relation to it; or
- *extrinsic* – focusing on the rewards that result from academic study in terms of vocational or social advantage.

These are elaborated further as four categories of "academic" or "personal," and "vocational" or "social" forms of motivation, which have remained fairly stable in the literature (Beaty, Gibbs, and Morgan 1997; Entwistle, McCune, and Hounsell 2003). Intrinsic academic orientation is the one that teachers will identify with most, because it refers to the study of the subject for its own sake, for the intellectual challenge and fascination it offers, and a hunger to understand how the world works. Taken to extremes, it is the kind of orientation that leads students away from the specific demands of the course, to follow their own lines of interest, so unless balanced with a degree of extrinsic vocational motivation, the students may even fail in their exams. Most students have a mix of orientations, and for many the focus is not the subject, but the other advantages of a university education. They may even fulfill their personal goals without satisfying course demands – this is often a concern at the Open University, that students are content to study the course assiduously without taking the exam because, for example, they were not interested in the qualification, but in learning about French. Motivation to study is not an immutable property of a student, but describes "the relationship between the individual, and both the course of study, the institution and indeed the world beyond the university. It can also change and develop over time" (Beaty, Gibbs, and Morgan 1997: 86).

The implication is that the course of study itself can influence the way the student perceives their expectations. This work does not imply that students need different types of teaching according to their form of motivation, but that teaching can shape their motivation, to become more balanced across both intrinsic and extrinsic forms, and across personal, social, intellectual, and vocational outcomes.

The Role of Emotional Engagement

Knowing who our students are, and what sense of self-efficacy and motivation they bring to a course, means we can adapt to their needs more readily. A study of young entrants from families with no history of HE, for example, shows that the categories "intrinsic" and "extrinsic" motivation have to be elaborated to account for the feelings associated with early experiences of university study (Haggis and Pouget 2002). There were negative feelings of alienation resulting from school experiences, linked to the absence of effective strategies for dealing with formal learning, even though they wanted to work hard and do well. Unable always to find an intrinsic interest in what they were studying, these students had no study techniques to fall back on to sustain their extrinsic motivation to do well. The study showed that an access course, which helped them reflect on the process of study, and provided support in the form of companionship with other students in the same position, was successful in turning around the negative feelings, and enabled the students to develop stronger study strategies.

> With a much wider range of students, there is arguably a need for a shift from assumptions about ability, support and "spoon-feeding" towards the recognition of a need for much greater clarity and explicitness about the approaches and attitudes that higher expectation teaching currently assumes. Teaching that engages in explicit discussion and modelling of desired approaches and styles of thought could ease the pressure on the perceived need for "support" by dealing with students' confusion and disorientation in the working contexts of specific subjects and actual writing tasks, at the time they are experienced.
>
> (Haggis and Pouget 2002: 332)

The process of acculturation to a particular style of thinking and discussing is what makes university life engaging and memorable for so many students who pass through it. The emphasis on "modeling" academic behavior is important here, because that is one of the principal ways of accessing what it means to be academic, for students who have not come from a clearly academic environment.

> "'Support', for these students, was not something 'extra', provided by a learning centre detached from their mainstream courses, but the way in which tutors both taught their subjects, and interacted with the students on an individual level.
>
> (Haggis and Pouget 2002: 333)

The value of the social role of the teacher for the large number of students who struggle with the process of formal learning suggests that we must make explicit these other ways in which teaching supports the acculturation to academic ways of thinking and practicing.

We must be careful in our interpretation of students' needs with respect to their orientation to study (Entwistle and Smith 2002; Honkimäki, Tynjl, and Valkonen 2004), as it may disguise the wide variation in learner experience that lies behind the "established 'academic/liberal' versus 'vocational/instrumental' framings" (Haggis 2004: 346). Individual students' stories are highly complex, entangling school, home, work, and social encounters in the individual's perception of self as learner. This is part of what they bring to learning. But adapting to diverse student backgrounds, knowledge and aspirations is problematic (Hounsell and Entwistle 2005), and would be unrealistic and unmanageable for the teacher of a large class. What we can take away from this profusion of diversity is the default assumption that all students would like to be successful learners, given the right conditions, but they may often need a lot more clarity, encouragement, and opportunity to discover how to be the learner they could be (Haggis and Pouget, 2002).

Engagement and Learning

Studies of "motivation" and "orientation" to study have been elaborated further by the broader concept of "engagement". Research on student engagement is underpinned by the constructivist view that education is fundamentally about students constructing their own knowledge, and it is the role of institutions and staff to generate the conditions that stimulate and encourage student involvement in learning (Umbach and Wawrzynsk 2005). This study used two large surveys to examine the relationship between teachers' accounts of their behavior, and the perspectives of their students. The conclusion was clear:

> The educational context created by faculty behaviors and attitudes has a dramatic effect on student learning and engagement. Institutions where faculty create an environment that emphasizes effective educational practices have students who are active participants in their learning and perceive greater gains from their undergraduate experience.
>
> (Umbach and Wawrzynsk 2005: 173)

The effective educational practices that were found to engage students more deeply in their studies are those where teachers:

- use active and collaborative learning techniques, and students teach each other, or work on projects together;
- offer a higher level of academic challenge to write more clearly, do repeated drafts of a paper, to integrate ideas and information from a variety of sources;
- emphasize higher-order cognitive activities, thinking critically and analytically, synthesizing ideas into new interpretations, solving complex real-world problems;
- engage students in enriching co-curricular experiences of community work, practicums, internships, fieldwork studies, foreign language coursework;
- engage in high levels of course-related interactions with their students, such as discussing assignment grades, using email for communication, and discussing career plans.

In several of these teacher practices we can discern the ambitions of the learning outcomes discussed in the Chapter 2. The surveys of student engagement demonstrate the unsurprising finding that students are more likely to engage in the kinds of learning activities that lead to higher-level outcomes if the teaching they experience demands and supports such activities.

Teaching and Student Engagement

Entwistle's conceptual model of influences on students' level of understanding brings teacher and student perceptions and actions together, with motivation mediating between *a student's perception of the teaching* and *the outcomes they achieve* with respect to the teacher's target outcomes:

> The teacher's target is interpreted by the students through the filter of their existing knowledge and personal histories, including their attitudes, beliefs, and self-concepts. All of these affect their motivation and approach to studying within the classroom, their comprehension of the target, and their perception of the learning context. These three components then influence the learning strategies, effort, and engagement that students show in carrying out the task, resulting in a personal understanding of the topic which is then evaluated by the teacher or examiner.
>
> (Entwistle and Smith 2002: 335)

There is a complex interrelationship, therefore, between the teacher's design and implementation of the course, and what the student brings to the course. The analysis offers a framework that clarifies what kind of influence the teacher has. We can place other educational research outcomes within the framework, to illustrate these influences in more detail. For example, the way teachers conceptualize their teaching affects how students respond to a course, in particular the extent to which the teachers appear to care about their students (Hannon *et al.* 2002). Teachers can play a nurturing role for the whole student group, creating the sense of belonging to a shared endeavor that can change student perception of the nature of academic work. In a constructive and cooperative learning environment the teacher can be demanding without creating a perception of high workload (Kember and Leung 2006).

The overall implication of this section is that the teacher can make a real difference to a student's emotional response to a course. If they foster a sense of self-efficacy, encourage a balance of orientations to study, and use educational practices that engage, nurture, and challenge their students, their students can develop the confidence to become effective learners.

Intellectual Characteristics

The previous section highlighted the close relationship between the emotional and intellectual aspects of formal learning. Now we look at studies of the intellectual aspects in more detail. From the teacher's point of view the most important intellectual characteristic is what a student knows about their subject, although the range of conceptions and misconceptions that students exhibit is not itself the focus of these studies. What students know is seen as an emergent property of how they come to know it. So research studies have coalesced around two main aspects: the student's conception of the nature of formal knowledge (whether it is dualistic or relativistic), and their approach to study (what contribution they expect to make to the process of learning).

Conceptions of Knowledge

It was an interesting idea to make a study of what students thought about the nature of knowledge. This is the concern of philosophers, and probably would not have entered easily into educational research without the insights of Harvard student counselor, William Perry. From his work with students who needed support during their studies he developed a longitudinal account of the intellectual development they went through, formalized by selecting a group who were interviewed at length, once a year for four years. This long term methodology enabled Perry to discern a clear maturational process in how students thought about knowledge, and the sense of responsibility they had for what they knew – the intellectual and ethical dimensions of development (Perry 1970). The understanding he derived from a large group of individuals he came to know well over the years enabled him to define a scheme of nine distinct stages of development, to describe the many different individual pathways he observed among his students. This heavily nuanced account of intellectual development is too complex to have survived as a useful tool for teachers to use, but the fundamental insight is important: that students progress, broadly, from

1. a dualistic position of knowledge as right or wrong being the responsibility of an authority, to
2. an open view of knowledge as a multiplicity of positions of equal value, to
3. a relativistic view of knowledge as contextualized, requiring a personal commitment to aligning it with one's own values.

Progress was not necessarily forwards: sometimes it was possible to find students who regressed to earlier stages in the light of their perceptions of the teaching. This three-stage simplification of the Perry stages has been taken further in the literature, and has informed the development of further studies.

If the teacher wants to develop an inquiring mind in a student, they must be aware that some students see themselves as having no part to play in challenging the received view. This point is established by more recent studies that build on Perry's work to find out how students' conceptions of knowledge relate to the teaching context (Marra and Palmer 2004). Students answered survey questions about their conception of knowledge, and through interviews related this to their perception of the teaching. The critical difference between different types of students seems to be how the student describes their role in relation to what they are learning:

- If a student perceives a vast body of knowledge to be acquired, then mastery of it is seen as a struggle, for which they need help from the teacher to minimize what needs to be done.
- If a student sees knowledge as a means for acting in the world, where there are alternative ways of conceptualizing a particular context and their role is to take responsibility for how they use knowledge in that context, then they are in a good position to know what they need from the teacher.

This contrast is reminiscent of the work on self-efficacy, because the intellectually more immature student has not yet developed the confidence that enables them to take more control of what and how they learn. The result is that students with lower ratings on the Perry dimensions (PL) are less likely than those with higher ratings (PH) to take advantage of an education that encourages a broader contextual view of what is being taught:

> This difference is understandable given their differing levels of intellectual development. The PL students are still holding on to a view of the world that ultimately has right and wrong answers. In such a world, a knowledge of context is unnecessary. The PH students have made the shift to viewing knowledge as relative and contextual, so therefore, exposure to

experiences, both inside and outside the classroom, that contribute to their understandings of contexts are valuable and indeed, for these students, worth investing energy and time.

(Marra and Palmer 2004: 121)

And better still, the study drew the cheering conclusion that both groups benefitted from teaching and learning experiences where they were guided through work that put the new knowledge into real-world contexts; and students valued the sense of progressing from dependency on the teacher to independent responsibility for using the knowledge they were gaining. To have a sustained impact on students who are still developing towards the higher levels of orientation, however, the teaching has to continue to provide these project-based opportunities as otherwise it will encourage a return to the lower levels, as Perry documented himself (Wise *et al.* 2004).

There is no difference between the disciplines here – as we saw in Chapter 2, teachers' intentions are similar: the learning outcome "achieve a greater awareness of the contested nature of knowledge" is relevant to all subject areas. Is this carried through their teaching to be reflected in the student body?

Another study in this area sought to investigate the difference between disciplines by looking at a group of students in science and engineering who were also studying humanities subjects. Survey items located the students' level of orientation on the Perry dimensions, and then did follow-up interviews. The study showed that the epistemological shift from dualistic to multiple perspectives was harder to achieve in science than in social science for half the students (26/52), but that the shift from this to the relativistic level was more common in science. Only four students were at the upper end of orientation towards a more contextualized view of knowledge in both areas, which is what a good education should be aiming for (Palmer and Marra 2004). The teaching in the two areas did not have the same impact across this group of students, suggesting that a Perry level of orientation may not characterize a student, but a student in the context of a particular style of teaching. Their own intellectual development is contextualized – it builds according to the learning opportunities provided.

Science and engineering are taught with much more emphasis on what is known, than on the contextualized perspectives that are common in the teaching of the social sciences. One student quote captures this neatly: "In engineering there's always an answer. And in philosophy there's never an answer". This is a reflection of the way students are asked to engage with those subjects, which in turn reflects the way the development of knowledge is practiced – engineering seeks a workable solution to a problem while philosophy seeks ways of conceptualizing a problem. A student's epistemological orientation may not be consistent across the different subject areas they encounter at any one moment in time.

We know then, that our students are continually developing their intellectual and personal orientation towards the knowledge they are gaining, and their role in using it. We know also that teaching has an impact, but that intellectual development takes place over years, and is an iterative process of maturation in response to the teaching and learning opportunities that present themselves. Above all, this cannot be taught in a didactic way. Perry puts it best:

> We cannot push anyone to develop, or "get them to see" or "impact" them. The causal metaphors hidden in English verbs give us a distracting vocabulary for pedagogy. The tone is Lockean and provocative of resistance. We can provide, we can design opportunities. We can create settings in which students who are ready will be more likely to make new kinds of sense.
>
> (Perry 1988: 159–160)

The intellectual characteristics students bring to learning are forged by their previous educational experiences. This is important because their conception of knowledge influences how they use the teaching available, but they will also have developed cognitive skills and ways of approaching their study, which we look at next.

Approaches to Learning

There is a wide literature now that sets out to capture the approaches to learning that can be found in a student population. The stability of these for any individual student is unclear, but we should expect that. The point of education, after all, is to develop the individual; it should be possible for every student to go beyond one particular approach to study, inspired by the teaching and by the learning activities they engage in, and become an independent, inquiring, and versatile learner.

A recent comprehensive study compared several categories of learning styles defined in the literature, and points out that while a mismatch of learning style with teaching may be uncomfortable, a match does not stretch the student. The optimal teaching style provides a balance that both supports and stretches all the students in a class, to enable them to develop (Felder and Brent 2005). Some students will need support from the teacher to adapt to an unmatched style of teaching. This is clear from a study of approaches to discussion learning, for example. Students who are not aware of the benefits of discussing, or reflecting on, and revising their ideas "tended not to approach either face-to-face or online discussions in ways likely to improve their understanding or their levels of achievement" (Ellis *et al.* 2007). Students do choose to avoid these teaching techniques:

> Because of their conceptions of learning and instruction many students are not willing or able to carry out the activities presupposed in many learning environments based on constructivist principles, preferring

instead to cope with learning situations using strategies suitable for more direct instruction and teacher control.

> (Lowyck, Lehtinen, and Elen 2004: 403)

Students may take from the teaching only what suits their existing habits, ideas and preferences for learning and study (Vermetten, Vermunt, and Lodewijks 2002). But where do these habits and ideas come from? The student is continually interacting with their context of study, and the way the learning environment is organized around them. Their habits and ideas about what it takes to learn develop within this context, which clearly helps to influence the direction of that development.

The Role of the Teaching Environment

The main work on the role of the teaching environment concludes that the principal influences on quality of learning are students' approaches to learning and studying, and their perceptions of how the teaching-learning environment is designed (Entwistle and Peterson 2004). The illustrative diagram of these influences in Figure 3.1 shows that approach affects learning.

The diagram also shows that the nature of the teaching affects approach, as we saw in the study of engagement and learning:

> University teachers using approaches indicating a student-oriented approach to teaching and a focus on student learning (as opposed to a transmission approach) are more likely to have, in their classes, students who describe themselves as adopting a deep approach in their studying.
>
> (Entwistle and Peterson 2004: 422)

Similar studies agree that students' perceptions of their learning context are not stable, but develop continuously in response to that context (Lowyck, Elen, and Clarebout 2004). Because of the recognition that "students can also adapt their ways of tackling academic work to circumstances" (Entwistle and McCune 2004: 333), recent survey studies of these relationships have included questions relating to reflection, meta-cognition, and self-regulation, which track the extent to which students adjust their study strategies to their perceptions of the teaching and assessment context.

The overall conclusion from the comparison of six study inventory surveys (Entwistle and McCune 2004) is that three principal dimensions are needed to describe the intellectual characteristics that students bring to learning, each of which encapsulates intentions, motives, and processes of learning and studying:

- The "deep approach" is focused on understanding, aiming for meaningful learning, using critical thinking, relating and structuring ideas, reflective/ elaborative processing, constructing knowledge, and use of evidence.

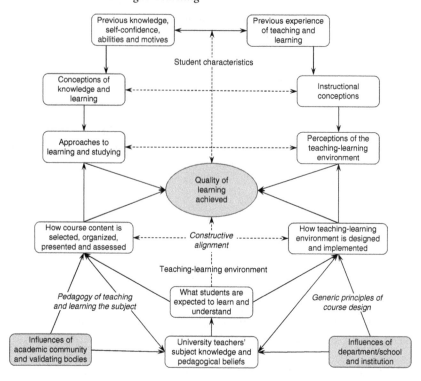

Figure 3.1 Conceptual framework showing influences on student learning.

Source: Redrawn from Entwistle and Peterson, 2004.

- The surface approach is focused on reproducing, where learning is the intake of knowledge, memorizing without understanding, repeating analyses already carried out, unthinking acceptance of ideas, syllabus-bound fragmented knowledge, extrinsically motivated by external regulation.
- The strategic approach to studying is focused on achieving, being aware of study requirements, self-regulating through careful time management, concentrating, and on working hard and systematically.

This research programme is important because it illuminates for the teacher how their students' intentions, perceptions, and motivations influence their approaches to study. The research demonstrates that teaching methods and forms of presentation can affect all these dimensions. The most effective teaching methods seem to be those that:

- guide students towards independent learning;
- situate the application of knowledge in different contexts;
- stretch students beyond their preferred styles; and
- encourage reflection and self-regulation.

The teacher is responsible for much more than the knowledge and skills to be taught – they have to create an environment that nurtures all their students through all the stages of intellectual development mapped by Perry's original work.

Formal and Informal Learning Contexts

Having put the onus on the teacher to develop the right context for developing intellectually, we now have to acknowledge that the student's environment for learning extends well beyond the formal institution. Two types of learning environment, formal and informal, are beginning to merge as the use of social technologies blurs the boundaries between learning within and beyond the institution. So are students now bringing new contexts to their studies, which could distort or perhaps complement the learning environment their teachers offer?

Formal and Informal Learning

One thread that runs through all these discussions is the distinction between the learning we do in the context of education, and the learning we do for ourselves. This has most recently emerged as the contrast between "formal" and "informal" learning, especially in the context of workplace learning (Eraut 2004; Marsick 2006), although the idea has been discussed by learning theorists for some time.

Vygotsky, writing in the 1930s, and critiquing Piaget, recognized a fundamental difference between the two types of learning: "It goes without saying that learning as it occurs in the preschool years differs markedly from school learning, which is concerned with the assimilation of the fundamentals of scientific knowledge" (Vygotsky 1978: 84).

While Piaget referred to "spontaneous" and "non-spontaneous" concepts to differentiate the two, Vygotsky usually referred to the latter as "scientific" concepts, in the broadest sense of "scientific", aligning these concepts with "systematic knowledge" in all disciplines. He argued that scientific/non-spontaneous concepts need special investigation, as we cannot assume that they are learned in the same way as spontaneous concepts. However, although the two types of concept are distinct, and "may be expected to follow different developmental paths from their inception to their final form" (Vygotsky 1962: 86), unlike Piaget, he also argued that they were interdependent, and "must influence each other's evolution" (Vygotsky 1962: 87). Vygotsky saw scientific formal learning (of concepts such as slavery, exploitation, or civil war) as different but not separate from spontaneous informal learning, and expressed the unity of the two in terms of their interdependence and mutual value. For him, the nature of formal learning is that its concepts are systematic and need to be mediated by a teacher, because they do not come from spontaneous experience.

We have to differentiate between studying *informal learning* about the world, which is the domain of the psychologist or sociologist or anthropologist, and studying *formal learning* about others' descriptions of the world, which is the educationist's domain (Laurillard 1987).

Formal learning is made possible through language, which is how we get access to the concepts that others have developed. Research in cognitive neuroscience tells us that the human brain has evolved to enable us to communicate successfully, so that we can learn from the experience and ideas of others:

> In a successful communication the point is reached where my model of your meaning matches my own meaning ... By building models of the mental world, our brains have solved the problem of how to get inside the minds of others.
>
> (Frith 2007: 175)

This is precisely what teacher and student are trying to achieve. And from the cognitive scientist's point of view this is what education succeeds in doing:

> Some people are experts who clearly have better models of some aspects of the world. By putting together the models of many people, we can construct a new model that is better than any model produced by a single individual. And our knowledge of the world is no longer derived from a single lifetime – knowledge passes from one generation to the next.
>
> (Ibid.: 181)

It makes education sound like an impressively successful process. From the educationist's point of view, however, we have to look more deeply into what this means. The idea of education as the transmission of knowledge from one generation to the next may be a reasonable approximation at this general level of description, but if we focus on the individual learner trying to grapple with the complex ideas put together by the experts, we have to recognize that for many students the knowledge does not transmit very successfully. Frith's characterization helps to clarify why learning about the world is so different from learning about others' descriptions of the world: it takes an expert to develop a model that the rest of us have not been expert enough to develop, and then it takes combinations of these models to develop the account we then have to learn as students. It is no wonder the knowledge is not always transmitted successfully. That is why it takes more than telling to teach. Language alone is not enough.

Why Formal Learning is Difficult

The point about academic knowledge is that, being formalized and articulated, it is known through exposition, argument, and interpretation. Knowledge derived from experiencing the world at one remove must be accessed differently from that known through a first-order experience. As neuroscience tells us, our brains have evolved to develop our first-order knowledge of the world from the earliest stages of infancy. The developmental psychologist's view of learning accounts for the ways in which we all succeed in developing our first-order knowledge of the world we experience. The educationist's view tries to understand why we do not fully succeed in learning the second-order knowledge of the world as described by others (Laurillard 2002). While the psychologist will investigate and celebrate the power of every human brain to learn how to apply the correct force to the muscles of the arm and hand to pick up a cup, the educationist has to grapple with the problem that very few human minds ever grasp the proper Newtonian concept of force. This fundamental scientific idea cannot be accessed in the same way as the everyday concept of force, and our brains have not evolved to cope. Informal, spontaneous, developmental learning is immensely successful. Formal, scientific, educational learning is at best only moderately successful.

For the psychology of learning to influence education, researchers and teachers have to work out how to organize the learning environment in such a way that the learning mechanisms we have evolved can be recruited to deal with these complex and sophisticated descriptions of the world. Telling the learner the account of the new knowledge will often not be an effective way for them to learn. This is why we need teachers, not just books. Learning in an educational context, formal learning, requires more than mere telling. Teachers have to understand what it takes to learn in this different context. As Säljö points out:

> Institutional learning is, to a large extent, to be understood as a systematic shortcut to insights that may never occur in individuals unless there is a rather systematic assistance in the processes of foregrounding perspectives, introducing concepts and discussing models.
>
> (Säljö 2004: 492)

That "rather systematic assistance" is the special contribution of the teacher, sometimes called "pedagogy," sometimes now called "learning design." The need for it shows that formal learning remains fundamentally different from informal learning.

What does this mean for the posited "blurring of the boundaries" between formal and informal learning, and the role of the teacher? In the informal learning environment of work or leisure, the learner is the key agent, conducting the progress of their own learning in relation to their personal goals and peer interactions, and the teacher has no direct influence or responsibility (Laurillard 2007). The teacher's responsibility is to be aware of that informal learning environment, value it, and make use of it, but also be aware that it is not necessarily in alignment with the formal learning environment they are trying to construct. Precisely because there are strong internal relationships between environment, behavior and outcome in which "people are each others' environments" (Bandura 2006), the boundaries do not blur completely. The two types of learning environment, formal and informal, each constitute a coherent blending of goals, activities, people, opportunities, and outcomes. Students learn different things in different ways in the two contexts, and may not be able to build a bridge between the two. The apparent technical link provided by the virtual world we all now inhabit does not necessarily blur the intellectual boundaries of formal and informal learning. So the teacher still has to work hard to help the learner make connections between their formal learning and the contexts it must draw on, and in which they hope it will be applied. In Chapter 10 we look at the ways in which the technology can assist them to do this.

What students bring to their studies is a mix of conceptions, skills, and motivations from their experiences of informal learning. The point of formal education is to help students develop greater efficacy in the physical and social world outside the institution. The teacher creating the formal learning environment has the responsibility to make that connection, but must do so in the knowledge that informal learning environments are an effective and powerful force for learning, and have their own quite separate agendas. The theory of the relationship between formal and informal learning is still undeveloped (Sharples, Taylor, and Vavoula 2007). We need one, because the virtual environments in which students operate in education, work, and leisure are more easily integrated than their equivalent physical environments. That simple fact means that these boundaries will certainly begin to break down, and teachers need to find ways to use this intriguing opportunity rather than be marginalized by it.

Summary

This chapter has shown that in designing courses and teaching it is important to be aware of the characteristics students bring with them, because they act as a filter that comes between our careful designs and the way these are experienced by the students. The interrelationships are complex, and mutually interdependent.

The emotional characteristics a student brings to their study change in response to the way the teacher interacts with students, and the way they nurture a sense of belonging and group cohesion. It seems that students are more likely to engage in learning activities that lead to higher-level outcomes if the teaching they experience demands activities such as collaboration, critical thinking, and practical applications, which explicitly model the high-level learning outcomes we sought in Chapter 2.

A student's intellectual characteristics may be shaped by their previous educational experiences, but these are not immutable because they will continue to be shaped by what they find in their current educational context. Effective teaching guides students towards independent learning, and situates the application of knowledge in different contexts, thereby stretching students beyond their current approach to learning, and encouraging reflection and self-regulation. The teacher has to create an environment that nurtures their students through all the stages of intellectual development from a reliance on authority for the truth to a sense of personal responsibility for what may be known within certain contexts.

What students also bring to their studies is the mix of conceptions, skills, and motivations from their experiences of informal learning. The teacher can help the learner make connections between their formal learning and the contexts they must draw on, and in which they hope it will be applied. To the extent that technology is a common environment for both formal and informal learning it may become possible for teachers to make clearer connections between theory and its practical applications in more direct ways, as we discuss in later chapters.

The generalized relationships discussed here do not immediately suggest a plan of action for the teacher trying to provide the best for each individual student, because their developmental trajectory may not conform to the norm (Haggis 2004). It is valuable instead to use these studies to be aware of the complexity of different attitudes, motives, and ways of thinking likely to be represented in the student cohort. However, the conclusions from all these studies are very similar: students' intellectual and emotional development will be strongly influenced by what teachers provide and demand, and this in turn will shape their ability to become the confident independent learners we want them to be.

4 What it Takes to Learn

Introduction

We know from the studies in Chapter 3 that what happens during the process of a student learning is dependent on what they perceive and expect of the learning environment designed by the teacher. But what is actually going on during that process? Before we can develop an effective approach to learning design in Chapter 5, we need a sense of the student's experience of learning – what are they doing, what are they trying to do, why are they doing it that way, and what are they not doing? The chapter is titled "what it takes to learn" to emphasize the focus on what the learner has to *do*, if they are to learn effectively.

Chapter 3 elaborated the relevant features a student might bring to a learning session. We now consider what happens in the process of learning itself, in order to understand the role the teacher can play in optimizing the experience for the learner. The teacher as designer has to shape the learning environment to ensure that effective learning takes place, but what counts as effective learning?

What Happens in Learning

The last century or so of research in psychology and education has seen the gradual development of a consensus around what it takes to learn in formal education. In Chapter 3 I argued that a peculiarity of academic learning is to focus, not on the world itself, but on others' descriptions of that world. There is a profound division between the psychologist's interest in how humans learn in general, and the educationist's interest in how humans learn to read, or do arithmetic, or understand physics, or analyze historical data. Psychology is the science of how we all learn about an environment from which we are adapted to learn (Frith 2007). Education is the design of an environment which will help others learn what experts have articulated (Laurillard 1987).

Theories of learning in psychology are not easy to adapt to the classroom, because they did not originate there. But these alternative ways of conceptualizing learning as a fundamental aspect of human cognition contribute to our understanding of formal learning in education. Each theorist takes care to differentiate their approach from those that have preceded them, of course, but we gain most from an integrated account of formal learning that harnesses as many perspectives as possible in our attempt to understand and improve this highly complex human activity.

Although there have been battles between the successive "isms" of learning theories, they are not strictly mutually exclusive. It is possible to build on the ideas and findings from behaviorism, instructionism, constructivism, social constructivism, situated learning, and constructionism to develop a reasonably coherent and comprehensive account of learning in formal education. It can be argued that the time has come, after a century of distinctive strands of learning theories, to seek a greater synergy across studies of learning in different disciplines.

> What we witnessed a decade ago was paradigm debates between information-processing theorists and situated learning theorists. However, the debate seems to have ended with a discussion of how theories are more alike than different.
>
> (Lajoie and Azevedo 2006)

By bringing together what we know about the different approaches to understanding learning we should be able to build a more robust understanding of what it takes to learn in education (Bransford *et al.* 2006). Each of the principal theories of learning has something to contribute, and together they provide a comprehensive account of what it takes to learn. To what extent can they be synthesized?

Behaviourism

Because Behaviourism concerns itself with the product and not the process of learning, it has a different focus from formal learning. It is about learning to exhibit certain behaviors, and it tells us that behavior can be manipulated through "operant conditioning" without needing to understand how the mechanism of learning takes place. That is of use to education only to a limited extent. But educators cannot dismiss Behaviourism as irrelevant. We certainly use marks, grades, credits, and qualifications as rewards intended to motivate students to focus on studying and revising. When exam scores and league tables are the principal goal, then it does not matter how those grades are achieved. If students find a way of passing exams by using the mechanisms of memorizing and parroting, that is sufficient. But formal learning has higher goals, as we know from Chapter 2. Our intention is to help students become independent learners, confident in what they know and responsible for how they come to know it. To be able to do this, teachers must take responsibility themselves for the process of coming to know, and need to know what it involves. Behaviorism gives us no help with this.

Associative Learning

Associative learning is of more interest to educators because it derives from the work of Pavlov and Thorndike, who did concern themselves with the process of learning as a physiological mechanism. The famous experiments with Pavlov's dog tell us that when a stimulus, such as a sound, is experienced prior to a desired goal, such as food, the brain learns to associate the sound with the expected consequence, which leads to the conditioned response of salivating prior to eating. A similar process leads to learned actions to achieve a goal. Thorndike's cat could learn to pull a string to access food through trial and error, after trying many other behaviors, such as scratching, biting, squeezing; when it accidentally pulled the string once, this became an action that was more and more likely to be repeated on subsequent trials, until it became a learned action to achieve the goal. This "connectionism" account is more useful than "operant conditioning" because it does offer an account of the process of learning.

The trial-and-error learning process that enables associative learning is now the basis of neural network models that successfully model phenomena such as learning to recognize different images, or to distinguish phonemes. This has clear relevance to education in the early years of learning basic skills. An understanding of how the brain learns to accomplish these skills efficiently can help us work out the optimal sequence of tasks to give young learners as part of the pedagogy of teaching reading and arithmetic. This would benefit adult learners with learning difficulties as well. There are many high-functioning dyslexics and dyscalculics in academic life, for example, who have somehow overcome the early learning difficulties that neuroscience is now helping us to understand (Frith 2011). Intelligent and ambitious people often find compensatory strategies for dealing with inherited disabilities, but many do not. The whole-class teaching methods in primary school leave behind many pupils with low numeracy or low literacy capabilities. It is possible that associative models of learning could give us a better understanding of how to help learners with a learning process that is not automatic for them. They seem to need more than mainstream teaching methods offer.

There are many basic skills that affect our ability to take part in expert-level thinking – word processing, number-sense, envisaging three dimensions, hearing musical notes, hand-eye coordination – an inability in any of these areas could prevent adult learners from continuing their education along a certain path in their domain of study. Current developments in cognitive neuroscience could help to improve our understanding of how these fundamental capabilities are acquired, and the different ways they can fail to be acquired. That could enable teachers to assist learners in developing the compensatory strategies they need to overcome natural cognitive disabilities. Even university-level teaching, which has got beyond basic skills, has to assist students with specific cognitive disabilities that are not related to intelligence. It is important that all teachers are aware of this fundamental aspect of the way the brain learns, and in some areas fails to learn, irrespective of the learner's age or wider potential.

Cognitive Learning

The principal counter to the behaviorist approach to learning began with the Gestalt psychologists who emphasized the importance of a cognitivist approach that would account better for the success of associative learning. How could trial and error alone be sufficient as a mechanism? Why is the cat more likely to pull the string in later trials? They accounted for this by suggesting that the learner uses a success to think differently about the situation: to make a holistic structural reorganization of it that allows a link to be made between the action and its consequence (Wertheimer 1959). Modern neuroscientists answer the same question by suggesting that the connections in a neural pathway strengthen in response to the success of a random trial action, making it more likely that the same pathway will connect when the same situation reoccurs (Frith 2007) – which is a nicely explicit version of the idea of a holistic structural reorganization of that experience.

Gestalt psychologists extended the idea of structural reorganization to focus on the importance of meaningfulness to the learner. This was not an unconscious neural mechanism, but a conscious process that enabled the learner to make sense of the relationship between the goal, their action and its result. This kind of approach to learning had much more to offer teaching. Wertheimer in particular applied the structural approach to teaching, and was able to offer explicit recommendations, e.g. that the rule for finding an area of a rectangle should not be taught directly; instead the learner should be offered a meaningful problem to solve, such as how to determine which farmer has the larger field, as part of which they may discover, or be helped to discover, a way to determine the respective areas of the fields. This enables learners to build their own structural organization of the situation in which the solution path becomes apparent.

Experiential Learning

To take this idea even closer to the implications for teaching, we have to go back in time to Dewey's characterization of learning through experience, earlier in the century. The reader who prefers a quick introduction to the nature of the formal learning process should simply read anything written by John Dewey, whose insights have scarcely been improved upon in the subsequent near-century of educational research. There is surprisingly little to be found in the literature today that has no counterpart in his writings.

Dewey, like Wertheimer, argued that the learner's own organization of the problem situation is what enables them to develop new knowledge within a curriculum, just as they do in their untaught, informal learning about the world: hence his focus on experiential learning. Education must find the materials for learning within the learner's own experience. No matter what their age or stage, the learner will continually develop their knowledge through attempting to work through realistic experiential problems involving "the formation of ideas, acting upon ideas, observation of the conditions which result, and organization of facts and ideas for future use" (Dewey 1938: 88). These new facts and ideas form the basis for further experiences in which the teacher can present new problems, to be dealt with in the same way, the process being a continuous spiral guiding the learner through the ever-expanding curriculum of that domain. The task for the teacher is to plot the appropriate sequence of realistic experiential problems for their learners.

Can the learner do it without the teacher? The brain has developed to learn through imitation, in the sense that our perception of an action triggers a pattern of brain activity in the same motor areas that will control the action itself. We interpret the goal of the action and mentally rehearse what we have to do to achieve it, which is a very efficient way of dealing with the problem, much better than trial and error. When we then generate the action we will often find that it misses the mark – the sound I make by drawing a bow across a violin string is distressingly different from my teacher's – but there is sufficient similarity that it is now possible to focus on improving the gap. That works well as a form of experiential learning when the learner is able to discern and encompass the holistic structure of the action. But we often need the teacher's help with this. The way you hold the bow or the angle of your arm is not necessarily apparent to the learner as being a salient feature of the action, and the good teacher will deconstruct the action to help focus attention appropriately. Experiential learning requires the learner to undertake an analysis of the activity in a way that makes the appropriate structural reorganization possible. For simple tasks, like turning the page of a book, humans are very good at learning through imitation without the help of a teacher. For complex activities like reading we need help, and the task of the teacher is to work out how to deconstruct the activity so that learners become aware of what is salient to achieving the goal.

Social Constructivism

Learning happens automatically in the brain for our evolved capabilities. But the skills and knowledge that have been developed by other individuals, must be learned through imitation, discovery, or communication. Imitation gets difficult when the complexity of the expert activity does not reveal itself to the novice. Discovery will be slow if we each have to recapitulate the work of the millions of individuals who have contributed to the accumulation of human knowledge. Fortunately, we have communication through language that can express complex ideas.

Dewey and Vygotsky were probably the first educational theorists to emphasize the role of language and social interaction in development and learning. For Dewey education is a social process in the sense that the individual is acculturated through social interaction, which in a democratic society or group will aim for a variety of mutual shared interests, to secure in individuals "a consciously socialized interest", rather than having to control their beliefs and customs (Dewey 2001). For Vygotsky the role of language, as fundamental to thought, enables a process of "continual movement back and forth from thought to word, and from word to thought" which is itself an aspect of cognitive development (Vygotsky 1962). He further argued, in an approach that has been termed "social constructivism", that learning through discussion is important, and distinct from learning through practice, because the act of articulating an idea is itself a contribution to what it means to know that idea. As learners discuss with their teacher and with each other, they develop their ideas in ways that are different from the learning they do through practice and experience. The exchange may not always be equal, but the less experienced learner is enabled to move into their "zone of proximal development", i.e. a level of development they cannot achieve alone, but that is within their current practice capability (Vygotsky 1978).

The same idea of a continual iteration runs through the cognitive neuroscientist's account of how the brain deals with learning through communication. For learning about objects in the world the brain makes predictions about what will happen next, and uses the error to refine the prediction until it has a good model. Similarly, in communication person A's brain constructs a model of person B's idea, compares it with what B should do as a result, and uses any error in that prediction to see where the difference lies between the two models, and adapt their communication accordingly:

> I can know that my communication has been unsuccessful when my prediction about what you will do next is not quite right...The nature of the prediction error tells me how to change my communication: which points I should emphasize and which are not important [...] By modelling the mind of the person we are talking to we are able to alter the way we communicate with them.
>
> (Frith 2007)

This neatly summarizes the task of the teacher in adapting their communication to the learner, and Frith goes on to celebrate the value of communication as enabling us to move beyond the slower processes of learning through imitation and discovery. The quote used in Chapter 3 is worth repeating:

> Some people are experts who clearly have better models of some aspects of the world. By putting together the models of many people, we can construct a new model that is better than any model produced by a single individual. And our knowledge of the world is no longer derived from a single lifetime–knowledge passes from one generation to the next.
>
> (Frith 2007)

And this neatly summarizes the role of education. However the teacher's opportunity to adapt their explanation depending on how the learner interprets it, is a rare luxury in a mass education system. Precisely because communication is not a one-way process, teaching should not be a matter of simply telling. The classroom of learners is a collection of individuals on the other end of that communication process, each one trying to model the mind of the teacher, making sense of what their goal might be, trying to predict what they will do next, and modifying their model of the teacher's mind according to what happens. The problem for education is that these are not dialogues: the teacher has little opportunity to discover their prediction error for each individual until they come to mark their work; the learner has to work very hard to keep realigning their personal goals with what they think the teacher's goal might be, as well as modifying their model of the teacher's mind. Perhaps this explains why Dewey, Wertheimer, and Vygotsky all focused on the value to the learner of their own articulation of an idea in learning through discussion, not just the value of what their interlocutor says.

The focus here is on the use of language-based communication for "articulation". This is not the same as other forms of communication such as gesture or facial expression, or tone of voice. Language expresses complex propositions and relationships between concepts that are not practicable in other forms of communication.

Conceptual Learning

In formal education, the process of building an appropriate "organization of facts and ideas", i.e. knowledge, is a tough assignment for the learner because the context is so different from that of the physical and social world we are adapted to learn from. The facts and ideas in question are not those built up from the goals and actions of the learner, but those built up by scholars and experts over many years of careful study. This is where the educationist is abandoned by the neuroscientist who celebrates the capacity of the brain and can treat the fact that "knowledge passes from one generation to the next" as unproblematic. In that one celebratory phrase lays all the struggle of students and the effort of teachers. We will find little help from current theories in cognitive neuroscience as we try to work out how students are to learn the complex and alien facts and ideas coming from the minds of others. Even educational theorists, as we have seen, prefer to rely on experiential learning and the learner's attempt to articulate ideas. But in formal education, especially where the concepts are developed by experts, we need to understand how the learner might learn through communication from the teacher.

Discerning Structure

One of the most influential ideas on how students learn from teaching is a dichotomy of two different approaches to learning, originally characterized as "deep and surface level processing", derived from studying how students read a text (Marton and Säljö 1976a, 1976b). The key finding was an internal relationship between the approach to study and the learning outcome achieved – between the *how* and the *what* of learning. This work led to a long-term research program in many countries, investigating the qualitative differences in how students approach the task of learning others' ideas from reading texts and listening to lectures, and in how they conceptualize what they learned as a result (Marton, Hounsell, and Entwistle 1997). The finding common to all these studies is that some learners attend to the discourse in a way that distorts its intended meaning, and so the communication fails. Much of this work is brought together in a recent book, where Marton and Booth argue that only when learners are aware of the different structural levels within a text can they interpret and discern its intended meaning (Marton and Booth 1997).

The research program was convincing partly because it was able to relate the way students worked on a text – established through interview data – to the way they were able to summarize it, or use it to solve a problem. Qualitative differences in approach to reading or lectures led to differences in the level of complexity in the summary. Without accurately discerning the structure of the text students distort the meaning and end up with faulty conceptual structures. For example, if a student fails to perceive the *principle-example* structure in a text their summary is about the illustrative examples and misses the principle completely (Marton and Wenestam 1979). The same result was demonstrated for students learning from a text that took the form of an educational television program (Laurillard 1991). This kind of research helps to explain the importance of the "meaningful learning" that learners do for themselves informally, outside their school experience, and which Ausubel contrasted with the "rote learning" he found to be so common in schools (Ausubel 2000).

We know from the work on conceptual change and concept mapping, conducted mainly in the context of science and social science (Chi and Roscoe 2002; Novak 2002), that students develop clearly identifiable forms of misconception when they distort the structure of the text or discourse. The research program inaugurated by Marton's phenomenographic method of describing how students understand formal concepts in science, social science, and engineering, established the "outcome space" of the family of misconceptions that students were capable of developing around the target conception (Marton 1981; Marton and Pong 2007). The phenomenographic method has the powerful value, therefore, of discovering the structures of misconceptions in a topic area. If the teacher is aware of the likely misconceptions it is possible to pre-empt them when they explain a topic, or spot them in what their students produce, and then adapt their further explanations accordingly.

Developing Conceptions and Misconceptions

How are conceptions developed and misconceptions changed? Why do some students interpret Newton's third law of motion as referring to equilibrium, and only a small proportion interpret it correctly as the inverse proportion of mass and acceleration of two bodies? The simple answer is that the correct interpretation has a more complex logical structure, and to discern it requires the cognitive activities involved in the deep approach to study, defined as:

- seeking meaning;
- looking at the broad picture;
- relating ideas to previous knowledge and experience;
- looking for patterns and underlying principles;
- checking evidence and relating it to conclusions;
- examining logic and argument cautiously and critically;
- monitoring understanding as learning progresses;
- engaging with ideas and enjoying intellectual challenge (Entwistle and Peterson 2004).

These are the cognitive activities that elaborate what it takes to learn from communication. They are the activities that protect the learner from misinterpreting texts and discourses about formal concepts, many of which can lay traps for those not paying full attention. The idea of "pedagogic errors" (i.e. errors generated by the pedagogue) refers to the traps often present in teachers' explanations (Laurillard 2002). Newton's third law is often confused with equilibrium because it is stated as "every force has an equal and opposite reaction" – it *sounds like* equilibrium (the balance between two forces on an object), because the statement does not clarify that it is about the forces of two bodies acting on each other. There is no logical relationship between the correct and incorrect conception, because they are two entirely different situations. The origin of the misconception is not in the situation being described by the law, but in the context of the learning environment in which it is being taught. The definition is not well phrased.

Marton and Booth argue that only when learners are aware of the different structural levels within a text can they read it as it is meant to be read, and discern its intended message. Some students perceive the text as a hierarchical structure, whereas others "horizontalize" the structure, and therefore distort the meaning. They suggest that the features of a text that are designed to afford discernment of its structure may be missed by some students. If the title, sub-headings, connecting phrases such as "this example illustrates our main point that…," and other helpful markers of structure are absent or too subtle, then students are less likely to discern the internal structure, and hence the intended meaning.

From these examples, we can see that "discerning structure" is important because formal concepts and teaching texts have a complex internal structure, and by distorting their structure, students will distort their meaning, and fail

to achieve the intended learning outcome. An effective teaching strategy therefore must:

- clarify the internal structure of the concept;
- clarify the internal structure of the text;
- develop the student's skill in discerning the structure of any concept
  or text.

Interpreting Forms of Representation

For many of the concepts and systems of concepts that students confront in
academic study, the forms of representation they use, whether they are special
terms, symbols, notations, diagrams, or graphs, often compound the difficulty
of understanding the texts. These formal representations while helpful to the
cognoscenti present another interpretive challenge for the novice.

In a comprehensive review of the research on learning from formal representations, Ainsworth gives an account of the complexity of coming to understand an idea mediated this way. Formal representations can easily create a
barrier to understanding. She lists the cognitive tasks involved as being to
understand:

- the form of representation;
- the relation between the representation and the domain;
- how to select an appropriate representation;
- how to construct an appropriate representation.

These are the additional learning processes involved in gaining access to the
ideas and concepts mediated through formal representations, while also trying
to discern the structure and meaning of what they express. To some degree the
learner needs to already have some understanding of the concepts to be able to
make sense of the representations – the holistic structural organization for
these concepts can only be known fully through an iterative process that
gradually strengthens the right links, i.e. that makes the conceptual structure
meaningful. Reading and listening is not enough. The active processing
involved in a "deep approach" to learning is required, either facilitated by the
teacher, or contributed by the learner. The latter are the students who succeed
in getting the point of Newton's third law.

We know that complex conceptual learning is difficult because every exam
tells us that students do not easily understand the full complexity of the
concepts they have to learn. The research literature suggests that this is because
learners have to interpret the structure and meaning of various verbal,
symbolic, and visual representations if they are to build their own organization
of this knowledge. A great deal of teaching relies on students doing conceptual
learning from texts (mainly presentations by the teacher, and texts available

through print, and digital media), so we have to find ways of enabling teachers to discover and counter the approaches to conceptual learning in which students distort structure and meaning.

Constructionism

From Dewey onwards, learning and instructional theorists, no matter what their discipline focus, have been unanimous in emphasizing the importance of learning through experience (Bruner 1961; Dewey 1938; Kolb, Boyatzis, and Mainemelis 2000), learning through practice (Romiszowski 1999; Senge 2006), learning by doing (Schank, Berman, and Macpherson 1999; Schön 1987), learning by constructing (Kafai and Resnik 1996; Papert and Harel 1991), or situated learning (Brown, Collins, and Duguid 1989; Lave and Wenger 1991).

I use the term "constructionism" to characterize these similarities because Papert's term was linked explicitly to his idea of a "microworld", an environment designed to afford the learning of some system or set of concepts and powerful ideas (Papert 1980). All forms of learning through practice require a practice environment that has this property of affordance, so the microworld is a significant idea to make use of, despite its relative under-exploitation in the learning literature. A microworld that affords the construction of a concept gives more structure to the basic idea of experiential learning, and this could help in tackling the problem of making complex conceptual learning more intelligible for students.

Constructing

The focus on "constructing" aligns it with the idea of social constructivism, where the construct is developed through language. The nature of the doing in "learning by doing" depends on the discipline, but in all cases the assumption is that generating an action in pursuit of a conceptual goal helps the learner to construct their experience of the academic world:

> The idea that effective generation involves overt production reflects a common interpretation of constructivism in which 'learning by doing' means some form of hands-on or external activity ... responsible for helping the students learn more deeply.
>
> (Schwartz and Bransford 1998: 492)

This is the form of "constructivism" that Papert identifies as "constructionism" because the actions construct something, an "overt production", or a "public entity" of some kind (Papert 1980). Social constructivism concerns the special case when the overt production is the articulation of an idea, although the role of feedback on the development of the idea is not typically discussed. The idea that makes constructionism distinctive is that students learn more deeply because the actions they take to produce something elicit results that feed back information about how to improve their next action. This is similar to the idea of "situated learning", defined originally in a key article by Brown, Collins, and Duguid, which argues that learning must be "situated", in the sense that the learner's activity is located in a situation which itself plays a role: "Situations might be said to co-produce knowledge through activity. Learning and cognition, it is now argued, are fundamentally situated" (Brown, Collins, and Duguid 1989: 32).

The central idea in this tradition, though not stated this way, is that the teacher recruits for academic learning the "unsupervised" learning process that their learners have already developed for learning about the world without a teacher. Supervised learning uses guidance and feedback from the teacher to keep the learner on track. However, if the learning is situated in a meaningful context with a meaningful goal in view, the learner should be able to cope with less teacher direction and rely solely on the direct feedback from the environment on their actions. As in the discussion of experiential learning above, the learner must be able to interpret the feedback, they must be able to "discern and encompass the holistic structure of the action" to be able to use the feedback for learning. The value of this kind of contextualized learning is a powerful idea, and it keeps returning in the education literature under different guises, as experiential, situated, problem-based, constructionist learning, and no doubt there will be more such descriptors.

Types of Feedback

It is worth distinguishing the two types of feedback implied in the discussion of constructions. Although they are both formative, because they are used to "form" the learner's action, they are explicitly different types. Feedback from the environment and feedback from the teacher – intrinsic and extrinsic respectively – play different and distinctive roles in learning:

- "Intrinsic" feedback is internal to the action; it takes the form of a natural or authentic consequence of the action in relation to the intended goal, from which the learner can work out how to improve their action without teacher intervention.
- "Extrinsic" feedback is external to the action; it takes the form of an evaluative comment on the action, or guidance that the learner can follow to improve their action with respect to the intended goal.

The intrinsic/extrinsic distinction has been identified also as "consequences of actions" vs "coach" (Schank, Berman, and Macpherson 1999), and "knowledge of results" vs "knowledge of performance" as commented on by an instructor (Romiszowski 1999). There is also a construct equivalent to intrinsic feedback in the neuroscience accounts of certain computational models of learning, where the "critic" element of the learning mechanism uses information from the results of the previous actions generated: the information is intrinsic feedback on the actions, not guidance from an external element such as a coach or supervisor (Dayan and Abbott 2001). The value of intrinsic feedback is well established as a critical element in learning because it enables the learner to make progress in achieving the goal without the presence of a teacher, and is fundamental to the idea of constructionist, situated, and experiential learning.

Clear examples of intrinsic feedback are abundant in our normal, everyday life. We experience it every time we move a mouse, and adjust the movement to its manifestation on the screen. It is what we would get if we looked for books about feedback in learning by typing "feedback" into Google Scholar, and found only books about engineering systems. Intrinsic feedback gives you more information about your action than simply that it was inappropriate, enabling reflection that generates a cognitive rethink of how to generate a better action. In such a case you do not need a "coach' to provide you with "knowledge of performance" – the feedback you receive is meaningful, and therefore sufficient to trigger reflection on how you need to change your action, e.g. to try searching on "feedback learning" instead.

These examples contrast with "extrinsic" feedback, which does not occur within the situation but as an external comment on it: right or wrong, technical evaluation, advice about how to improve. It is not a necessary consequence of the action, and therefore is not expressed by the world of the action itself. Extrinsic feedback operates at the level of descriptions of actions, and is therefore predominant in education. It is the type of feedback discussed in the literature on formative assessment, aimed at "reducing discrepancies between current understandings or performance and a desired goal," where students can reduce the discrepancy by using more effective strategies or increasing their effort (Wiliam 2010). However, this does not give a cognitive account of how the right kind of feedback can generate an appropriate rethink of the action or idea.

Extrinsic feedback is potentially more efficient than intrinsic feedback, because it guides the student towards the optimal answer. But if the guidance is too helpful, it stops the learner doing their own active reflection.

These issues will reappear again in the following chapters, especially Chapter 10 on learning through practice. At this stage I hope to have established, from the student's point of view, the unity between, on the one hand, action with intrinsic feedback in the world as experienced directly, and on the other hand, action as description of the world with extrinsic feedback in the form of comment, guidance, or re-description by the teacher. To use feedback, students must be able to make sense of it. Students trying to understand an abstract organization of concepts and ideas are helped by a microworld, or modeling environment, that affords learning without a teacher, i.e. their situated actions construct an entity that elicits meaningful *intrinsic* feedback. Or in a practice environment, the teacher guidance provides meaningful *extrinsic* feedback they can follow to improve their actions and so develop their practice and the concepts that informed it.

Collaborative Learning

The final element in this analysis of what it takes to learn is the learner's production of some representation of what they have learned. The nature of "learning through production" has not been thoroughly researched, despite the importance in formal education of insisting that learners produce something to show they have learned. There is some attention to it, however, in the relatively recent interest in collaborative learning (Stahl, Koschmann, and Suthers 2006). Collaboration between students as a process of learning adds to the idea of social constructivism the idea of experiential learning that requires the learner to produce an output by acting on the world in some way (Laurillard 2009). It demands more than discussion, argument, question and answer: it demands also group consensus on producing an output.

The output may represent in many different ways what they currently know: as an essay, a report, a design, a diagram, an analysis, a presentation, a performance, a proof, a media product, a recommendation – it can be many things, depending on the nature of the learning outcome being represented.

A group collaboration works towards a clear end-point, or output in the form of a shared understanding that requires the participants to confront any discrepancies or contradictions in their discussions. In a group discussion it is often possible to get away with imprecise language to disguise or diminish a difference in conception, whereas constructing an agreed output – like a joint communiqué or a common visual representation – demands negotiations, explanations, process regulation, argumentation, and conflict resolution, which in turn require that each learner reflects on the other's ideas in order to critique or extend them, and on their own in order to defend or develop them (Dillenbourg and Traum 2006).

The same effect *may* happen in learning through discussion, in which the learner has to articulate their idea, recognized by Vygotsky and others as valuable in itself for learning. Each learner may be pushed by their peers to elaborate and defend their idea until they all reach a better understanding. But this takes some skill, a skill we do not often teach, although it can be taught (Wegerif 2007).

The discussion group may not act as a social way of constructing a concept, as we will see in Chapter 9, and often allows each member to keep their current personal construction unchallenged. Producing the articulated idea requires some reflection by the learner, but there the process stops. We have established that reflection is important, but what motivates it? In discussion alone a learner's peers may not wish to challenge what they say, but if they have to each produce an output and then collaborate to construct an agreed and shared external product, this motivates negotiation at least, which is likely to promote further reflection and reorganization of each learner's initial construct. In that sense, collaborative learning engages both social constructivism and experiential learning. It is a powerful form of learning.

Making Learning Happen

What do we take from this to inform the task of teaching? Psychologists and cognitive scientists have explored the full complexity of human learning throughout the last century, and those insights are still valid. Their findings are now being explained by the underlying neuroscience, and this helps to illuminate the extraordinary complexity of the learning process that our brains have evolved for managing our interactions with the natural and social world. Interestingly, none of these developments are changing very much the broad conclusions about what it takes to learn in formal education. In a survey of the research in cognitive science that took psychology into computational models of information processing, Shuell drew conclusions about the implications for teaching that would not have surprised John Dewey:

> effective teachers must know how to get students actively engaged in learning activities that are appropriate for the desired outcome(s). This task involves the appropriate selection of content, an awareness of the cognitive processes that must be used by the learner in order to learn the content, and understanding of how prior knowledge and existing knowledge structures determine what and if the student learns from the material presented.
>
> (Shuell 1986: 430)

Neither would they have surprised most teachers. More recently, one of the most comprehensive accounts of learning in formal education is the report from the Committee on Developments in the Science of Learning in the US (Bransford, Brown, and Cocking 2003). It is a valuable narrative of many of the ideas and findings of the past fifty years or so, and acts as a solid foundation for understanding learning. A later analysis of what learning theories bring to education quotes the National Academy of Sciences distillation of the research findings into three fundamental principles of learning:

1   Students come to the classroom with preconceptions about how the world works. If their initial understanding is not engaged, they may fail to grasp the new concepts and information, or they may learn them for purposes of a test but revert to their preconceptions outside the classroom.
2   To develop competence in an area of inquiry, students must: (a) have a deep foundation of factual knowledge, (b) understand facts and ideas in the context of a conceptual framework, and (c) organize knowledge in ways that facilitate retrieval and application.
3   A "metacognitive" approach to instruction can help students learn to take control of their own learning by defining learning goals and actively monitoring their progress in achieving them (Bransford, Brown, and Cocking 2003: 14–18).

The three principles are compatible with the general account given from the theories reviewed above, although they do not cover discussion and the collaborative aspects of learning. These are covered in a later analysis that compares the contributions from studies of "implicit learning" in psychology and neuroscience, "informal learning" outside the classroom, and "formal learning" in education. They are useful distinctions because the areas of research are carried out almost entirely independent of each other, and yet, as the analysis shows, they are still broadly compatible (Bransford *et al.* 2006).

It seems that our understanding of the fundamental mechanisms involved in what it takes to learn is surprisingly coherent across the contrasting approaches to studying it. With all the dramatic social and cultural changes over the last century, there has been no revision of the fundamental character of human learning, rather confirmation or elaboration of earlier theories. The teacher thinking about how best to design teaching and learning activities needs to have a model in mind of what it takes to learn, and needs to draw on whatever research and theory can offer. The different theorists defend their differences, because they each illuminate important insights into the process of learning, but that does not make them incompatible. For the teacher designing, it is valuable to try and develop as broad and inclusive a consensus as possible.

The main concepts and relations involved in learning as an active process, drawn from these different texts, are summarized in Table 4.1. This is compiled from the point of view of the learner learning, and as it draws on a range of theories it is phrased to be relevant in any context, implicit, informal, or formal.

The statements in Table 4.1 provide common ground for describing the learning process, whether it concerns an infant responding to the goal of exploring novelty, where the action is controlling their gaze, or an

Table 4.1 The Concepts and Relations Involved in Learning

1	Learning as an active process is triggered by a personal goal that requires action
2	the goal is partly individual and partly socially determined
3	the learner has access to a model of the relevant actions and their outcome
4	the action required for the goal is within their current practice capability
5	and is informed by their current conceptual organization
6	the articulation required represents their current conceptual organization
7	which results from access to another's articulated conceptual organization
8	or from the use of feedback on previous actions and articulations
9	or from another's comment on their own articulated conceptual organization
10	and the feedback is used to modulate future actions
11	and to modulate the conceptual organization that generated the action
12	and to modulate the goal

undergraduate wanting to impress their tutor, where the action is constructing a good argument.

These essential elements are brought together in a single representation in Figure 4.1. It shows the learner learning by using their personal goals and current conceptual organization to select from their current practice to generate actions on the external environment. The learner can use an action modeled by a teacher, or use results from their own action to modulate and build their practice capability. What they get from the teacher or the environment may modulate their current concept, their personal goals, or current practice capability, and so generate new actions in a continual iterative process of development and learning.

If a teacher is present, there is also the opportunity to learn through communication, from the teacher's explanations of their conceptual world, i.e. the curriculum. The learner may generate their own articulation of the teacher's explanations, or may use information from their interaction with the external environment to modulate their concept and generate articulations of it, again in a continual iterative process of learning and development. If other

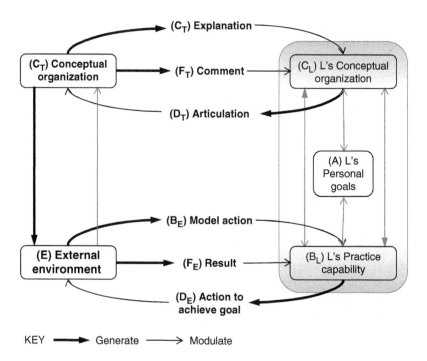

Figure 4.1 Consolidation of theories on what is involved in learning from the external environment, and in learning from a teacher. Shading identifies the internal cognitive components the learner depolys during the process, which the teacher is trying to influence.

learners are present then the modeled action and explanations may come from them, which may or may not be equivalent to the teacher's, of course. Figure 4.1 is a way of combining and representing all the formal descriptions of learning so that teaching design can benefit from all these insights.

Learning happens when each connection drives the next. Each one has to *generate an output from its origin to modulate its destination component*, which in turn provides an impetus or capability for that component to produce the next connection, so that the iteration continues. The teacher's concept generates an explanation to modulate the learner's concept; the learner's concept generates an articulation to inform the teacher; the teacher now generates a new explanation or comment to modulate the learner's concept, and so on. Similarly, the environment generates a model action to modulate the learner's practice; the learner's practice generates an action to match the model action; the environment generates the result of that action to modulate the learner's practice; and so on. The cycles may also begin with the learner's goal generating an articulation to elicit a response from the teacher, or generating an action to elicit a result in the environment. If concepts call on experience and actions call on conceptual understanding this motivates the internal cycle of goals, concepts and actions. This is a complex account, inevitably, given the nature of learning; and it demonstrates how many different ways it can break down, especially when the one-to-one iteration between learner and teacher is so rare.

Learning as change or development of the individual's goals, knowledge, and practice capability is captured in the final three points in Table 4.1, and the teacher also learns. The extent to which the learner does use their experience to modulate their current goal, action, and concept is what the teacher has to use to modulate their own goals, knowledge and capabilities as a teacher.

Because learning is an active process, it follows that the learner will be learning from whatever they are doing – if they are sitting quietly in a class listening to a teacher, they are learning about social acculturation, and learning about algebra only insofar as they are successfully modeling the teacher's mind. So if the teacher is aiming for the development of formal knowledge and skills, then each of the statements in Table 4.1 has consequences for how they approach and learn about their teaching. Table 4.2 proposes what this means for how the teacher facilitates active learning.

The requirements for the teacher, listed in the second column of Table 4.2, show the complexity of taking these fundamentals of learning into their teaching.

It becomes more complex still when we have to interpret what the fundamentals of formal learning mean for the new contexts of learning technologies. Psychologists and neuroscientists have not yet turned their attention to whether learning through discussion, practice, and experience operates differently when it is mediated by digital technologies. Historically, and even currently, our accounts of human learning have been developed in the context of the natural forms of interaction we have in the external environment of the

Table 4.2 Consequences for the Teacher of the Conditions for Active Learning

What is involved in active learning	How the teacher promotes successful active learning
Learning is oriented towards the personal goal of the learner (1, 2)	The personal goal of the learner has to be aligned with what the teacher needs their goal to be Dewey suggests aligning them by grounding the task to be learned in the learner's own experience, and by securing the learner's socialized interest (A)
The learner uses the model action and their practice capability to generate their action to achieve the goal (2, 3, 4)	The learner's current practice capability must include those needed to achieve the goal So the teacher has to model and deconstruct complex actions (B_E), setting a task goal that requires actions that are currently within the learner's zone of proximal development
The learner uses another's concepts and their current concepts to generate their articulation (2, 3, 5, 6, 7)	The learner needs access to the teacher's conceptual organization (C_T) So the teacher has to clarify the internal structure of the concept, and clarify the internal structure of the text (C_T)
The learner uses feedback to modulate their concepts and practice capability in relation to the goal (2, 8, 9)	Building a repertoire of appropriate actions requires the teacher to provide an external environment (E) that gives the learner sufficient feedback for testing actions (D_E) in relation to their goal (A) to build an improved practice capability (B_L) and concepts (C_L) The teacher has to monitor learner actions in the environment (D_E) and articulations of their concept (D_T), as a representation of their current practice capability (B_L) and conceptual organization (C_L)
The learner uses feedback from an action or articulation to modulate their current conceptual organization, practice capability, and personal goal (10, 11, 12)	The teacher has to ensure that the learner receives meaningful intrinsic feedback from their actions in the external environment (F_E) and meaningful extrinsic feedback comments or guidance from the teacher (F_T)

Note: Numbers refer to statements in Table 4.1, and letters to components in Figure 4.1.

physical and social world, but digital technologies are changing these forms of interaction. Explorations of the fundamental mechanisms of learning have not developed into a theory that embraces social and emotional factors in a way that allows us, for example, to predict the effects of an absence of these in a communication medium that relies on text alone.

Much of this interpretive work will have to be done by teachers, which is partly what this book is about, but we do not start from nothing. We can use what we know from psychology, cognitive science, and neuroscience, because the learning mechanisms humans have evolved will still play a fundamental role in the way learners operate in the new educational media and environments we create for them, just as they did for the once innovative environments of books and classrooms. This is why I set out to express the fundamentals of the learning process in a way that will help us understand what happens when the characteristics of the learning environment change.

Summary

This chapter has sought to gain an insight into the learning process from the student's perspective. As a complex human interaction, formal learning has been studied from several different perspectives, and I have drawn on the principal lines of argument to find the common ground. Each theorist focuses on a particular aspect of the learning process, but the idea of a synergy in our understanding of learning can succeed, I think, if we treat the contrasting theories as complementary rather than oppositional, where each offers a different kind of insight into what it takes to learn.

From the research currently available, from cognitive science, cognitive psychology, educational psychology, cognitive neuroscience, and education, this chapter expressed the general consensus around what it takes to learn in the form of the diagram in Figure 4.1. To summarize, learning is a process of using concepts and practice to generate articulations and actions that elicit communication from the teacher and information from the environment to modulate those concepts and practice.

5 What it Takes to Teach

Introduction

The previous three chapters looked at the nature of formal learning as distinct from other kinds of learning, what students are likely to bring to the learning process, and what it takes to learn in the context of formal education. The general conclusions in each case drew on a range of empirical and conceptual studies to provide an account of what is known about formal learning. There is a great deal of material to draw on, but by considering some of the key texts in each area, and taking an inclusive approach to seeing commonalities across studies wherever possible, I believe we have a good basis for deriving a principled approach to designing the teaching-learning process.

Factors Influencing the Design of Teaching

To put the focus of this chapter in its context, Figure 5.1 shows a representation of the principal factors that make up the context for designing teaching and learning.

The contextual influences on the overall curriculum requirements are represented in the greyed out parts of Figure 5.1, because the focus in this chapter is on the design of the teaching itself within that unchangeable context. The diagram is compatible with Figure 3.1 showing how factors in the learning context influence student learning (Entwistle and Peterson 2004). However, given the importance of the alignment of teacher and learner goals, discussed in Chapter 4, the influence of learner goals is explicitly included here. Figure 5.1 presents the context within which the teacher is designing in order to influence students' learning outcomes.

Students bring their motivations, knowledge, and skills to their learning activities, which help to define their personal goals, although these may vary across different courses, given their background and the nature of the course. The learning activities they undertake are influenced also by their perceptions of the teaching methods and assessment, and their actual learning outcomes (Entwistle and Peterson 2004).

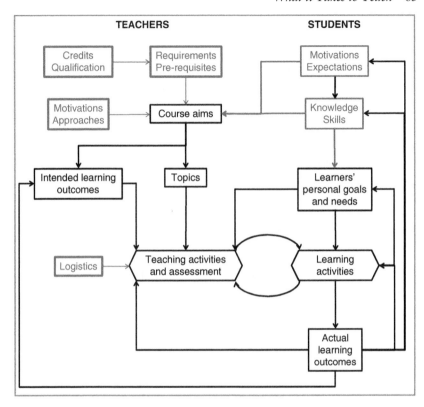

Figure 5.1 The principal context factors influencing the design of teaching and
learning.

From the teacher's point of view, the design begins with their aims for the
course, influenced by their own motivations, interests, and ambitions for how
they want their students to learn. But these are tempered by the need to take
into account any requirements set by a standards body, or professional body,
or quality agency, and the prerequisites of the knowledge and skills it is reasonable to expect of their students. These are dependent in turn upon the level of
qualification, and the duration of study time available, defined, usually, in
terms of scheduled learning hours, course credits, hours of study, or the
equivalent. The course aims are constructed to appeal to students' likely interests and expectations.

The logistics of study (student numbers, learning environment, location of
study, part-time or full-time, etc.) will impact on how teaching methods are
selected for their logistical characteristics, but this chapter focuses on the intellectual aspects of teaching methods and assessment.

Against this background the teacher makes decisions about the design of the
teaching-learning process. Figure 5.1 shows that the teacher carries out their

initial pedagogical design on the basis of two kinds of proximal influence: their intended aims, learning outcomes and curriculum topics (Chapter 2), and their perception of the students' motivations, expectations, knowledge, and skills that influence their approach to study (Chapter 3). The students' likely learning goals and needs in relation to the intended outcomes (Chapter 4) form the basis of how the teacher designs the teaching and learning activities and assessment.

Figure 5.1 also shows that there are feedback loops between learning activities and teaching activities, indicating the iterative character of the teaching-learning process. The actual learning outcomes demonstrated in the assessment can be used not just as an evaluation of the students' capability, but also of the effectiveness of the teaching methods. In the larger cycle of teaching and curriculum review, the students' performance in assessment also impacts on an evaluation of the curriculum, learning outcomes, aims, and even the nature of the assessment itself.

In this chapter I am keeping the focus on the design of learning that an individual teacher or small team would be responsible for. This is where the literature on instruction, or learning, or teaching, or pedagogic design typically begins. But for the practicing teacher the contextual background is important, as it actively constrains what they can do. The factors and interrelationships for teachers in Figure 5.1 are similar to those in most books that cover the planning and design of teaching and learning (Entwistle and Smith 2002; Fry, Ketteridge, and Marshall 2003; Prosser and Trigwell 1999; Ramsden 2003; Reigeluth 1999a). The factors also coincide with the principal information required by course proposal documents now in use in most universities and colleges, which therefore have considerable impact on what actually happens during the teaching-learning process. But course proposal documents do not typically ask for an analysis of students' learning needs in relation to the aims of the course.

Approaches to Designing for Learning

This section is about "designing for learning" because the teacher's focus is on learning. The term is preferable to "instructional design" or "teaching design" or "pedagogy design" because it maintains the focus on the learner. And "designing for learning" is more apt than "learning design," which carries with it a sense that we can design learning; we cannot. But we can do our best to design *for* learning, in the sense that we create the environment and conditions within which the students find themselves motivated and enabled to learn. I take all these terms to mean the same.

This chapter revisits some of the work covered in Chapter 4, from the perspective of what it means for teaching. Chapter 4 worked through different aspects of the learning process from the point of view of educational psychology, cognitive psychology, cognitive neuroscience, and education, and distilled their separate insights into a single account of what it takes to learn that is applicable to formal education. This chapter looks at how educational theorists working in the field of instructional design use their understanding of learning to generate principles for the design of teaching.

The problem for teachers is that the instructional design literature, as it is generally called, displays a plethora of different representations of advice and guidance. In Reigeluth's extensive volume on instructional design theories and models, the 40 contributing researchers offer some 20 different diagrammatic models of the process of teaching and learning, and the lessons learned from research studies are summarized for each chapter in over 200 guidelines for teachers (Reigeluth 1999a). A further problem is the lack of consensus, as the authors in this field rarely reference the same underlying theorists; those who score best in this volume are Anderson (J. R.), Bereiter, Bloom, Bruner, Dewey, Gagné, and Vygotsky, but each is mentioned in only four of the 27 chapters. This is celebrated as a "rich array of approaches to the design of instruction". For the practicing teacher, however, it is a field in disarray if it cannot integrate those ideas into a workable set of guiding principles. In a similarly wide-ranging volume edited by Duffy and Kirkley, relating instructional design to distance education (Duffy and Kirkley 2004), only Vygotsky is salient, along with Duffy, Jonassen, Bransford, and Wenger, each of whom is referenced in fewer than half the chapters. A UK handbook for university teachers favours Biggs, Boud, Gibbs, and Ramsden, each referenced in one-fifth of the chapters (Fry, Ketteridge, and Marshall 2003). In a more recent UK volume explicitly focused on digital methods (Beetham and Sharpe 2007), only Vygotsky is salient again, with non-US researchers Dalziel, Engeström, Laurillard, Oliver, and Sharpe, alongside Wenger being referenced in a third of the chapters. We are now half-way through the "decade for synergy", foreseen by Bransford and colleagues (Bransford *et al.* 2006), who make a well-supported and extensive case for synergy between cognitive neuroscience, informal learning, and educational psychology, as the disciplines that contribute to an understanding of learning. However, they do not yet offer a synthesis, and do not extend the embrace to instructional design. They do make several references to Vygotsky.

Perhaps we can all agree on Vygotsky as a shared source of inspiration, but clearly we do not yet have a unified approach to designing for learning in the sense of a clear set of guidelines for teachers that builds on a consensual understanding of the learning process. Entwistle and Smith made a similar observation:

> The aim of all these theories has been to produce ideas with wide generality, and many have been used to suggest ways of improving the effectiveness of learning within education. They do, however, all too often appear to contradict each other, and may also seem unrealistic. The teacher is faced with an array of principles, all of which claim to improve learning, yet few of which have their origins specifically within classroom contexts.
> (Entwistle and Smith 2002: 322)

There are several precedents in the literature for establishing guidelines for teachers. Each one aims to derive from our understanding of learning a principled approach to teaching. I am attempting to do the same. Perhaps the attempt is doomed. But without it there is no basis for the comparative analysis of the range of conventional and digital teaching methods that will tell us how they may best be used to support student learning. That is an imperative for our education systems now, so we have to try.

Chapter 4 distilled the form of the learning process to a set of iterative cycles of change within the learner and between the learner and the teacher and their external environment. Each part has implications for how the teacher can assist the learner in completing those cycles of developing capability successfully. Table 4.2 set out the requirements for what the teacher must do to facilitate successful active learning, suggesting they

- align teacher-learner goals;
- set task goals that use concepts and actions that are available to the learner;
- clarify the structure of concepts to assist the organization of knowledge;
- construct an appropriate practice environment;
- monitor learner actions and articulations of their concepts;
- ensure meaningful feedback.

The sections that follow cover the principles of design developed in the instructional design literature – or the "educational design literature" – that set out to address these kinds of teacher roles.

Aligning Goals, Activities, and Assessment

The principle of alignment derives from the recognition that the teacher must align the learner's goals with their own for them to succeed in achieving the intended learning outcomes. This led to the preference for experiential learning methods over more didactic approaches, because learners are more likely to be engaged in trying to achieve a goal that makes sense to them. Didactic teaching has to work harder to engage the learner's interest. Ausubel's "advance organizer" is the most widely known principle for recruiting the learner's interest to share the teacher's goal: the teacher uses an analogy in the learners' own experience, or an intriguing issue, or a puzzling question, for which the didactic teaching then provides a pleasing explanation (Ausubel 2000). Dewey took the more radical view that the goals should be negotiated with the learners, and emphasized: "the importance of the participation of the learner in the formation of the purposes which direct his activities in the learning process…" (Dewey 1938).

The teacher may suggest the goals of learning, although "the teacher's suggestion is not a mold for a cast-iron result, but is a starting point to be developed into a plan through contributions from the experience of all engaged in the learning process" (Dewey, 1938).

To follow Dewey strictly, we would need to adapt Figure 5.1 to allow learners to influence not just the Aims, which they can perhaps do post-16 through the market research process for college courses, but also the intended learning outcomes for a particular course. A negotiated curriculum is rare in education below PhD level, and non-existent at the school level Dewey was trying to influence. It is left to the individual teacher to manage that negotiation of goals.

The educational design literature is concerned more with a different kind of alignment: of learning outcome, teaching method and form of assessment. This principle is reflected in several texts:

> The curriculum is stated in the form of clear objectives, which state the level of understanding required ... the teaching methods are chosen that are likely to realize those objectives ... Finally, the assessment tasks address the objectives ... they should be learning.
>
> (Biggs 2003: 27)

> aligning goals for learning with what is taught, how it is taught, and how it is assessed.
>
> (Bransford, Brown, and Cocking 2003:151)

> constructive alignment has been examined as a way of thinking strategically about what and how we want our students to learn (conceptual change, student focused, or information transmitting, teacher focused?).
>
> (Fry 2009: 146)

> Ensure constructive alignment of aims with teaching, assessment and student support.
>
> (Entwistle and Peterson 2004: 424)

> The necessity of pedagogical alignment cannot be over-emphasized. There are multiple dimensions that must be aligned when designing and implementing any undergraduate course ... At a minimum, these dimensions include: course objectives, course content, pedagogy, task characteristics, instructors' roles, students' roles, technological accordances and assessment strategies.
>
> (Apedoe and Reeves 2006: 336)

The imperative of design logic in any context says that it is important to align what you intend to achieve with the way you go about it, and with the way you will judge your success in achieving what you set out to do. So in one sense this principle offers rather little. The final quote above looks more challenging than the others, but in fact the course content is contained within the objectives, and the teaching methodology has been unpacked into pedagogy, task characteristics, roles, and technological affordances. They all advocate essentially the same principle.

Alignment is an unobjectionable principle, but the question is, how to achieve it? One answer is that "you get students to do the things that the objectives nominate" (Biggs 2003: 27), literally: it is the "verbs" that are aligned. The table of objectives against learning activities shows two identical lists of verbs such as "reflect", "explain", "argue", etc., duly aligned (ibid.: 57). This rather unhelpfully finesses the problem of alignment. These verbs do not constitute learning outcomes, which are better framed as capabilities or capacities the students will achieve through their study activities. It is not the case that, if we want students to "understand how evidence is used in argument" (see Chapter 2), we can simply translate this into the learning activity "understand how evidence is used in argument". And if you try turning it into "use evidence in an argument" it tells you nothing about how to help the students do that. Teachers need an answer to the question "what does it take to understand?" As we shall see in later sections, it is more complex than aligning verbs.

The representation of the learner learning in Figure 4.1 shows that the actions generated are informed both by the goal the learner is trying to achieve, and their current concepts; and that the information that results from the feedback on their action then modulates their conceptual knowledge in order to improve the next action, and may also modify their goal. The cycle of *goal–knowledge–action–feedback–modulation* constitutes what is learned and how. What the concept of alignment recognizes is that unless the teacher addresses the full cycle the intended learning outcome may not be achieved. It *might* be achieved, if the learner is able to build for themselves the alignment between intended learning outcomes ←→ teaching–learning activity ←→ assessment, but the principle of alignment says that it is the teacher's role to ensure it.

Monitoring Alternative Conceptions

The principle of alignment, while it is a good general design principle, omits the idea of the learner's readiness to learn. This derives from the learning theorists' insight that the teacher must ensure that the task being set uses concepts and actions that are available to the learner – i.e. are close to their "zone of proximal development". Their current concepts, action repertoire, and access to concepts and model actions are sufficient for doing the task. Curriculum design in education, in every subject, is an exercise in finding the appropriate sequence of concepts and skills. It is an uncertain process, often lacking in good information about which concepts are especially difficult, and what prior capabilities, concepts, and knowledge structures are needed at each stage. This is compounded by the fact that students arrive at each stage of their education with a wide range of formal academic knowledge, including some serious misconceptions, which means the teacher may always be building on sand. The best way to insure against this is to discover what the students already know, especially where this may be critical for making sense of the new concepts. It is one of the guidelines to teachers for designing learning environments that support a deep approach, distilled from the educational research literature by

Entwistle and Peterson: "Relate teaching directly to prior knowledge and to the 'understanding aims'" (Entwistle and Peterson 2004: 424).

The principle of discovering students' preconceptions is also one of the key teaching principles advocated in *How people learn*, a comprehensive report on a wide range of learning-related studies drawing on findings from the disciplines of cognitive, developmental and social psychology, learning theory, learning technologies, education, anthropology, and neuroscience (Bransford, Brown, and Cocking 2003). From this analysis the authors have derived three congruent *teaching* principles, to match the research findings on learning quoted in Chapter 4. The first is that "teachers must draw out and work with the pre-existing understandings that their students bring with them" (Bransford, Brown, and Cocking 2003:19).

This is further elaborated as requiring the teacher to:

- actively inquire into students' thinking;
- create tasks and conditions under which student thinking can be revealed;
- use frequent formative assessment to make students' thinking visible to themselves, their peers, and their teacher;
- provide feedback that can guide modification and refinement in thinking;
- use assessments that tap understanding, not facts or isolated skills;
- recognize students' preconceptions that make the topic challenging;
- draw out preconceptions that are not predictable;
- work with preconceptions so that students challenge and replace them.

These points are the means by which the teacher can cover the requirements illustrated in Table 4.2 as "monitor learner actions", "ensure meaningful feedback", "set tasks that are within learner's zone of proximal development", and address the expectation specified in Figure 5.1 that the teacher must take into account the prior conceptions, and therefore the learning needs of their students. It is the idea advocated in the scholarship of teaching, that teachers should have an awareness of the "central position of the perceptions of students" (Trigwell *et al.* 2000).

The same principle is advocated by Marton and colleagues in an edited collection of theory and practice-based case studies on teaching and learning that give the teacher the task of creating "the necessary specific conditions" that make it possible to learn (Marton and Tsui 2004). Rather than abstract from the specific findings of the case studies to a generic statement of the principles of teaching design, Marton argues that the teacher must discover the "specific conditions" for each curriculum topic, and this includes knowledge of what students bring to their study, i.e. the students' current capabilities and prior knowledge

This work is grounded in interview and observation studies of the experience of learning, which used "phenomenography" as the method for eliciting and describing the phenomena of learning from the students' points of view.

The methodology is successful in demonstrating the link between the student's approach to learning and their personal learning outcome, which is why it has been influential, as discussed in Chapter 4. Through eliciting students' ways of describing a concept, or the meaning of a text, or the interpretation of a problem-solving exercise, it is possible for researchers to map the outcome space of the different possible ways of conceptualizing a topic in the group of learners studied (Marton and Tsui 2004).

The consensus in educational design is that as teachers we must discover the prior conceptions of students if we are to support their intellectual journey towards the intended conceptual structures. The focus on *prior* conceptions suggests that it is only prior conceptions that we need concern ourselves with. Unfortunately, our own teaching can also generate inappropriate conceptions, which is why monitoring the learner's articulation is a key teacher role in Table 4.2, so that "monitoring alternative conceptions" is a truer description of what is needed than simply eliciting prior conceptions.

Scaffolding Theory-Generated Practice

Chapter 4 documented the importance of giving learners a practice environment that enables them to learn from experience. With the right type of task environment they can translate their concepts into practice, evaluate how well they achieve the goal, and use this to improve their practice and further develop their knowledge. The analysis generated a challenging set of requirements (see Table 4.2) for the teacher to:

- model and deconstruct complex actions to set a task goal requiring actions that are currently within the learner's zone of proximal development;
- provide a practice environment that offers sufficient practice for testing and improving their repertoire of actions;
- ensure that the learner receives meaningful intrinsic feedback from their actions.

There is evidence for all these. Deconstructing complex actions is the essence of "scaffolding", i.e. the supporting structures the teacher creates (Bransford, Brown, and Cocking 2003), such as "reducing the number of steps required to solve a problem by simplifying the task, so that the learner can manage components of the process and recognize when a fit with task requirements is achieved" (ibid.: 104).

Sufficient practice is important because this is how the learner tests and modulates the concepts that generated their actions, and the more complex the concept, or the more unfamiliar it is, the more time they will need: "time on task is a major indicator for learning and … deliberate practice is an efficient way to promote expertise (Bransford, Brown, and Cocking 2003: 173).

But deliberate practice requires the feedback and modeling that helps the learner work out how to improve on their actions:

- marking critical features of discrepancies between what the learner has produced and the ideal solution;
- demonstrating an idealized version of the act to be performed (ibid.: 104)

... where deliberate practice is goal-oriented and provides feedback to enable improvement. The feedback is a critical element, and Bransford and colleagues argue for the importance of "having a 'coach' who provides feedback for ways of optimizing performance ... it is not efficient if a student spends most of the problem-solving time rehearsing procedures that are not optimal for promoting skilled performance" (ibid.: 176).

The type of practice environment being described here is the typical one used in formal education, where students are set a number of problems, or tasks, or exercises, so they can put into practice what they have learned. This does not provide "intrinsic" feedback, where students see the results of their actions and can learn independently. The students working on a traditional writing or problem-solving task have no informational feedback from the environment to make use of, which is why Bransford and colleagues advocate the "coach," who gives extrinsic feedback which guides them to improve their performance.

There are two difficulties with this. One is pedagogical: the coach must be careful to "fade" their support and ensure the student does the work of interpreting and analyzing how to improve their performance (Pea 2004), e.g. by asking them to look at the difference between their output and a model answer. The ideal practice environment would offer a carefully calibrated set of exercises, each in the learner's zone of proximal development, and each providing the formative intrinsic feedback that enables learners to interpret results and work out how to improve for themselves – the essence of the learning process. The second problem is logistical: in the context of a mass education system few students can hope to receive the detailed and timely feedback they need while working on tasks.

The principle of scaffolding, as defined in the educational design literature, does not differentiate between intrinsic and extrinsic feedback. Extrinsic feedback in the form of advice and guidance from a teacher or coach is valuable, but a practice environment that gives intrinsic feedback on the results of their actions enables the learner to be independent. Designing such an environment is non-trivial, of course, and we return to this in Chapter 10.

Fostering Conceptual Change

Scaffolding students' learning in a task practice environment is intended to develop conceptual understanding, but the more common approach is to use teacher presentations, texts, and specialized forms of representations to describe and explain the concepts to be learned. Creating a good environment for learning through practice is important, but is difficult and time-consuming. Class presentations, lectures, books, and digital media are seen as the most efficient teaching method in terms of teacher time.

Educational design theorists agree about the importance of knowing students' prior conceptions as a starting point. There is still too little research of the kind carried out using the phenomenographic methodology, that would map the space of student misconceptions in the main curriculum topics, sometimes referred to as "threshold concepts" or "troublesome knowledge" (Meyer and Land 2005) – those concepts that are foundational to a robust understanding of the field, but can be in conflict with natural assumptions, or are highly complex, or are counterintuitive (examples are "force", "natural selection", "recursion", and "short-term memory"). To effect successful conceptual change, the teacher has to understand the relationship between the learner's likely conceptual knowledge structure and the intended knowledge structure, and from this derive the teaching-learning activities that enable learners to move from the former to the latter. The educational design literature proposes the use of "bridging," "cognitive conflict," and "the architecture of variation." Each approach is essentially aiming to recreate in the teacher-student language-based dialogue the goal–action–feedback–modulate cycle of experiential learning.

The *bridging strategy* uses intermediate analogous examples to help students discern the concept in focus as similarities between instances; the teacher chooses familiar initial situations, progressing to those that are more advanced, less intuitive, but still subject to the same principle or involving the same concept. This is often exemplified in science topics (Brown 1992; Clement 1993), but applies equally well to other topics (Clement 1993).

The idea of *cognitive conflict* is to find what a scientist would call the "critical experiment," i.e. the one that is capable of deciding between two conflicting theories. The familiar teaching strategy "*predict–observe–explain*" uses this idea: the teacher sets up a situation designed to get students to predict a known typical misconception, or inappropriate interpretation, to be confounded when the student observes the actual consequence, and has to modulate their conception as a result:

> To promote learning, it is important to focus on controlled changes of structure in a fixed context … or on deliberate transfer of a structure from one context to another.
>
> (Bell 1985: 72)

> Create constructive friction within the learning environment to encourage development.
>
> (Entwistle 2004: 424)

For example, the art history teacher wanting to jolt students' assumptions might ask them to guess who painted a landscape or portrait to demonstrate the range of styles used by a Picasso or a Mondrian in their early years.

The teacher has to think about the logical relationship between the structure of the concept and the sequence of controlled changes the learner has to go through if they are to discern the concept in question. This is what Marton refers to as "*the architecture of variation*" (Marton and Tsui 2004). If students are to discern the structure of a concept or system, and its relationship to the goal, which they must if they are to understand it, then, Marton argues, they need to experience it in a particular way. The key to this is that the teacher must be aware of "the architecture of variation" of a concept, because students can only discern what they are enabled to discern, and "can never discern anything without experiencing variation" (ibid.: 43). Rudyard Kipling made the same point poetically: "he cannot know England who only England knows".

It is a common finding in the studies of students reading texts (see Chapter 4) that the internal structure of some texts has almost been disguised, so difficult is it to discern, whereas other texts, more easily understood, make the structure salient and offer an experience of variation that makes the meaning of the concept discernible (Laurillard 1991; Marton and Wenestam 1979).

Working out the architecture of variation for each topic is the same kind of design challenge that the microworld presents (see Chapter 4). I have watched learners trying to use a physics microworld where they have no idea how to interpret what is happening on the screen, so they cannot use the feedback to modulate their actions. The same can happen in a teacher-learner dialogue. In both cases there is a logical relationship between the structure of the concept to be known, and the learner's ability to use the information the situation presents to refine and improve what they produce. When the teacher gets the design right the situation "co-produces" the knowledge through the learner's activity.

All three techniques, *bridging, cognitive conflict,* and *the architecture of variation,* specify the form of interaction that must take place between teacher, student, and subject matter. We must think about the learner iterating through the learning sequence, having the opportunity to develop perceptions and approaches, creating new experiences that become background for the next in the sequence. And for this to be possible, they must be explicitly aware of variations and contrasts that bring the conceptual structure into focus. Dewey put it well:

> It is part of the educator's responsibility to see equally to two things: First that the problem [intended goal] grows out of the conditions of the experience being had in the present, and that it is within the range of the capacity of students; and secondly, that it is such that it arouses in the learner an active quest for information and for production of new ideas. The new facts and new ideas thus obtained become the ground for further experiences in which new problems are presented. The process is a continuous spiral.
>
> (Dewey 1938: 79)

The continual iteration between teacher, student, and content makes this kind of teacher-student dialogue akin to the process we see in learning through practice. The teacher is not simply describing the concept, but is setting up the learning environment as a kind of language-based microworld, designing the series of instances of the concept to afford the learning of the concept in general. The intended outcome is an improved conceptual structure, the learner's task goal is to use their current knowledge to make an accurate prediction for an instance of the concept, their action is a prediction (e.g. a guess at who painted a portrait), and the feedback is an unexpected result, which requires a rethink of the conceptual structure that produced the prediction, elicited in the form of an explanation. That is how the teacher fosters a robust conceptual change process.

Encouraging Metacognition

The sections above have several times referred to the activity of "reflection". The representation of "the learner learning" in Figure 3.1 shows all the opportunities for the learner to modulate their cognition – conceptual organization, goal, repertoire of actions – by reflecting on the feedback from either the external environment or the teacher. Without it there will be no learning, and yet it is a process that the learners themselves must be responsible for, and which the teacher can only encourage, not observe. They have to deduce its presence or absence from their observation of the learner's actions or articulations.

Educational design theorists are agreed about the importance of reflection as part of the process of active learning. It is referred to as "meta-cognition" because it is referring not to a "trial-and-error" response to a failed action, but to a response that considers the action itself and its relationship to the knowledge structure that generated it, as well as the extent to which it achieved the intended goal. Teaching meta-cognitive skills of this kind is explicitly advocated:

> A "metacognitive" approach to instruction can help students learn to take control of their own learning by defining learning goals and actively monitoring their progress in achieving them.
>
> (Bransford *et al.* 2006: 66)

and it is the teacher's role to try to elicit these skills, either through encouragement, or modeling:

> Encourage reflection, metacognitive alertness, and self-regulation in studying.
>
> (Entwistle and Peterson 2004: 424)

An effective way of encouraging meta-cognitive skills is to enable students to articulate and share them, through peer group learning:

Provide opportunities for group discussion of both content and learning processes.

(Entwistle and Peterson 2004: 424)

Educational design theorists are agreed on the general principle of encouraging meta-cognitive skills, but it is often the detail of teachers' specific examples that provides greater value as teaching design guidelines, than the more general principle:

> a teacher and a group of students take turns in leading the group to discuss and use strategies for comprehending and remembering text content ... take turns presenting their ideas to the group and detailing how they use prompts in planning to write. The teacher also models these procedures. Thus, the program involves modeling, scaffolding, and taking turns which are designed to help students externalize mental events in a collaborative context.
>
> (Bransford, Brown, and Cocking 2003: 67)

This detail could be a lot more helpful to a teacher than the more abstract guideline. It expresses clearly the learning design pattern the teacher used for helping students become more aware of developing meta-cognitive skills. This is the point of patterns, first raised in Chapter 1, and we will come to it again in Chapter 6. Patterns spell out the detail of the pedagogic principle.

The educational design literature must always contend with the balance between the specific and the generic. Meta-cognition is an important aspect of learning that must be encouraged, but as a general principle it provides little help to the teacher. On the other hand, general principles are important for distilling the vast literature on educational practice. We return to this dilemma in later chapters in the discussion of learning design patterns.

Teaching as Design

There is consensus that a good understanding of learning should inform the design of teaching; there is a natural logic to the point. But the nature of the relationship, and the process by which we derive the one from the other, remains problematic. Educational research necessarily uses specific instances of teaching-learning activities targeted on specific learning outcomes. But the general guidelines distilled from these studies, and the literature on good teaching practice, tend to distil out all the value – one example is "Learners have to be brought to 'engage' with what they are learning so that transformation and internalization can occur"; another is "Teachers must reduce the amount of didactic teaching". They provide no help or guidance in how we might do this, or they seem obvious and unremarkable, so it is easy to believe we are already obeying them as we teach.

There is clearly agreement that designing for learning is not an exact science, and that we need a continual iteration of ideas and experience to generate the knowledge in the field. All teachers should be able to do continual professional development: "Teachers are learners and the principles of learning and transfer for student learners apply to teachers" (Bransford, Brown, and Cocking 2003: 242).

The quote is a beautiful encapsulation of the inevitable consequence of the complexity, uncertainty, and non-deterministic nature of learning design – teachers must be learners too. It acknowledges that teaching is a "design science," more akin to engineering than it is to physics, because it is aiming explicitly for change towards an intended outcome: "Engineers are not the only professional designers. Everyone designs who devises courses of action aimed at changing existing situations into desired ones" (Simon 1969: 129).

Teaching has to make use of what is known about learning and teaching from research, but must also develop heuristics, skills, and practitioner knowledge to create effective learning designs, rather than relying on the science alone. This is still a principled approach.

Marton came to the same conclusion. Because of the specificity of conditions in each curriculum topic, discovering the insights into what constitutes the architecture of variation for each topic is part of the teacher's professional role. He proposes that teachers become engaged in what is termed a "learning study", or design experiment, which includes the familiar stages in educational technology:

- Define the set of educational objectives in terms of the capabilities and values to be developed.
- Design the teaching [using] feedback from the previous teaching experience, and findings from research.
- Teach according to this plan.
- Evaluate the extent to which students achieved the objectives.
- Document and disseminate the design lessons learned (Lo *et al.* 2004: 193).

This is very close to the process represented in Figure 5.1, with the exception of the final point, which explicitly places teachers within their own professional learning community.

Reigeluth also argues that education should make more use of design-based research focused on improvement, rather than descriptive research focused on comparison of methods (Reigeluth 2003). This is expressed by the feedback loops in Figure 5.1. The methodology requires formative research that generates data capable of improving the efficiency, effectiveness, and appeal of the teacher's design (Reigeluth 1999b). The knowledge generated by such work would be embedded in improved instructional formats, and in generic design principles. It would be a significant innovation if teachers did their own research: "faculties seem inclined to use research and experimentation to

Table 5.1 Teaching Principles and the Strategies Proposed to Meet Them

Principles	Guidelines for teacher's roles and actions
Align goals, activities, assessment	draw on learners' experiences to align their goals with the teacher's; use assessments that tap understanding, not facts or isolated skills; test deep conceptual understanding rather than surface knowledge
Monitor alternative conceptions	actively inquire into students' thinking; ask about internal relations within the structure; recognize students' preconceptions that make the topic challenging; draw out the preconceptions that may not be predictable; use formative assessment to make students' thinking visible to themselves, their peers, and their teacher
Scaffold theory-based practice	simplify the task, so that the learner can manage components of the process and recognize when a fit with task requirements is achieved; provide feedback and modeling that can guide modification of actions and the concepts that generated them; design exercises within the learner's zone of proximal development; design exercises that provide the meaningful intrinsic feedback that learners are able to interpret and use to revise their actions; create tasks and conditions that reveal student thinking; give learners the means to build an external representation of their knowledge to share with others
Foster conceptual knowledge development	use examples to help students discern the concept in focus from the similarities and contrasts between instances; analyze the architecture of variation that reveals conceptual structure; develop a "discursive microworld" for conceptual learning; work with preconceptions so students challenge and replace them
Encourage meta-cognition	encourage students to practice and discuss metacognitive strategies; model the use of meta-cognitive strategies; encourage students to practice and discuss these strategies; engage students in grading their own and their peers' performance; encourage group discussion of both content and learning processes; show students have different conceptualizations; compare descriptions and highlight differences and inconsistencies

understand and improve every institution, process, and human activity except their own" (Bok 2006: 317).

Turning teaching into a design-based research activity is an acknowledgement that teachers need to practice a form of experiential learning themselves, rather than rely wholly on a structured body of formal knowledge. Few teachers make reference to the educational research literature, and no doubt make use of their own heuristics, but this is not the same as taking a design-based approach, which demands a more rigorous and collaborative approach. Treating teaching as a design science would be a radical move in all sectors of education.

A Principled Approach to Designing for Learning

This chapter has attempted to unpack the core of the diagram in Figure 5.1 – the teaching activities needed, given the intended learning outcomes and students' likely study approaches and learning needs, to elicit the learning activities that will result in learning outcomes that come close to those intended.

Chapter 4 ended by summarizing what we know to be the key activities involved in what it takes to learn. The texts referenced in this chapter provide assistance to teachers who wish to address those learning needs. I have organized their guidelines for teachers around the five main design principles that come closest to addressing the requirements generated in Chapter 4: aligning goals, activities, and assessment, monitoring alternative conceptions, scaffolding theory-generated practice, fostering conceptual change, and encouraging meta-cognition. These are collected together in Table 5.1.

Summary

Table 5.1 distils the conclusions from the literature that constitute design guidelines for teachers. There is a consensus across the different schools of thought on one fundamental issue: that since the learning process and its context is so complex, we cannot be prescriptive about the principles of teaching, and therefore teaching should itself be an iterative process of learning. In design science terms, teachers would be doing the "progressive refinement" discussed in Chapter 1 that makes improvement possible.

The required learning activities summarized at the end of Chapter 4 are broadly addressed by the literature on educational design summarized in this chapter. Educational design theorists have also introduced more reference to learners engaging with their peers as a way of scaffolding the learning process. There is a risk however, that the guidelines generated from research tend to be too generic to be of real practical value.

Teachers wanting to improve the quality and effectiveness of the learning experience for students need a principled approach that distils theory and practice on formal learning in a way that informs and guides their design, links the generic pedagogy to the specific teaching and learning activities relevant to their subject, and helps them test it in practice.

The next chapter sets out to do this, aiming to achieve a workable consolidation of what the field can say about what it takes to teach.

6 Motivating and Enabling the Learning Cycle

Introduction

Previous chapters have looked at what formal learning is, what students bring to the process, what it takes to learn in a formal context, and what it takes to teach. This, broadly speaking, is one principal thread of the story so far:

- Formal learning – learning about experts' descriptions of the world – is different from the way we learn about the world for ourselves, which makes it much more uncertain and difficult to research, hence the reluctance of educational design theorists to be specific and prescriptive, no matter how ambitious the demands on, and aspirations of, our education systems.
- Students need help with motivation to learn because formal learning has distant rewards, except for the intrinsic reward of intellectual curiosity. They need help with how to approach the learning of something that is the product of someone else's thinking, and teachers do not naturally provide an environment that affords learning of this kind.
- What it takes to learn in formal education has processes in common with what it takes to learn in the natural and social world, but is not the same. What we know from the disciplines contributing to education is complementary and gives a complex picture of what the learner needs to do.
- What it takes to teach cannot be determined directly from what it takes to learn, which means that teachers must be willing to treat the process as essentially problematic, iterative, and always improvable; we must stop assuming that teaching can be theorized like a natural science, and treat it as a design science.

There is a considerable gulf of uncertainty between knowing what it takes to learn and knowing what it takes to teach, and the educational design world has not yet bridged it.

The aim of establishing workable guidelines for teachers brings us to the principal focus for this book. The design of teaching and learning has become far more complex in the last decade or so because the technologies available to education have expanded dramatically, a trend that looks likely to continue. Digital technologies are now ubiquitous in education, and have transformed the range of teaching-learning activities available. They should, therefore, be subjected to a critical evaluation alongside all the existing conventional methods if we are to use them effectively.

The Under-Performance of Learning Technologies

The promise of learning technologies is that they appear to provide what the theorists are calling for. Because they are interactive, communicative, user-controlled technologies, they fit well with the requirement for social-constructivist, active learning. They have had little critique from educational design theorists. On the other hand, the empirical work on what is actually happening in education now that technology is widespread has shown that the reality falls far short of the promise.

The measures used to assess progress by both UK and US public funders of digital technologies in education, have often focused on input parameters, such as the ratio of students to computers, rather than output parameters, such as the benefits and value to the students. Larry Cuban in the US has argued that the promised revolution in schools is illusory, since the evidence suggests that teachers "adapt technology to fit the familiar practices of teacher-centered instruction" (Cuban 2001). He and his colleagues list some possible reasons:

1.   Teachers have too little time to find and evaluate software.
2.   They do not have appropriate training and development opportunities.
3.   It is too soon – we need decades to learn how to use new technology.
4.   Educational institutions are organized around traditional practices.

In the UK the government agency Becta collected data over several years, which showed continual progress in the access and use of technology, and a gradual shift towards "enthusiastic" and "e-enabled" use, but these are also essentially input parameters measuring changes in self-description by schools and colleges, rather than effectiveness (Becta 2006). This kind of data does not assess the extent to which technology is changing teaching practice, or changing the way learners learn. The latest report echoes Cuban's reasons for lack of change in teaching practice: "lack of awareness of the benefits of different practice for learning, lack of practical pedagogical skills, and possibly lack of time and incentives to develop practice" (Becta 2008).

Similar issues are apparent in higher education, where the technology has been available even longer than in schools, and yet has not revolutionized the quality and effectiveness of the learning experience, partly because of the nature of our education systems (Laurillard 2008b). These are wide-ranging systemic issues, such as the politics of education, methods of assessment and quality assurance processes, which the focus of this book does not touch. But if they were all to change, as they will over time, and create an institutional and cultural environment more conducive to innovative teaching, there would still be the problem of exactly how to optimize the design of learning technologies.

While we cannot expect that a revolution in the quality and effectiveness of education will necessarily result from the wider use of technology, we should expect the education system to be able to discover how to exploit its potential more effectively. It has to be teachers and lecturers who lead the way on this. No-one else can do it. But they need much more support than they are getting.

The aim of this chapter is to establish a way of guiding and testing all forms of teaching-learning activity, conventional and digital, in a way that generates a workable methodology for teachers as designers.

A Framework for Analyzing Formal Learning

Figure 4.1 brought together in one representation seven different accounts of the learning process: associative, cognitive, experiential, social constructivist, conceptual, constructionist, and collaborative learning, and Table 4.2 used it to show how teachers can make an impact on the process. This single representation depicts what seem to be the irreducible components and the iterative connections between them, of a learning process involving a teacher.

One version of this cyclical process would be "learning without a formal teacher", the "unsupervised" learning that neuroscientists refer to, or the "developmental" learning of cognitive psychologists, or the "informal" learning of educationists. Table 6.1 illustrates the successive stages that might be involved in learning without a teacher, and shows two contrasting interpretations: (a) a baby learning to grasp an object, and (b) a student learning to use a new specialized concept appropriately in analyzing a socio-political situation in discussion with other students.

The two examples are chosen to show that the same representation is capable of being applied to two very different types of learning situation. They also show that the initial goal may not determine the outcome of learning. The learner can react to negative feedback in many different ways, including adjusting their goal and strengthening the action that failed, rather than changing the action. This is why teachers have to work to align learner goals with their own, unless they are content with learners developing their own goals. The learner's initial goal–action–feedback cycle takes place in the external environment, which includes both the physical and the social world, and both can modulate goal, action, or concept. The social science student is acting in the academic environment of analyzing a situation with fellow students, but what begins as the goal of applying a concept then becomes a social goal of winning an argument. The learning process does not have uniquely determinable outcomes.

Table 6.1 The Mechanisms Involved in Learning without a Teacher, Interpreted for (a) a Baby Learning from an Action, and (b) a Student Learning from their Peers

Learning processes	Interpretations in contrasting examples
The learner develops their goal (A)	(a) To pick up a toy (b) To apply the concept of "vandalism" to a given situation
The goal generates an action from their practice capability (B_L), modulated by their conceptual interpretation of the task (C_L)	(a) It involves moving the arm and coordinating this with moving the fingers (b) The term "vandalism" is applicable to a certain class of situations, but the given situation is not one of them
The action generated (D_E) modulates the external environment (E)	(a) The baby's hand knocks the toy over, which amuses the adults (b) The student's interpretation contrasts with that of other students
The action produces some form of result from the environment (F_E)	(a) The toy falls over, the adults laugh (b) The other students argue that concrete office blocks can be a form of vandalism
The result acts as informational feedback on the extent to which the action achieved the goal (A)	(a) and (b) The result was unexpected as the action appears not to have achieved the initial goal
If it is achieved the conception (C_L) and action (D_E) is modulated to strengthen it	(a) and (b) The initial goal was not clearly achieved so this does not modulate the selected action
If not, the failure of that action is used to modulate the conception (C_L) and the goal (A) that generated it	(a) The action needs to be gentler to pick up the toy, but if you want to make adults laugh, knock it over (b) The concept needs to be nuanced to achieve agreement with others
This produces either a new goal or reactivates the same goal but using a new action generated by the modulated conception	(a) It's more fun to make the adults laugh, so the baby repeats the same action to achieve that goal, modulating both action and goal (b) It's more interesting to defend their initial concept, so the student modulates their goal to do this, and modulates their action to elaborate their defense of their argument

Ways of Facilitating Learning

The primary interest in this book is the process of formal learning with a teacher, and how the teacher can design the teaching-learning environment to facilitate learning. What Table 6.1 does not represent is what makes the student's learning situation distinct from the baby's, i.e. the role of language, the ability to communicate that Frith identifies as the means by which "knowledge passes from one generation to the next" (see Chapter 4).

Chapter 4 worked towards a representation of the learning process as a consolidation of the main theories of learning. Figure 6.1 shows an elaborated representation of the internal learning process that was developed in Figure 4.1. The learner interacts with the teaching-learning environment at two levels: by generating articulations of their concepts, and by acting on the external environment; and they receive feedback on both. The teacher's role, to put it most simply, is to motivate the internal cycles generating and modulating the learner's concepts and practice, which is what facilitates learning. The teacher designs the way the learner engages with their intended concepts and practice in the teaching-learning environment – but how?

The links in Figure 6.1 are drawn as double lines to indicate the continual iterative cycles that enable the learner to develop their concepts and practice in the way the teacher intends. In the cut and thrust of teachers and learners interacting with each other there will be many different ways in which these iterative cycles work, some over short periods of a few minutes but often long periods of several weeks. The interactions take place as discussions that link teacher concepts and learner concepts, practice tasks where the teacher provides the practice environment for learners to apply their concepts, and ways of mixing both. The teacher is not always present, so the learner is work-ing independently, supported by the teacher represented in the form of pres-entations in books, documents, websites, videos, and working in the practice or modeling environment the teacher has designed as practice exercises, projects, labs, programs.

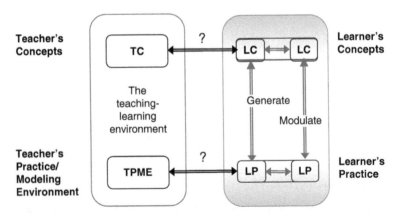

Figure 6.1 The learner learning, represented as a cyclical iteration within their conceptual organization, within their practice, and between the two, while interacting with the teaching–learning environment.

Whatever the particular circumstances of the interaction between teacher and learner, the simplest way of capturing the fundamental form of the teaching-learning interaction is the diagram in Figure 6.1. Teacher and learner are the essential participants; concepts and practice are the interrelated capabilities being developed; there are two ways of interacting between teacher and learner, through language and representations of the concepts, and through applying the concepts as practice.

Having stripped down the teacher-learner interaction to a framework of its bare structural essentials, we now have to put back the detail of how this plays out in the classroom, the tutorial, the lab, the assignment. What are the different ways in which teacher and learner work together in education, and to what extent do they succeed in motivating the internal learning cycle?

We begin by looking at three distinct cycles of interaction between teacher and learner: the teacher communication cycle, the teacher practice cycle, and the teacher modeling cycle.

Teacher Communication Cycle

In Chapter 5 we looked at what the learning design literature proposed for the roles the teacher could play in facilitating learning. The *teacher communication cycle* represents what Table 5.1 summarized as the teacher's role in aligning goals, monitoring conceptions, and fostering conceptual knowledge:

- draw on learners' experiences to align their goals with the teacher's;
- use assessments that tap understanding, not facts or isolated skills;
- test deep conceptual understanding rather than surface knowledge;
- actively inquire into students' thinking;
- ask about internal relations within the structure;
- recognize students' preconceptions that make the topic challenging;
- draw out the preconceptions that may not be predictable;
- use formative assessment to make students' thinking visible to themselves and their teacher;
- use examples to help students discern the concept in focus as similarities and contrasts between instances;
- analyze the architecture of variation that will reveal the conceptual structure;
- develop the "discursive microworld" that affords the learning of the concept in focus;
- work with preconceptions so students challenge and replace them.

Figure 6.2(a) represents this social constructivism and conceptual learning through the cyclical iteration between the teacher's and the learner's concepts. The arrows in the diagram depict the teacher influencing the learner's internal cycle at the conceptual level by:

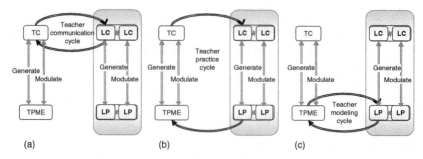

Figure 6.2 The learner learning concepts (LC) and practice (LP) through interaction in (a) the teacher communication cycle, (b) the teacher practice cycle, (c) the teacher modeling cycle, from the teacher's conceptual organization (TC), and the practice/modeling environment set up by the teacher (TPME).

1. explaining a concept through language or other forms of representation,
2. eliciting learners' questions or the way they articulate their concept or reflect on their experience,
3. responding to learners' questions and commenting on their articulations.

The "teacher's conceptual organization" stands for whatever representation of the curriculum is appropriate for the current learning context – it may be a class presentation, a lecture, a book, a handout, a video, a diagram, a PowerPoint slide, a web resource – whatever the teacher is using to help the learner to learn by attending to their explanations and demonstrations. Or the teacher may be giving hints and guidance to learners as they work, or giving comments on an essay or report – the many ways the teacher helps their learners to learn by commenting on how they express their understanding.

The figure represents the iterative links as double lines again because the number of cycles is an important pedagogical criterion. How many does it take for each member of a conversation to be sure they share the same idea? One cycle, such as:

T: Plurality in government means that parties compete for votes to govern
L: I understand

would not be sufficient for either teacher or learner to be sure they share the same idea. They need a second cycle for the teacher to elicit the learner's interpretation, and the learner needs some assurance they are on the right lines:

T: What would be an example of a government that is not pluralist?
L: A dictatorship?
T: Good.

This second cycle assures both parties that they share the same idea. The teacher communication cycle does not normally operate one-to-one, of course, and the more typical cycle would be:

T: explains concepts
Ls: write essays
T: marks essays.

But most essays will not have achieved the intended learning outcome, so this cycle will not assure both teacher and learner that they share the same idea, and would need a further cycle:

Ls: improve essays in the light of teacher comments
T: re-marks essays

This is a "formative assessment" cycle, and is very labor intensive, of course. Is there a better design? The most efficient cycle a teacher could hope for is to give a class presentation, use an audience response system to elicit learners' choices of answer to a question about the presentation, and receive 100% correct responses from the class – this cycle would assure teacher and learners alike that they share the same idea (unless learners are guessing – it is still not infallible). The number of cycles is important pedagogically because this is how teacher and learner both know the learner has learned what was intended. And of course it is clear from this how difficult it is for teachers with large classes to assure the success of the teacher communication cycle for the individual student.

Teacher Practice and Modeling Cycles

The teacher can also influence the learner's internal cycle at the practice level that reflects the ideas of experiential learning and constructionism, by:

1   providing a practice environment in which the learner can generate actions from their practice repertoire with feedback from the teacher, and
2   providing a modeling environment that can itself respond with meaningful informational feedback on the actions they take.

The *teacher practice cycle* in Figure 6.2(b) represents some of the teacher's roles in scaffolding theory-based practice summarized in Table 5.1 as:

* design exercises within the learner's zone of proximal development;
* create tasks and conditions under which student thinking can be revealed;
* give learners the means to build an external representation of their knowledge to share with others;

- provide feedback that can guide modification of actions and the concepts that generated them.

These roles will be familiar to every teacher who sets exercises for their students to practice their skills and to link theory to practice, in homework and assignments for teacher marking. Again at least two cycles are needed to assure both teacher and learner that the learner is learning, e.g.:

T: sets task to explore how healthy their normal diet is against given criteria
L: investigates real world properties of diet against criteria and properties of food types
T: the practice environment specified by the teacher provides the data for the learner to analyze
L: the learner analyzes and reports on the data collected and interprets the extent to which this is a healthy diet
T: the teacher comments on the report to indicate to the learner how well they have done the analysis and interpretation.

The sequence is a mix of practice and communication, where the learner needs the extrinsic feedback on their report from the teacher to be sure of the extent to which they have learned because their home eating environment responds to their actions with information, not feedback.

An environment that does provide feedback reduces the demand on the teacher, but is more challenging from a design point of view. This is the *teacher modeling cycle,* shown in Figure 6.2(c), which represents what Table 5.1 summarized as the remainder of the tasks in the scaffolding role:

- simplify the task, so that the learner can manage components of the process and recognize when a fit with task requirements is achieved;
- provide feedback and modeling that can guide modification of actions and the concepts that generated them;
- design exercises that provide the meaningful intrinsic feedback that learners are able to interpret and use to revise their actions.

Creating a modeling environment that models the task in such a way that the learner can see the result of their actions in comparison with the intended model is one of the most powerful ways of learning, and enables the learner to "learn without being taught" – when the tasks are within their capability and they are able to interpret the feedback, i.e. it is meaningful to them. The modeling environment enables the learner to learn through generating actions to achieve a goal and using the feedback to modulate their practice as revised actions to improve the fit with the goal. For example, if the modeling environment is an interactive model of family eating, the learner can test their understanding without teacher intervention. Here the cycles also have to repeat to assure learning, e.g.

T: the program sets a task to design a daily menu that achieves given criteria for a healthy diet
L: the learner selects food types and amounts for a daily intake
T: the program displays the learner's menu scores against alternative menus with better scores
L: the learner uses the comparison to design an improved menu
T: the program displays the extent to which the menu achieves a better score.

For both teacher and learner, the great advantage of this adaptive microworld is that the learner can keep working on improving their menu design without feedback from the teacher because they are getting intrinsic feedback on their actions from the model in the program, and this enables them to see how to improve.

For non-quantifiable topics, where there are often many acceptable answers, a program can provide a comparison with alternative good models of an output, such as alternative ways of translating a text into a second language, or alternative ways of interpreting child behavior exhibited on a video clip – the learner's action may not be wrong, but "model answers" like this enable them to see how well they have done by comparison, and where they can improve – again, without teacher intervention.

Peer Communication and Modeling Cycles

The framework we use to analyze formal learning must also represent the role of other learners. As Vygotsky suggests, they play the important role of eliciting the learner's concept as one aspect of social constructivism, and, as Chapter 4 discussed, of encouraging learners to produce and exchange outputs of their practice. The other learner does not take on the teacher's responsibility of initiating explanations of theory or models of practice, and they cannot be held responsible for meaningful information feedback and accurate comment – they may happen to do this, but may not be able to. Each learner plays the same role for each other learner, of eliciting the expression of an idea and its instantiation in practice (i.e. each of the peer learners is also represented in LC and LP). They can offer critiques, ideas, comments, questions, and alternative outputs, and so motivate the iterative cycles between concepts and practice, and assist each other's meta-cognition. The peer communication and modeling cycles represent what Table 5.1 summarized as the teacher's role in encouraging meta-cognition, and the means to exchange ideas and practice with their peers:

- use formative assessment to make students' thinking visible to their peers;

- give learners the means to build an external representation of their knowledge to share with others;
- encourage students to practice and discuss metacognitive strategies;
- model the use of meta-cognitive strategies;
- encourage students to practice and discuss these strategies as they learn to use them;
- engage students in grading their own and their colleagues' performance;
- provide opportunities for group discussion of both content and learning processes;
- show students have different conceptualizations;
- compare descriptions and highlight differences and inconsistencies.

Figure 6.3 represents the role of peer learners on the same framework by complementing the teacher-learner interactions with the *peer communication cycle* and the *peer modeling cycle*.

As learners exchange ideas through discussion and exchange their outputs from the practice or modeling environment through collaboration, these cycles also need to repeat until the learners have negotiated an agreed understanding, or, perhaps more interestingly, have been unable to agree and have a question to put to the teacher.

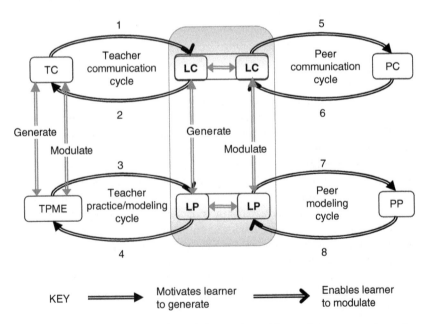

Figure 6.3 The learner learning through interaction with peers' concepts and practice (PC, PP), exchanging concepts and the outputs of their practice (numbered components are defined later in the text).

The Conversational Framework

The framework in Figure 6.3 is the Conversational Framework, which was developed as a way of challenging the use of new technologies in learning (Laurillard 2002). It was derived from the then current research on student learning, and inspired by the example of Gordon Pask's *Conversation Theory*, a cybernetic model of teaching and learning (Pask 1976). The framework is used here to represent the analysis of formal learning that derives from the wider literature on learning discussed in the previous chapters.

It is significant that our understanding of the formal learning process still references the work of Dewey, Piaget, and Vygotsky, nearly a century later. What it takes to learn has not changed, despite the profound cultural and technological developments over that period. The basic account of formal learning as an iterative process, linking both knowledge and skills (theory and practice), and engaging the learner with teachers and their peers remains unchanged. What does change is how we motivate and enable formal learning.

The aim of the Conversational Framework is to represent, as simply as possible, the different kinds of roles played by teachers and learners in terms of the requirements derived from conceptual learning, experiential learning, social constructivism, constructionism, and collaborative learning, and the corresponding principles for designing teaching and learning activities in the instructional design literature. This is the simplest possible static visual representation that can capture the complexity of the collective ideas in the literature on what it takes to learn, and therefore what it takes to teach.

Some of the critiques of the Conversational Framework have focused on its complexity. I wish it could be simpler, as elegant as the Kolb Learning Cycle, or as memorable as Senge's Double-Loop learning, but although these representations of learning are compatible with it, I think they omit too much. Formal learning has to take account of what both teacher and learner do. It has to acknowledge both theory and practice. And it has to embrace both individual and social learning.

Alternative frameworks are compatible, but can be even more complex (Conole 2004). The conceptual framework proposed by Noel Entwistle and Colin Smith provides a useful way of thinking about education, and can be readily adapted because it is so general, but although it focuses teachers' attention on what influences a student's understanding, it does not seek to clarify the nature of the iterative relationship between teaching method and learning activity, which together influence the learning outcomes. This is an important relationship for designing teaching because that is where the pedagogical power of digital technology lies. Similarly, the analysis of theories of learning carried out by Bransford and others, referred to in Chapter 5, built a synergy across the disciplines to provide a better foundation for designing teaching, but did not represent a synthesis that could be used by teachers for design.

The idea of the Conversational Framework is to try to use the salient ideas in the principal theories of learning to give us the basis for understanding how to design teaching and learning now that digital technologies are making more impact on education. It cannot claim to be a complete synthesis perhaps, but it can offer a practical framework for design.

The Formal Framework

The representation in Figure 6.3 shows all the ways in which the teacher and other learners motivate the iterations in the internal learning cycle. To make these explicit they are defined as follows, where numbers refer to the activities in Figure 6.3.

The teacher communication cycle (TCC)

(1)   enables each learner to modulate their concept by giving them access to the teacher's concept,

(2, 1) motivates each learner to generate questions or articulations of their concept and practice because the teacher is giving them extrinsic feedback.

The teacher practice cycle (TPC)

(4, 1) motivates each learner to modulate their practice by generating actions that elicit extrinsic feedback from the teacher.

The teacher modeling cycle (TMC)

(4, 3) motivates each learner to modulate their practice by generating actions that elicit intrinsic feedback from the modeling environment.

The peer communication cycle (PCC)

(6)   enables each learner to modulate their concept by providing access to their peers' concepts,

(5, 6) motivates each learner to generate articulations because they are getting extrinsic feedback from their peers.

The peer modeling cycle (PMC)

(4, 7) motivates each learner to generate actions in the practice environment because they are sharing the output of their practice,

(8)   enables each learner to modulate their practice by using the model of their peer's output.

These are the cycles in the external learning context that contribute to the learner's internal learning cycle. There are many more complex cycles present in these iterative loops, difficult to express in a static diagram, but enacted every day between teachers and learners in all sectors of education.

To sum up the principles embedded in the formal framework: the teacher's design is aiming:

- to *motivate* or *enable* the learner
- to *generate* their *articulations* and *actions*
- that *modulate* their *concepts* and *practice*

and they do this by designing a teaching-learning environment for learners that provides design elements for each of the activities in each teacher/peer communication, practice and modeling cycle, detailed in Table 6.2

Any one teaching-learning event will use different combinations of these design elements. The overall teaching design principle is to use as many design elements as possible to motivate the iterative internal learning cycle that develops learners' concepts and practice.

By phrasing the teacher's design tasks in these terms, we can now see more easily what roles the technology could play.

Technologies for Teaching-Learning Activities

From the perspective of the individual learner, this framework for theories of formal learning proposes a rich mix of activities fuelling the impulse to build a more effective knowledge structure, and more skilled ways of using it. For the teacher as designer it explains why one design might be better than another in terms of the mix of teaching-learning activities, and the amount of iteration the designs motivate.

It takes several types of teaching–learning activity to cover the framework. Those commonly found throughout education, i.e. learning through

Table 6.2 Design Elements Mapped to Activities within the Conversational Framework Cycles

Design elements for activities in the Conversational Framework	Cycles
Access to the teacher's concepts	TCC1
The means to articulate their concepts and reflections on practice	TCC2
Extrinsic feedback on questions or articulations of their concepts	TCC3
A practice environment that facilitates their actions	TPC1
Extrinsic feedback on their articulations of their actions	TPC2
A modeling environment that elicits their actions	TMC1
Intrinsic feedback on their actions from the model	TMC2
Access to peers' concepts	PCC1
The means to articulate their concepts and reflections on practice	PCC2
Extrinsic feedback from peers on articulations of their concepts	PCC3
Sharing practice outputs with peers	PMC1
Access to peers' outputs as a model for their practice	PMC2

"acquisition", "inquiry", "practice", "production", "discussion", and "collaboration", together support the theories of learning discussed in Chapter 4, and cover the Conversational Framework. They are listed in Table 6.3, which shows that each one can use a range of different technologies and methods,

Table 6.3 Types of Learning and the Different Types of Conventional and Digital Learning Technologies that Serve Them

Learning through	Conventional technology	Digital technology
Acquisition	Reading books, papers; Listening to teacher presentations face-to-face, lectures; Watching demonstrations, master classes.	Reading multimedia, websites, digital documents and resources; Listening to podcasts, webcasts; Watching animations, videos.
Inquiry	Using text-based study guides; Analyzing the ideas and information in a range of materials and resources; Using conventional methods to collect and analyze data; Comparing texts, searching and evaluating information and ideas.	Using online advice and guidance; Analyzing the ideas and information in a range of digital resources; Using digital tools to collect and analyze data; Comparing digital texts, using digital tools for searching and evaluating information and ideas.
Practice	Practicing exercises; doing practice-based projects, labs, field trips, face-to-face role-play activities.	Using models, simulations, microworlds, virtual labs and field trips, online role-play activities.
Production	Producing articulations using statements, essays, reports, accounts, designs, performances, artifacts, animations, models, videos.	Producing and storing digital documents, representations of designs, performances, artifacts, animations, models, resources, slideshows, photos, videos, blogs, e-portfolios.
Discussion	Tutorials, seminars, email discussions, discussion groups, online discussion forums, class discussions, blog comments.	Online tutorials, seminars, email discussions, discussion groups, discussion forums, web-conferencing tools, synchronous and asynchronous.
Collaboration	Small group project, discussing others' outputs, building joint output.	Small group project, using online forums, wikis, chat rooms, etc. for discussing others' outputs, building a joint digital output.

both conventional and digital. None of the technologies provide the design elements that serve all types of teaching-learning activity.

The first four types of learning – acquisition, inquiry, practice, and production – describe individual learning, while discussion and collaboration describe social learning, where the learner engages with at least one peer. Figure 6.4 shows how the Conversational Framework represents the types of individual learning.

For learning through *acquisition* (Figure 6.4(a)), the learner is reading, hearing or watching an explanation of the teacher's concept, or the teacher's model actions. This enables the learner to modulate their own concept, and see a demonstration of the teacher's practice, but does not require them to generate any action or articulation. Technologies and methods used are typically lectures, class presentations, books, documents, videos, and web resources.

For learning through *inquiry* (Figure 6.4(b)), the learner is prompted to investigate the texts, documents, and resources that reflect the concepts and ideas being taught. The learner is more in control, but is being guided to

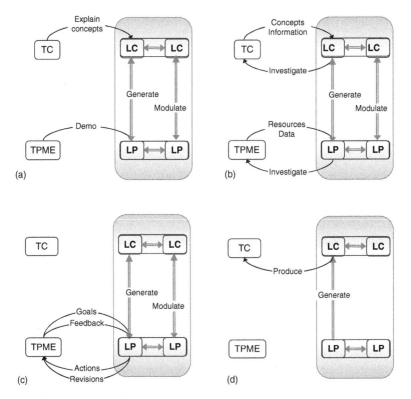

Figure 6.4 Types of individual learning mapped to the Conversational Framework (a) learning through acquisition, (b) learning through inquiry, (c) learning through practice, and (d) learning through production.

investigate and compare concepts or information, investigate and use resources and data, and so modulate their conceptual organization by generating these investigations and using what they find to articulate their changing concepts, i.e. learning through finding out. Technologies and methods used are collections of material and digital resources, fieldwork, site visits, and virtual reality environments.

This contrasts with learning through *practice* (Figure 6.4(c)), where learners are using their developing concepts to improve their actions: to put the theory into practice in working to a goal, generating an action to achieve it, and using the feedback to modulate their action or their conception. Examples discussed in Chapter 5 include analyzing a poem or trying to optimize a model of climate change. The teacher's role illustrated here is to provide a modeling environment that requires action and provides intrinsic feedback. Technologies and methods used are model answers, worked examples, interactive games, simulations, microworlds, and adaptive models.

Learning through *production* (Figure 6.4(d)) is the way the teacher motivates the learner to consolidate what they have learned by articulating their current conceptual understanding and how they used it in practice. It is an aspect of the learning process that is hardly discussed by learning theorists, but it plays an important role in education. Producing an essay, for example, is meant to motivate the learner to pull together and organize their exploration and critique of the literature; the project report motivates them to draw conclusions from their inquiry and practical work, and account for how they arrive at them; producing a design or performance motivates them to present their practice in the form of a public output. Producing an output generates a representation of the learning enabled by the other types. In its simplest form it is the learner's articulation of their current thinking, which enables the teacher to respond with extrinsic feedback, guidance, and further explanation.

The types of individual learning show the internal conversations the learner conducts as they think through what they are trying to learn, reflecting on what they are hearing or reading or receiving as feedback, and modulating their concepts (LC–LC) and practice (LP–LP) accordingly.

Figure 6.5 shows how the Conversational Framework represents the types of social learning. For learning through *discussion* with other students, the teacher provides some stimulus in the form of a question, or issue, and the learners generate ideas and questions which in turn create a demand for each learner to modulate their ideas, and generate further ideas and questions. Technologies and methods are small groups, seminars, asynchronous online discussion forums, and synchronous chat.

Learning through *collaboration* incorporates learning through discussion, practice, and production. Learners exchange the products or outputs from their practice, which motivates them not only to modulate their actions, but also to generate a discussion of the reasons for them. The teacher's role here is to provide the means to create shareable outputs, the task goal to produce a joint product, and a practice/modeling environment for developing

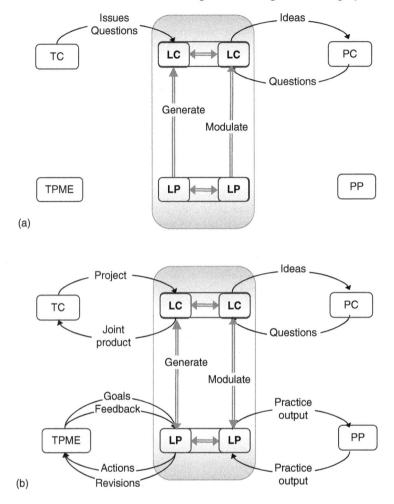

Figure 6.5 Types of social learning mapped to the Conversational Framework (a) learning through discussion, and (b) learning through collaboration.

their output. This type of learning is likely to motivate more iteration between the learner's concept and practice than the other types discussed, because it combines both learning through practice and learning through discussion. Technologies and methods are group projects, group work with modeling environments, wikis and other online knowledge-building environments.

These mappings represent how the learner experiences the types of learning. We alternate them in lessons and courses precisely because they have different kinds of value for the learner, so we should be able to express the nature of that value. Teachers aim for an optimal mix of these common types of learning appropriate to their context. The Conversational Framework provides a comparative analysis of what each type contributes to supporting the learner.

The Framework as a Design Analysis Tool

Since it describes what it takes to create an effective learning design, the Conversational Framework can also act as a design analysis tool. It provides a way of analyzing a learning design in terms of the mix of activities and the likely amount of iteration it motivates. In the move to greater use of learning technologies we should be able to account for why we expect them to improve the learning experience. For example, the framework has been used to show why mobile technologies (Cook *et al.* 2007) are able to enhance the learning experience in a public space such as an exhibition, museum, or art gallery, in comparison with a conventional approach (Laurillard 2007). Here is an illustration of how it works.

The learning outcome is that students should be able to articulate the thesis being presented in the exhibition. The teaching methods for the initial design combine class work and fieldwork to help the students make the most of their visit to the gallery. The first column in Table 6.4 outlines this conventional approach. The second column annotates the initial design with the associated components of the Conversational Framework. Since this reveals that the design covers only some of the components, the third column redesigns the learning experience by making use of students' mobile phones to provide a more effective practice environment, and to give students the means to collaborate. The fourth column annotates the new activities with the associated components of the Conversational Framework. The redesign is a much richer learning experience, fuelling more iteration of all dialogue forms and, in that sense, is more likely to be effective for the students.

The reason for using the digital technology is clear from the improved coverage of the Conversational Framework it achieves and from the opportunities it creates for learners to repeat the learning cycles of generating and modulating their concepts and practice.

By setting out the learning design in this way it should be possible to show how it can answer the questions:

- What motivates the learner to keep generating actions and articulations?
- What enables the learner to keep modulating their concepts and practice?

Table 6.5 shows the extent to which each cycle in the Conversational Framework addresses these two questions, where the design criteria are linked to the types of learning listed in Table 6.3.

The effectiveness of any teaching-learning design has to be tested with learners to find out whether it succeeds in eliciting the intended activities from students, and whether they achieve the intended learning outcome.

Table 6.4 Using the Conversational Framework to Show how Digital Tools Create a Richer Learning Design Pattern

Initial design (conventional)	CF components covered	Redesign (adding digital technology)	CF components covered
Teacher introduces the work of the artists; Teacher provides extracts of the catalog linked to key paintings for students to read in advance	*Enables* the learner to *modulate* concepts (TCC1)	Same, plus: *Teacher provides extracts of the presentation for students to download to their mobile devices*	*Enables* the learner to *modulate* concepts (TCC1)
Teacher provides access to gallery and study guide for students to work in pairs on the key paintings and the relations between them; Instructions to take notes to bring back to class	*Motivates* each learner to *generate* analyses that will elicit later feedback in class (TPC1, 2)	Same, plus: *Guide provides digital codes for each painting; Instructs students to identify features in paintings, and upload answers; Students can check their inputs against the teacher's model answer*	*Motivates* each learner to *generate* actions that elicit immediate feedback to each learner (TMC1)
Students to work in pairs in the gallery, using the guide to make notes	*Motivates* the learner to *generate* a comment that will elicit feedback in class (TPC1)	*Students to generate challenges and responses for other student pairs;* *Students record and upload their ideas and observations to a shared website*	*Motivates* each learner to *generate* actions that elicit alternative actions (PMC1) *Motivates* each learner to *generate* a comment that will elicit feedback to each learner (PCC1, 2)
In the next class discussion, students are asked to report on what they noticed and the notes they took	*Motivates* each learner to *generate* a comment that elicits feedback in class (TPC2)	Same, plus: *Students use the whiteboard to display their records and notes from the gallery*	*Motivates* each learner to *generate* a comment that elicits feedback to each learner (PCC2)
The teacher summarizes students' comments in terms of the intended thesis	*Enables* learner to *modulate* concepts (TCC3)	Same, plus: *Students' outputs are a collaborative digital catalog of the exhibition on the school website*	*Enables* learner to *modulate* concepts (TCC3) *Motivates* each learner to *generate* a shared output (PMC1, 2)

Table 6.5 Design Criteria for the Teaching-Learning Cycles to Motivate and Enable Learning

What motivates the learner to generate actions and articulations? *What enables the learner to modulate their concepts and practice?*	
Teacher Communication Cycle (TCC) Learning through acquisition and production Figure 6.4(a) and (d)	*Enables* the learner to *modulate* their conception by providing access to the teacher's concept, and *motivates* them to *generate* an articulation that elicits extrinsic feedback
Teacher Practice Cycle (TPC) Learning through inquiry Figure 6.4(b)	*Motivates* the learner to *generate* an action that elicits extrinsic feedback, *enabling* them to *modulate* their concept
Peer Communication Cycle (PCC) Learning through discussion Figure 6.5(a)	*Motivates* the learner to *generate* a comment that elicits a comment from a peer, *enabling* them to *modulate* their concept
Teacher Modeling Cycle (TMC) Learning through practice Figure 6.4(c)	*Motivates* the learner to *generate* an action that elicits intrinsic feedback from the model, *enabling* them to *modulate* their concept and their practice
Peer Modeling Cycle (PMC) Learning through collaboration Figure 6.4(b)	*Motivates* each learner to *generate* an output to negotiate as a shared output, *enabling* each learner to *modulate* their concept and their practice

Note: For codes See Table 6.2.

The framework used in this way provides an explicit account of what is expected, so it sets the criteria for a formative evaluation of the design.

The Idea of Pedagogical Patterns

Chapter 1 argued that teachers could be seen as design scientists, working in the way designers and reflective practitioners do in all such professions, to keep improving their practice, in a principled way, building on the work of others, and developing the knowledge base of the field. Unlike other professionals, we have few tools for representing, testing, and sharing teaching designs. Sharing the resources developed through the Open Educational Resource movement is good, but this only shares the practice; teaching journals, conferences, and magazines are good, but only articulate the principles. And none of these properly develop our knowledge of the optimal use of technology for learning.

The idea of "pedagogical patterns" is to develop a way to articulate, test, and share the principles and practice of teaching that builds our knowledge of how to use digital technologies (Laurillard and McAndrew 2003). The name "pedagogical pattern" differentiates this format from the more generic "design patterns", from the more technical "learning design", and from the less structured "learning pattern" (McAndrew, Goodyear, and Dalziel 2006), and attaches it to "pedagogy" as the means of facilitating formal learning. Chapter 1 proposed the categories of description a pedagogical pattern would need to include, at the heart of which was the link between "a sequence of teaching–learning activities" and the warrant for the design in terms of how they related to "design principles."

To articulate the practice of teaching, the design pattern must be able to "capture the pedagogy" that a teacher has found to be effective (Laurillard 2008). A "sequence of teaching–learning activities" (see Chapter 1) can be a simple narrative account, but that would not link to learning design principles. The Conversational Framework provides a way to do this. It specifies the roles to be played by teachers and learners in terms of the principal ideas in theories of learning, so the teaching–learning activities in a pedagogical pattern can be mapped to types of learning or learning cycles in the framework.

We have seen an example in Table 6.4 of a sequence of teaching–learning activities specific enough to be useful to a teacher, mapped to design principles, and showing the beneficial role of the technology.

Summary

This chapter set out to consider how we might evaluate the different teaching–learning activities in the teacher's repertoire against the requirements derived from theory. The Conversational Framework is intended to act as a challenge to the way both conventional and digital teaching–learning activities are designed to motivate and enable learning.

The collective understanding from over a century of educational research is that formal learning requires a complex set of iterative transactions between teachers and learners, and between the concepts and practice of the individual learner. The professional teacher takes all these into account in designing for learning:

- to *motivate* or *enable* the learner
- to *generate* their *articulations* and *actions*
- that *modulate* their *concepts* and *practice*.

Without that, the learners are left to their own resources. They may succeed. In fact the framework provides an effective definition of the outcome of "learning to learn":

> Skilled learners conduct their own internal learning cycles by setting up the means to interact with the environment and with others to generate the articulations and actions that elicit the feedback needed to modulate their concepts and practice.

The ideal for many teachers in schools, colleges, and universities is to develop such independent learners, but when the institutional focus is on passing exams, rather than on ways of thinking and practicing, the responsibility rests with the individual teacher to provide the scaffolding environment that develops independent learners.

The format for a pedagogical pattern that can represent its pedagogic design principles with reference to the Conversational Framework would meet the criteria set at the end of the last chapter.

The framework is as simple as possible given what we know about teaching and learning, and neutral with respect to the range of conventional and digital methods now available to teachers.

This last point is important. Digital technologies have been around for a long time now in all sectors of education. It should now be commonplace to include them in an analysis of how teachers should help students learn. However, in most of the books on theories of learning and instructional design, there is still a separation between conventional and digital technologies. There are theories that are common to both, but conventional and digital methods are discussed in separate chapters. The blend of teaching and learning methods that constitutes the practice of probably now the majority of teachers is not yet reflected in the literature that aims to support them.

To summarize: the Conversational Framework attempts to encapsulate what we know about the nature of formal learning, what students bring to learning, what it takes to learn, and what it takes to teach. The vertical iterative cycle represents what theories of learning claim about what happens in the mind of the learner, whereas the horizontal iterative cycles represent what educational design principles prescribe as the activities by teachers and learners and their peers that lead to productive learning. The teacher's vertical iterative cycle generates and modulates the teaching–learning environment they create.

On this basis, the next few chapters analyze the design of the teaching–learning process. Each chapter takes the perspective of the types of learning discussed here: through acquisition, inquiry, discussion, practice, and collaboration. Learning through production happens when learners generate articulations from all the other types of learning, as part of the teacher communication cycle. Each chapter shows how research on teaching and learning enables us to understand and challenge both conventional and digital methods, and through that analysis develop learning designs and pedagogical patterns that are optimized to be as effective as possible for our students.

7 Learning Through Acquisition

Introduction

This chapter works through studies of learning through acquisition – this is what learners are doing when they are listening to a lecture or podcast, reading from books or websites, and watching demos or videos. The process of learning through acquisition is probably still the most common in formal education. The student is playing a relatively passive role while the teacher uses the transmission mode of teaching.

Active learning has been an explicit intention of educational design since Dewey's advocacy of experiential learning a century ago, and yet students are still likely to spend a large part of their formal learning time in listening and reading. Learning technologies have simply shifted the narrative account of the subject matter from one medium to another, lectures to podcasts, and books to web resources. The multimedia capabilities now available through technology have been exploited well to improve presentational quality, using pictures, diagrams, animation, audio, video, and hypertext, but these attractive presentational formats still invite the learner to follow rather than initiate action, and language is still the dominant form of presentation.

The recent work on multimodality recognizes the importance of looking beyond language to acknowledge "the new multimodal configurations and genres (in both digital and print media) that are significant for creativity and learning" (Jewitt 2008). Jewitt argues that a multimedia environment, either physical or digital, with teachers co-present or not, is an opportunity for students to engage in many ways other than just following the storyline. A multimodal analysis shows that the affordances and constraints of a multimedia presentation can alter "as people strategically mix media and modes in performing concrete social actions" (Jones 2009). So the medium does not determine the form of learning. The teacher does that, by using it to convey what is to be done and what is to be learned (Jewitt 2008). In later chapters the same media mix will feature in more active forms of learning. In this chapter the focus is on what happens when the media are used to give a narrative account of the subject matter for learning through acquisition.

The narrative form is remarkably robust, no doubt because it is very efficient in terms of scarce and expensive teacher time, and remains a dominant form in teaching, even though students do not typically attain all the intended learning outcomes. And in higher education there has been no great clamor from students to change. In fact they have been known to complain when we stop lecturing and insist on them doing active learning. So in this chapter, because learning through acquisition plays such a significant role in formal education, the question is: "How do we make sure we use presentational teaching methods effectively?"

Learning Through Acquisition

The Conversational Framework shows all the types of teaching-learning activity we can use to make a learning design effective. It is a poor strategy to rely on just one, "teacher explains concept," which is the teacher side of "learning through acquisition," because it leaves so much for the students to do for themselves. We cannot avoid learning through acquisition. Students do need to learn what others have discovered, to hear about expert ways of thinking and practicing, and what is known already in their field. If Newton felt the need to stand on the shoulders of giants, the rest of us should probably do that too. It is this sense of enabling students to build on the work of others that is fundamental to formal education and the progressive development of ideas.

As we saw in Chapter 1, learning outcomes expect students to develop "awareness", "knowledge", "understanding", "perspectives", – we have many ways of saying we expect them to learn about the pre-existing knowledge of the discipline. We would disappoint our students if we did not. Many students are motivated, as Chapter 2 discussed, by an intellectual curiosity about why the world is the way it is, and how it works. From childhood onwards there is a hunger and curiosity to find out more about the world. Educators agree on the importance of understanding the key ideas and theories of our culture, science, and history, so learning through acquisition is important and inevitable. What educational theorists insist on is that simply telling the story of one's subject is not enough; hence the complexity of the framework that represents their theories. This chapter looks at the challenge of making learning through listening, reading, and watching – learning through acquisition – an active process.

Teaching Using Narrative Presentation

The media we naturally use to tell a story – present a theory, explain a concept, demonstrate a phenomenon, describe a perspective, or offer a point of view – are those that best support the narrative form: lectures, books, presentations, demonstrations, websites, podcasts, and videos. How can they support active learning?

Listening, reading, and watching are not the same as doing. They elicit a constrained form of thinking, requiring the audience to keep pace and follow the narrator, rather than follow their own ideas. Teachers are aware of these limits, and mix in questions and discussion in their class presentations, and exercises with model answers in readings, and audience participation in demonstrations.

Listening to presentations and podcasts, reading books and digital resources, and watching demos and videos are appropriate for learning through acquisition because they share the fundamental pedagogical feature that they require the student to follow the teacher's concepts and ideas through a structured narrative that has an intended meaning. For podcasts and digital resources the learner can control pace and sequencing, but the meaning and internal structure of the narrative are still there for the learner to *follow*.

The great value of the narrative form is its structure, and the cues that enable the audience to discern the author's meaning (Luckin *et al.* 2001). So this section looks at how a teaching method or medium uses structure to assist learner comprehension. The next section looks at ways of using digital technologies to augment these methods and improve their effectiveness. The following section considers how to prepare students well for learning from narrative presentations.

Structuring a Narrative Presentation

We know from Chapter 3 that academic discourse, whether presented in spoken, written or visual form, creates difficulties for students trying to follow the presentation. Students fail to discern the salient characteristics of the key concepts, and horizontalize the structure of the text, which distorts its meaning. To help in developing the skills of discerning structure, we concluded (see Table 4.2), that the teacher must:

1. clarify the internal structure of the concept;
2. clarify the internal structure of the text.

Because of the greater focus in the research literature on methods seen as supporting constructivism, there are rather few recent studies on how to design lectures, written texts, websites, podcasts, or videos for learning. The few there are confine their advice to reiterating the conclusion from student learning research, that it is important to make the structure clear, and suggest signposting and organizing devices such as headings, graphics, advance organizers, repetition, and summaries (Biggs 2003; Butcher, Davies, and Highton 2006; Duffy 2008; Fry, Ketteridge, and Marshall 2003; Horgan 2003; Mayer 1999).

The recent awakening of interest in audio and video podcasts, where lectures can be downloaded to mobile devices, has generated extensive use, but little evaluation and research. There is evidence that podcasts are effective for revision (Evans 2008; Lazzari 2009), which reflects the convenience of the medium more than its intrinsic pedagogic value, and that students in higher education value podcasts as a supplement to, rather than a replacement of traditional lectures, as they still want the contact with lecturers (Copley 2007). Lectures also fare well in comparison with web resources, where the straightforward transfer of the same material to its digital equivalent achieves no significant difference in knowledge acquisition. A study that compared a set of lectures with their equivalent on the web found that the requirements of the Conversational Framework, such as "Clear task goals, so that they know when they have achieved them … Intrinsic feedback that is meaningful, accompanied by access to extrinsic feedback" were "the very features for which our course members identified a need" (Frederickson, Reed, and Clifford 2005), namely, the interaction and feedback that learning theories propose, but that go beyond what the narrative form itself normally offers.

The digital equivalents of the traditional narrative methods used in education bring no special pedagogical advantage in terms of their narrative form, it seems, but are appreciated for their logistical convenience. How can the teacher optimize their pedagogic value? For that we turn to studies that address the two design requirements above.

Clarify the Structure of the Concept

Variation Theory is designed to address this issue. Chapter 3 recorded examples from several different disciplines of students who oversimplify the internal structures of concepts or fail to spot their salient features. The Conversational Framework, being derived from studies of how students learn, has nothing to say about *how* teachers should structure their presentation of the concept. Variation Theory does.

Variation Theory proposes how the text (in whatever medium) can help students focus on its structure, other than simply using good signposting and organizing devices (Marton and Booth 1997). The key is in building the "relevance structure" for their experience. Marton and Booth characterize learning as a "change in something in the world as experienced by a person" (ibid.: 139), an idea based on an experiment by Székely in 1950. The experiment gave a group of students a text on mechanics and moments of inertia followed by a demonstration showing the behavior of a torsion pendulum unwinding under different conditions. The second group was shown the demonstration and were asked to predict the effects of moving the weights; later they read the same text. The learning outcomes of the second group were much higher on a transfer task of predicting the outcome of a new experiment. Marton and Booth explain this in terms of the "relevance structure" of the learning activity, i.e. the learner's experience of a sense of a need to know. The learners in the second group, who saw that their prediction was wrong, had the great advantage of a wake-up call. Those in the first group, who were simply asked to follow the text and demonstration could slumber on in ignorance of their ignorance.

"Relevance structure" is an interesting idea because it gives some logical bite to the idea of "constructive alignment," and suggests how the learner's goal is shaped by the nature of the task and their interaction with it. It also recalls the idea of an "advance organizer", which uses the concepts the learner already has to build a bridge to the new, perhaps more complex concept, as a way of making it meaningful and relevant (Ausubel 2000). Although the precise form of the advance organizer may not always be clear, the value of advance organizers is to enable the learner to compare and contrast the new ideas with what they already know (Ausubel 1980). Marton takes this further to bring greater precision to the argument by focusing on the internal logic of the conceptual structure being learned.

Some concepts are more logically complex than others, which makes them more difficult to teach. A concept as a set of properties (e.g. coffee is made of x and costs y) is less complex than a concept that expresses a relation (e.g. the price of the coffee depends on the relationship between supply and demand). The teacher's task is to provide an experience of variation between instances of the concept that enables the learner to focus on its salient features. A nice example of this is the concept of "price", which can be seen as a property of a commodity, or as a relation that is dependent on demand (coffee got cheaper when everyone wanted one), or as dependent on supply (problems with the coffee harvest made it more expensive), or as dependent on the relationship between the two (the price of coffee varies in order to balance the relationship between supply and demand). Marton and Pang studied how teachers introduced the concept of price and concluded that the more successful pedagogical patterns focused more carefully on presenting an *experience of variation* of all aspects of the concept (Marton and Pang 2006):

- instead of using different commodities to illustrate variation of price with supply and of price with demand, they use the same commodity for each aspect of the concept;
- instead of showing the variation of price against just increases in supply and demand, they show the variation against both increases and decreases;
- instead of considering just cases where both supply and demand increase, they show also cases where they change simultaneously in opposite directions;
- instead of a static diagram to represent supply–demand curves, they use a computer animation to represent dynamically the relative change of magnitude in demand and supply so that the simultaneous movements between the two curves show directly how the balance between the two magnitudes changes.

These findings show how it is possible for the teacher to present a relational concept (price) more clearly by deconstructing it into all the forms of variation of its parameters (supply/demand, increase/decrease/relative change), and then reconstructing it to enable the learner to experience it as a simultaneous whole. The particular role of multimodal presentation was apparent in this study because it could show the simultaneous change in two magnitudes. This is a complex abstract idea that can only be visualized through computer animation, and could be critical to scaffolding the learner's full understanding. There are many other examples in Marton and Tsui's book, such as those already discussed in Chapter 5 (Marton and Tsui 2004).

The importance of the idea of variation in the way theoretical concepts are presented to students is also found in the work on representation. Many forms of non-textual representation are common in textbooks – symbols, diagrams, charts, graphs, icons, etc. Teachers often use multiple representations of a concept to assist the understanding of the text, because there are several advantages:

1. one may complement another so that together they provide a complete representation – visual and verbal versions of a story in a second language; words and diagrams describing the behavior of a system;
2. one may constrain the interpretation of another – an animation assists the interpretation of a graph; a symbolic form makes a verbal description more precise;
3. two different representations may together assist the construction of a deeper abstraction of the concept – a novel and an acted play depicting a political situation; an equation and a concrete instance of an event.

The disadvantage is that learners must be able to interpret the technical representations accurately, and integrate them with the meaning of the text, and this is a hard cognitive task in its own right (Ainsworth 2006). While multimodal theory celebrates the increasing multiplicity of forms of representation made possible by new technology, cognitive psychologists are showing that this may make the understanding of texts, and learning through acquisition more difficult, not less. Attractive visuals and dynamic animations may seem the most salient aspects of the presentation to the learner, but may not be the most important for understanding.

Cognitive load theorists, who come from a very different tradition, have investigated the issue most extensively, and provide a useful analysis. A teaching text creates three main sources of difficulty:

- the intrinsic complexity of the concepts;
- the extraneous complexity contributed by the way the text is presented; and
- the "germane cognitive load" (the cognitive activities relevant to making sense of the presentation).

We are stuck with the intrinsic complexity, but we can help with the other points. One way is to reduce the extraneous complexity, by introducing a static version of a graph or picture before a dynamic one, for example, to give the learner more time to process the information involved. Recent work has focused on the "germane cognitive load" by devising activities that make explicit the work it takes to interpret and integrate the different forms of representation. One example is to use "completion problems," where the student has to fill the gaps in progressively incomplete problem–solution paths. This technique is successful on transfer tests because the strategy helps students to abstract the generalized solution paths they need by working across variations in problem tasks (van Merriënboer *et al.* 2002), as Variation Theory would predict.

A second example is to direct students to link the textual and algebraic components of a screen presentation to their visual counterparts by drag and drop, so that learners can construct the integration of the two forms of representation themselves, and then check the accuracy (Bodemer *et al.* 2004). Here again we find the value of explicit variation across conceptual features, or situations, as a way of helping students focus on what is relevant. The teaching design does not rely on the presentation alone – it also directs learners to activities that deconstruct the concepts and their internal relationships.

To clarify the internal structure of the concept, therefore, the teacher must think about how to expose the whole complexity of the conceptual structure, and create tasks that coax the learner into focusing on what is salient, and thinking about how one part relates to the others.

Clarify the Internal Structure of the Text

We know that students using a surface approach to learning will fail to discern the structure, and therefore the meaning, of a text, whether given as lecture, or book. I found the same problem in a study of students learning from social science videos. The internal structure of the video was elaborate and yet obscured from the students, so they found it difficult to discern the overall meaning conveyed through that structure (Laurillard 1991). Their summaries of the videos focused on local meanings of particular sequences, especially those represented most evocatively through filming a vicarious experience and not just pointing the camera at talking heads.

The study built on Marton and Wenestam's work (see Chapter 4) on students' understanding of texts with a principle-example structure, and applied a similar methodology. The structural levels within five Open University videos were described in a similar way to that used for text, in terms of "the main point", which was made up from "component points", and illustrative "examples of components". Students' understanding of the videos was judged from their summaries, and the quality of these varied greatly across the five videos. The one on *Political Theory* generated summaries at the main point level from only 46% of the students; another, on *Social Integration*, generated summaries at the main point level from 80% of the students.

Why was the latter so much more successful? All the videos had the same principle-example structure as the text examples in the earlier study, but there was an important discriminating feature. The amount of time a video devoted respectively to the main point, the component points, and the examples, was distributed differently. *Social Integration* had a relatively high proportion of screen time on the main point, repeatedly clarifying the relation between it and the evidence cited at the example level. A feature of this kind would assist those students for whom the internal structure might otherwise be "horizontalized." The *Political Theory* video made the main point that there are alternative political theories to explain how society changes. The total time spent on this was very small in comparison to the time spent on the two contrasted theories, of Marxism and Pluralism, and their respective examples. The structure appeared to be sequential, not the hierarchical structure it in fact was, with the examples being illustrative of the more abstract relational point about alternative theories.

The implication is not that videos should devote a third of their screen time to the main point, but that they should offer ways of helping students discern the main point. The *Political Theory* video spent too much time on illustrating the two theories and too little time reflecting on the variation between them.

Whatever medium is used for a text, its meaning is revealed through its structure. So the first guiding principle for supporting learning through acquisition is that we have to make the structure clear, through using the usual organizational techniques, but also by helping students actively discern the structure.

Most studies that discuss the problems of surface approaches to learning recognize that efforts to clarify the structure will not always succeed. Students may still "horizontalize" the text or discourse, or be distracted by the power of the example and miss the point it is illustrating. This brings us to another way of supporting learning through acquisition, which is to augment it with other forms of learning that help to optimize its value.

How Can Digital Technologies Help?

There are many studies in the literature that run comparisons between one method of teaching and another, such as lectures versus print materials, or PowerPoint slides versus notes. Either they find no significant difference, or if they do, this is used to draw conclusions about the nature of the medium. For example, one study concludes that "whereas PowerPoint structures the content of lectures, it does not structure how students interact with the material outside of the classroom." There is no study that could possibly be done that could legitimately draw such a conclusion about a medium, because the instance cannot represent the medium in general, and in all educational situations there are many factors at work that cannot be isolated. With the right context and execution of the idea it would be perfectly possible to use slide handouts to structure students' follow-up work, as we see in the next section.

The studies discussed here do not attempt to make spurious comparisons, and instead focus on what has been achieved for students by extending a narrative presentation to include digital technologies and methods such as student discussion, handouts, and activities.

Enabling the Teacher-Student Dialogue

The classical way to improve on the form of a class presentation is to allow for questions. The approach has spawned many elaborate ways of engaging students: buzz groups and small group role-play exercises are good ways of interrupting the one-way flow, or getting students to work together to understand or comment on a point, so that the teacher can respond to the higher quality questions thus generated for the benefit of all students.

Cutts and his colleagues at Glasgow University show how the Conversational Framework can be used to challenge new digital technologies to take this further (Cutts *et al.* 2004). "Clicker" technology, or a Group Response System (GRS) contributes usefully by collecting a quantitative and anonymous representation of how a large class is thinking from responses to multiple-choice questions, without embarrassing the individual student. In responding to class thinking the teacher can enter into a large-scale dialogue with their audience. The same technology can be extended to groups, so that role-play or buzz group discussions generate a collective response from each group that is aggregated with all the other groups' responses. This pattern gives each learner a richer learning experience because they:

- have an iterative dialogue with other learners;
- generate an agreed response;
- see the variation in responses across all groups; and
- hear the teacher's discussion of each one.

The discussion cycle in the Conversational Framework is therefore addressed very well in comparison with a class presentation alone, by using new technology explicitly to augment learning through acquisition with learning through discussion: "As Laurillard's model predicts, these interventions have been shown to improve educational performance significantly" (Cutts *et al.* 2004: 1).

A more radical shift, from class presentations to a blend of these with interactive resources, showed that students' relative evaluation of the "narrative lecture" put it below text, interactive materials and the PowerPoint presentation (Dalsgaard and Godsk 2007).

Improving the Presentation of Structure

The visual support most commonly used currently in education is a slide presentation tool created for business presentations. The software can provide a pleasing professional result and slides are often made available on an institution's intranet. Prepared notes or slide handouts are a good way to supplement the class, as students can organize their notes better (Susskind 2005), and in class they can concentrate on understanding, not on simply recording the event in note form (Sutherland, Badger, and Goodith 2002).

Slides can improve the pedagogic value of the class by engaging the learner actively in some way (Kinchin 2006; Levasseur and Sawyer 2006). The same slide that illustrates a concept can include a question to the student, for them to complete at a later stage. This is especially useful if they only download the slides without attending the class, which is increasingly common in post-16 education as students take more control over how they study. Extending the record of the class event even further, some institutions make the slides available together with an audiovisual recording of the presentation and in-class annotations. In one study, evaluation suggested that it was the materials, not the lecture, that was most used outside the lecture itself (Winer and Cooperstock 2002). This would depend crucially on the quality of the slide design.

Activities and Feedback

There are many other ways of introducing student activities as part of learning through acquisition, especially as a result of new technologies. Jewitt makes the important point that digital media do not have to maintain a pre-determined storyline. Being able to contribute to the narrative takes it to a higher level, making it more appropriate for more contested subject areas where the learner can expect to contribute, or learn to contribute to the discourse:

> the facilities of new technologies make non-linear narrative more possible than the printed page does. The design ... serves to fragment the notion of linear narrative and to encourage readers to see themselves as writers. In doing so, these texts "undo" the literary forms of closure and narrative ... and offer the reader the potential to create (however partially) the text being read.
>
> (Jewitt 2005: 329)

We know from the discussion of "relevance structure" that the teacher must create space for the learner's contribution as they respond to the sense of a need to know by trying to complete their partial understanding. There have been many attempts to make learners active in reading a text by using *in-text questions*, e.g. students are asked to write down their point of view on a topic before reading on to compare the author's point of view with their own; students are set analytical tasks, or calculation tasks, as appropriate to the material. Unfortunately, evaluation studies of in-text questions have not been particularly encouraging, as students use them much less than the designer would expect (Fung 2005; Lockwood 1992; Marton and Booth 1997).

Ference Marton's studies of students' reading demonstrated this through the discovery of the surface approach (see Chapter 3), and he further confirmed that students may take an instrumental approach to reading even when the text included instructions to take a more active approach (Marton and Booth 1997).

Only a small proportion of students actually write something down when asked to do so in an activity (Fung 2005; Lockwood 1992). But in-text questions too often create quite difficult open-ended tasks that disturb the narrative flow of the text, or students treat them more like rhetorical markers, where the question posed will clearly soon be answered if you read on. Such tasks seem unfair. If a student works on an exercise, they feel the need for some feedback. Hannon reported this finding from evaluating a design for an online course based on both Gagné's sequential instructional model and on the iterative Conversational Framework, concluding that the latter was supported by students' comments: "Students want (and expect) quick and detailed responses to their questions and concerns, as well as timely, qualitative feedback on their work" (Hannon *et al.* 2002: 11).

Even for distance learning students active interaction with teachers is expected, and Hannon found that introducing techniques such as posting model answers and frequently asked question (FAQ) responses in a subsequent version of the course improved the satisfaction of both teachers and students.

This is just as true for the engaging medium of video, which is becoming increasingly important now that there are so many user-generated videos available online for use in learning and teaching (Duffy 2008). An evaluation study of videos of children doing mathematics, used for teacher training, concluded that students found it useful to have teacher notes setting task goals at the end of short sections of video, but also wanted feedback on their actions:

> There is also clear evidence that if questions and directives are highlighted ... they will need to be supported by some indication of the answers or observations students might make. Without such support many students felt both frustrated and anxious about the quality of their learning.
>
> (Durbridge 1984: 240)

Durbridge suggests ways in which "pre-emptive" extrinsic feedback can be offered: for example, the teacher's version of the answer, such as the identification of behavior in a certain part of the video that matches a defined category, or their comment on an expected wrong answer, is written at the end of the notes. The advantage of digital media, of course, is that this kind of feedback can be conditional – students are only given access to it when they have developed and submitted their own answer.

One interesting feature of narrative in a digital form is that interactive hypertext invites the learner to deconstruct the given narrative line, and construct their own. The reader does indeed have the potential to, in Jewitt's words "create the text being read." That frees the learner from the text, but it may also free them from understanding the intended meaning, which puts the responsibility back to the teacher to help them do this. The point was made in a study of learners' use of educational digital resources, which concluded that it is important for the designer to keep them focused on the development of the argument, i.e. to:

- clarify the overall goal;
- keep reminding them of the goal;
- help them define their own sub-goals;
- motivate their own articulation of what they know;
- motivate them to refine it; and
- enable them to assess for themselves the extent to which they are achieving the goal (Laurillard *et al.* 2000).

To augment the narrative form, these studies, culled from different educational research traditions, have all suggested using activities that together have the effect of extending learning through acquisition to learning through discussion, inquiry, practice, and collaboration as well. There are still remarkably few studies that help us with ensuring that the text itself is presented in a way that makes it reliably intelligible on its own.

Preparing Students for Learning Through Acquisition

In this section we look at the role of individual study prior to learning through a class presentation. Schwartz and Bransford found a way to prepare students for getting the best out of a class by giving them a particular kind of preparation activity.

Prior to a presentation on concepts of memory in classical psychology, they prepared a textual description of the target concepts and the experiments that exemplified them. Students were asked to make a summary of the text.

A second teaching design prepared students for the presentation by giving them a text that described data from experiments that provided contrasting cases to help students develop differentiated knowledge of the target concepts in the psychology of memory. The students were asked to analyze the data, generate distinctions between them, and graph their results.

Following these two forms of preparation all students then went to the same class presentation that explained the theory and concepts they had been studying. The learning outcome being tested was the extent to which the two different learning experiences enabled students to act like psychologists – had they internalized an appropriate way of thinking and practicing? Could they transfer what they had learned to making a reasonable prediction about a new hypothetical experiment in the same domain (Schwartz and Bransford 1998)? The two pedagogical patterns are shown Table 7.1 , where each stage of the pattern is mapped to the teacher modeling and communication cycles defined in Chapter 6. Posttests showed that the second group had a significantly higher probability of being able to transfer their learning to making a successful prediction.

As a result of the first design the learner does not do enough to challenge their initial concept, and so fails to transfer to the new task of prediction. In the

Table 7.1 Alternative Pedagogical Patterns Mapped to Conversational Framework Cycles with their Respective Outcomes

"Double telling" (Fig 7.1(a))	*Cycles*	*"Discovery and telling" (Fig 7.1(b))*	*Cycles*
(1) Teacher prepares short chapter that develops target concepts, and uses the experiments to exemplify those concepts	TCC1	(1) Teacher prepares simplified experimental designs and data from classic psychology experiments, *selected to show contrasting cases*	TPC1
(1) Student is set task to read the chapter on theoretical concepts and experiments	TCC1	(2, 3, 4) Student works on task to *analyze contrasting cases by looking for patterns* in the data and *generate distinctions* between contrasting cases	TPC1
(2) Student is required to produce a three page summary of the text	TCC2	(5) Student is required to *produce graphs* of the contrasting cases	TCC2
(3) Presentation on concepts, experiments and results of the same studies, with graphs that summarize the relevant data, and explain the meaning of experiments in terms of implications for human behavior in the relevant domain, with concepts to account for the variations in the data cases.	TCC1	(6) Presentation on concepts, experiments and results of the same studies, with graphs that summarize the relevant data, and *explain the meaning of experiments in terms of implications for human behavior* in the relevant domain, with concepts to account for the variations in the data cases.	TPC2
→ *Low probability of transfer* to making predictions using same concepts from contrasting cases		→ *High probability of transfer* to making predictions using same concepts from contrasting cases	

Note: Numbers refer to Figure 7.1. For codes see Table 6.2.

second design, the practice environment with teacher feedback (TPC) motivates them to modulate their concept and so succeeds in transferring to the prediction task. The "Discovery and telling" pattern, is more effective than the "Double telling" pattern because the teacher has designed a succession of stages each of which builds the motivation for the student to act at the next stage in the optimal way. There are several critical differences in practice apparent in the table:

• students analyze the contrasting data cases to generate distinctions, rather than just read about the data others have analyzed;

- students produce graphs to express these distinctions, rather than just produce summaries of the text;
- students attend to the explanations of the distinctions they generated, rather than just follow the account being given.

The study shows that the form of the contrasting cases text was crucial to enabling the students to work analytically, the graph was crucial to doing the analysis in such a way that it created a readiness to hear the explanation, and the class presentation was crucial to completing the gap in understanding they were now aware of.

Figure 7.1 shows how the six steps in the "Discovery and telling" pattern use both the teacher communication cycle and the teacher modeling cycle, whereas the "Double telling" pattern uses only the former. It offers the same time on task – that was carefully controlled. The more successful pattern works because it creates a readiness to hear the explanation, whereas writing a summary of a text requires only a reinterpretation of the text, and does not throw up any puzzling challenges to claim the learner's deeper attention.

Schwartz and Bransford point out the importance of making sure that the learning activities are aligned with the learning outcome, i.e. the contrasts in the case data should differentiate the features that exemplify the principle being taught, as in Variation Theory, so that as students analyze the data their attention is drawn to the anomalous cases, e.g. those that can only be explained using the concept of "recency effect", or "script intrusions".

The study demonstrates the power of the class presentation when the students are well prepared to learn from it. As Schwartz commented:

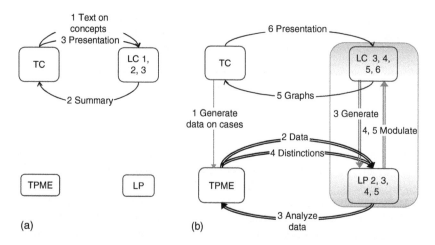

(a)   (b)

Figure 7.1 Sequences for the alternative learning patterns (a) "Double telling," and (b) "Discovery and telling," for learning through acquisition, mapped to the Conversational Framework (numbers refer to Table 7.1).

This result provides an important lesson for those who believe that direct teaching (e.g., a lecture) is contrary to constructivist ideals. As argued above, people construct their knowledge regardless of whether the input comes from the physical or linguistic world.

(Schwartz 1999: 211)

The successful preparation activity requires more creativity from the teacher because it is not just a matter of selecting an appropriate text and asking them to summarize it. The task for the teacher is to understand the relevance structure of the relationship between the concept they are teaching, and the kind of activity the learner must carry out to become aware of the need for that concept, or explanation. It is not a trivial task – but if it is hard for the teacher, how much harder it must be for the learner to think about the meaning of the concepts being presented in relation to their practical application, without the prior assistance of a challenging activity.

Capturing Pedagogical Patterns

What can we conclude from these studies that will help us make best use of the still dominant "narrative presentation" in education? One important conclusion from all these studies is that learning through acquisition must be supplemented before, during, or after, by other types of learning, as the Conversational Framework suggests. There is little help from the literature, except from Variation Theory, on how best to organize and present the conceptual structure of a domain whether in conventional or digital form.

The problem is critical now that so much informational material is available through the digital media of web documents, animations, podcasts, and videos. It would be absurd to imagine that because students can easily navigate them this will somehow make the internal structure and meaning of the myriad of digital documents more intelligible. Multimodal texts and new forms of e-learning have not been shown to be different or better than conventional forms. They are easier to find and to navigate; they still need careful effort by the teacher to make them intelligible. Access to a variety of different explanations of a concept, if the learner is prepared to look beyond Wikipedia, may offer useful alternative explanations, and links to information and concepts they already know, but this is simply relying on the wonderful ease of access to multiple narratives provided by the internet. If we have not yet worked out how to make the conceptual narrative itself clear and intelligible to the learner, then each narrative may still be poorly understood. The teaching community still has the responsibility of working out how to structure an intelligible presentation of a difficult idea.

Perhaps the development of Open Educational Resources will create a bazaar of multiple ways of presenting the difficult formal concepts of each domain of study, enabling the wisdom of the crowds of students and teachers using them to determine which are the best? For this to work the teaching community needs to articulate and exchange its best teaching ideas, as a way of building on each others' work, much as the research community does, to discover best practice (Laurillard 2008; Laurillard *et al.* in press).

We have seen that the narrative form, whether as lecture, book, digital resource, video, or podcast, needs to be accompanied by activities that help the learner to discern its meaning. There are no studies that demonstrate the relative value of different ways of sequencing elements such as principle–example, concept–instance, components–summary, but there are many, like those discussed above, that offer detail on types of structure, and on the kinds of activities that elicit the other forms of learning. The similarities between them suggest that we should be able to capture some of that detail in a generalizable way – by discerning patterns in effective methods for learning through acquisition.

Figure 7.1 shows that the presentation played a different role in the two versions of that particular teaching design pattern. The Conversational Framework represents the difference in the way the presentation impacts on the learner's conception: in the "discovery and telling" pattern the "analyze data" activity drives action at the practice level which motivates the internal generation and modulation of concepts and practice, which prepares the learner to use the presentation as informative feedback on their discoveries. The critical feature of the "analyze data" activity was that it demanded the discernment of important distinctions, as Schwartz and Bransford point out: "Before people can productively elaborate on features of the world, they need to discern those features. This discernment is the unique contribution of analyzing the cases" (Schwartz and Bransford 1998).

This is the point that Marton makes with the idea of "Variation Theory". The Székely pattern of "predict–observe" has some similarity with the Schwartz and Bransford pattern of "discovery and telling." In both experiments the learners were given a task that required them to attend to the internal structure of the situation in order to complete a task, and in both cases this led to the discernment of the salient concepts in such a way that the teacher's input then explained the phenomena they had discerned. Summarizing was not as good as analyzing in the memory domain; watching was not as good as predicting in the mechanics domain. Summarizing and watching do not challenge the learner to get inside the internal structure of the concepts being presented. But the curiosity generated by analyzing or predicting gives the learner the goal the teacher needs them to have when they approach the text – the expectation of finding the answer to a puzzle.

Summary: Designing for Learning Through Acquisition

We can make learning through acquisition an active process. Although the narrative media of class presentations, books, and videos are dominant throughout education, and retain their narrative character in the digital equivalents of podcasts, web resources, and online videos, they can all be modified and augmented to address more components of the Conversational Framework than simply "teacher explains concepts".

The chapter has argued that:

- learning through acquisition is an important part of the formal learning process;
- the narrative presentation media that dominate afford learning through acquisition;
- these media alone cover only one aspect of the Conversational Framework;
- the digital equivalents of the conventional media of class presentation, book and video are also essentially narrative media; and
- all these media can be augmented to cover more of the Conversational Framework by combining them with teacher–student dialogue, improving the presentation of the conceptual structure, and providing activities with feedback.

The following chapters consider what educational theorists and educators have to say about the other forms of learning represented in the Conversational Framework, and the extent to which their pedagogies can be enhanced by digital technologies and captured in pedagogical patterns.

8   Learning Through Inquiry

Introduction

This chapter works through studies of learning through inquiry. Inquiry learning makes use of resources that provide searchable access to information, data, knowledge, and ideas, both conventional and digital. The resources include books, pictures, spoken texts, diagrams, animations, videos, databanks, libraries, and repositories, in conventional and digital form. Resources may also be locations, such as museums, art galleries, and exhibitions, or sites of educational interest, such as historic buildings, archaeologic sites, factories, laboratories, communities, and other locations, depending on the discipline. Locations have always been brought into learning environments through descriptions in documents and videos, but the learning environment can now be brought to the location, through the use of mobile technologies. All these technologies, conventional and digital, support the learner in the process of inquiry. We can think of inquiry learning as the learning activity through which students turn the teacher's narrative into their own.

Learning through inquiry should be valuable to the learner because, rather than having to "follow the storyline", as in learning through acquisition, they are in control of the sequence of information, and can "follow their own line of inquiry", making them more active, and giving them a greater sense of ownership of their learning. They will be using narrative and informational media, but engaging more actively with the content by taking a critical and analytical approach, and thereby coming to a fuller understanding of it. The conventional technology of a library supports this form of learning very well, as it provides access to relevant texts, a catalogue system for searching, and support staff who are expert in information literacy, and can help students develop these skills as part of the activity. The conventional form of inquiry learning, still in use in masters courses, but not confined to them, is to send the students to the library armed with a reading list and an essay question. This is not sufficient to ensure that they practice a critical and analytical investigation of the resources, so we have to ask what it takes to help them do that, whatever the nature of the resources.

Beyond books and journals, every discipline makes use of the media most appropriate for providing authentic exemplars of the theory or concepts in practice: clinical cases for medicine, business case studies for management education, nature walks for botany, written texts for literature, databanks for social science, field trips for anthropology. The digital world now makes an impact on every discipline because it changes the nature of our access to these resources. But how does that change our approach to learning design? Do *digital* libraries change the quality of the inquiry learning process? Can we augment what conventional technologies offer by using their digital equivalents for an inquiry? Is there more we can do with either conventional or digital approaches to improve the coverage of the Conversational Framework, and support the "inquiry" aspect of the learning process more effectively?

Learning Through Inquiry

Inquiry-based learning is seen as important because it rehearses students in the fundamental skills of learning that are essential for developing their own knowledge, which should be continually adapted, and refined. This is the means by which students use their studies to learn how to learn. The perceived need for education to deliver the curriculum, however, has tended to bias the teacher's interest towards acquisition rather than inquiry learning, leaving the student to discover these skills themselves; or not, as often happens. So it became important for educational theorists to promote the value of inquiry as a learning skill, and forcefully, as Postman and Weingartner did in their monograph on "teaching as a subversive activity" in 1969. They argued for a fundamental shift in the teacher's approach from "telling" to encouraging the learners to "ask questions," because "regardless of source, unless the learner perceives an inquiry as relevant, no significant learning will take place" (Postman and Weingartner 1969: 47).

The process of inquiry they saw as a core skill of learning to learn:

> Good learners ... know how to ask meaningful questions; they are persistent in examining their own assumptions; they use definitions and metaphors as instruments for their thinking and are rarely trapped by their own language; they are apt to be cautious and precise in asking generalizations, and they engage continually in verifying what they believe.
>
> (Postman and Weingartner 1969: 30)

This is inquiry learning as the critical examination of descriptions of the world, of theoretical knowledge as presented by the teacher, where the student learns how to use existing texts and materials for their own intellectual inquiry, coming to a more contextualized understanding, and making it their own, not content with the mere acquisition of someone else's ideas. Since then inquiry learning has taken on a wide range of meanings. It may be termed also "inquiry-based learning" (IBL), or "problem-based learning" (PBL), or "project-based learning", but in all cases the aim is to get beyond the conventional pedagogy of class presentation + assigned readings + knowledge-based assessment in the form of short questions or essays (Schwartz *et al.* 1999). Inquiry learning makes students active participants in developing a response to a set problem or task:

> Inquiry-based learning describes a learning ... through research and investigation activities in response to set problems and tasks.
>
> (Oliver 2007: 4)

> Inquiry involves posing and exploring questions; gathering, interpreting, and synthesizing different kinds of data and information; and developing and sharing an explanation to answer the given questions.
>
> (Quintana, Zhang, and Krajcik 2005: 235–6)

> Student and tutor alike are involved in the revision and making of knowledge ... engaged with the construction and revision of bodies of knowledge, and ... bodies of practice.
>
> (Martin 2003: 303–4)

> Participate and practice the activities involved in inquiry, including using the language, tools, theories and methodologies associated with the particular discipline.
>
> (Apedoe and Reeves 2006: 324)

> A user-defined community of practice continually evolves through student interactions with problems, solutions and insights, and by building a common domain of knowledge that can be accessed jointly by all members.
>
> (Nathoo, Goldhoff, and Quattrochi 2005: 216)

> IL has its origins in the practices of scientific inquiry and places a heavy emphasis on posing questions, gathering and analyzing data, and constructing evidence-based arguments.
>
> (Hmelo-Silver, Duncan, and Chinn 2006)

> Learners are to unravel the relations between input and output variables through systematic experimentation. This process proceeds through five phases: analysis, hypothesis generation, experiment design, data interpretation, and conclusion.
>
> (van Joolingen *et al.* 2005: 674)

In all these cases the learner is not in fact branching out on a wholly new area of inquiry, as they would within a doctoral program. The essence of inquiry learning is to go beyond learning through acquisition alone, so it is relevant to all sectors of education. The aim is to foster an active approach to the subject content in texts and resources, so that students develop a richer understanding, and a more personal engagement with the ideas, including eventually a more relativist, and critical stance towards the knowledge.

There is an interesting internal relationship here. Students develop their knowledge by practicing the skills listed in the quotes above: questioning, investigating, analysing, hypothesizing, designing, interpreting, sharing, arguing, synthesizing. At the same time the motivation to practice these skills is the goal of developing their knowledge, so there is a symbiotic relationship between knowledge and skills in inquiry learning. The learning outcomes are still defined by the teacher, and the students' output is assessed as conforming or not to those outcomes, so teachers take care to set up a supportive environment to guide and scaffold the activity that learners undertake. Because the development of knowledge and skills is interdependent, students need guidance in taking an iterative approach, testing the knowledge they develop, and honing their skills to improve on what they find. They need some interim challenge to the quality of the conceptual knowledge they are developing, to be sure they are succeeding in developing both knowledge and skills.

Properties of Inquiry Learning

Clearly, inquiry as a learning activity broadly embraces a "family" of experiential pedagogic approaches (Hmelo-Silver 2004). Each is identified with different discipline areas, but they share the same underlying pedagogic aims, no matter what the name: inquiry-based learning (IBL), problem-based learning (PBL), cooperative learning, project-based learning, anchored instruction, case-based learning, experiential learning, service learning, or discovery learning (Coombs and Elden, 2004). These terms have also been aligned with constructivist, independent, and collaborative learning (Kirschner, Sweller, and Clark 2006). All these terms have been used to denote interesting forms of pedagogic design, and there are several common features of learning through inquiry that can be derived from the literature (Conole *et al.*, 2008; Coombs and Elden 2004; Hmelo-Silver, Duncan, and Chinn 2006) to provide a broad consensus on the main properties of this pedagogy:

1. It sets a challenging *task*, designed to assist the learner in linking theory to its application in a process approximating to authentic practice in the discipline, and relevant to the learner.
2. It provides specialized task *resources*, which may be: print and digital resources; a location, such as a lab or field trip or performance space; digital simulation or modeling environments.
3. The learner has some *guidance*, designed to model and elicit the skills of inquiry, investigation, interpretation, integration, analysis,

critique, evaluation, resolution, synthesis, and representation of a problem or issue.

All three features, task, resources, and guidance, are essential, no matter what name is given to the pedagogic form. Inquiry learning often combines both *individual* work and *collaboration* with other students, but researchers do not always characterize the latter as essential. There is little information about the exact nature of collaboration in this context, other than "negotiating ideas," so it is not seen as a key pedagogic feature. The other features are important to clarify.

Task

The task should be chosen to help the learner to link theory and practice, and develop Entwistle's "ways of thinking and practicing" discussed in Chapter 2. Inquiry learning complements learning through acquisition by changing *how* the knowledge is learned. Instead of listening to or reading about what is known, inquiry learning helps the learner emulate at least some of the practices of how the expert comes to know.

The nature of the task is important because the student's perception of relevance drives their motivation to work on it. If it is not their own question, or is not linked to their known interests and concerns, or there is no prior negotiation with them to establish it as an interesting and relevant question, then there is a risk that it will not hold their interest (Oliver 2007). If it *is* their own question, there is a high risk that the question is not tractable through the inquiry conditions available. Of course prior negotiation with the teacher to establish a researchable question is common at post-graduate level, but it could turn out to be a negotiation of the curriculum itself, so allowing the student freedom to decide the inquiry question is risky for most teachers, even though it is strongly advocated by researchers, even at primary level (Alexander 2004). Instead, because it is important to align teacher and learner goals, the teacher has to negotiate the task with the individual or the class, and establish a link with their interests and experience.

Inquiry learning helps learners make the link between theory and practice, and engage with the knowledge at a deep level through developing their thinking skills. Students need to experience the "ways of thinking and practising" within their discipline. In this respect, inquiry learning has similar objectives to the "problem-based learning" that was first developed in medical education:

> It is centered on the use of real-world or authentic problems that capture the complexity and ambiguity that learners will face in their careers rather than being structured around separate academic disciplines. These problems form the context for learning within which both content knowledge and skills or competencies are developed.
>
> (Coombs and Elden 2004: 527)

The sense of personal engagement with the inquiry is common to all these studies, emphasizing learning as a personal process: active, student-driven learning (Coombs and Elden 2004), and student-based exploration of an authentic problem (Wilke and Straits 2001).

Resources

The materials provided depend on what is available for students physically and digitally. Physical resources include books, documents, locations, artifacts, objects, recordings – they take many forms, depending on the subject area. Digital equivalents extend what is available to students, as we come to in a later section. Perhaps because resources are so subject-dependent there is little discussion in empirical studies of how they should be selected or provided, but clearly they have to fit the nature of the task.

It is interesting that although Hmelo-Silver and colleagues strongly advocate IBL and PBL, one of their key strategies for scaffolding is "embedding expert guidance" through lectures, texts, resources, and videos, all of which require learning through acquisition. Including such resources as a form of guidance, of course, begs the question of how well those resources support learning through acquisition. Embedding them within an inquiry learning task does not necessarily make them more intelligible. We saw in Chapter 7 an example of how it takes a particular learning sequence and task design to make the class presentation fully intelligible, so for learning through acquisition and inquiry to complement each other in inquiry learning we need to know more exactly how the expert guidance is designed and used.

Guidance

Guidance is essential, given the difficulty and complexity of the inquiry process. Sometimes referred to as scaffolding, or scripting, guidance is the planned support the teacher designs in to ensure that learners spend their time productively. This aspect of inquiry learning has generated some debate in the literature, where it has been criticized for offering only "minimally-guided instruction" (Kirschner, Sweller, and Clark 2006). In fact, as the response to this critique demonstrates at length, there are many examples of guidance in the literature of inquiry learning, such as:

- modeling the intended skills;
- adaptive coaching during the activity;
- collaborative problem-solving;
- eliciting explanations;
- support for interpretation and representation;
- prompts to use reasoning strategies;
- templates for explanations

...many of which are similar to the techniques advocated in the critique, i.e. the standard methods of worked examples and process worksheets (Hmelo-Silver, Duncan, and Chinn 2006). In fact these two articles derive from very different approaches to educational research; they have only six references in common out of a total of around 100 in each paper. Given that they cover exactly the same narrow topic this is a remarkable lack of overlap, and is a further indication of the problem identified in Chapter 5, of the lack of common ground in the theoretical underpinnings of learning design. The main debate is around either the need for instruction:

> in so far as there is any evidence from controlled studies, it almost uniformly supports direct, strong instructional guidance rather than constructivist-based minimal guidance during the instruction of novice to intermediate learners.
>
> (Kirschner, Sweller, and Clark 2006: 83)

or the need for more active learning:

> we argue that IL [inquiry learning] and PBL [problem-based learning] approaches involve the learner, with appropriate scaffolding, in the practices and conceptualizations of the discipline and in this way promote the construction of knowledge we recognize as learning.
>
> (Hmelo-Silver, Duncan, and Chinn 2006: 105)

We can resolve the issue quite simply, by noting that those advocating a constructivist approach do not advocate minimal guidance and do have many ways of scaffolding the learner's work. The controlled studies showing that constructivist methods fail may be picking up the fact that the task is poorly designed, just as instruction fails through poor design. It is not possible to carry out a controlled study that decides whether instructionism or constructivism is the most effective method in general, because the experiment will depend so much on the particular instantiation of each approach. Where "constructivist-based minimal guidance" fails, the response should be to improve the guidance, not reject constructivism.

Another way to resolve the issue is to note that none of the descriptions of the pedagogy of inquiry learning give sufficient attention to challenging the learners' developing knowledge as a way of getting them to critique their skills. This could be characterized as "appropriate scaffolding," where the form it takes is not more instruction, but the opportunity to test their developing knowledge and skills – and that implies an iterative approach. Students may challenge each other (making collaboration a key feature), or they could test their developing ideas against a model, or they could be challenged by the teacher. However it is done, they need feedback rich enough to enable them to improve their practice. For that reason, an iterative structure of the learning design should be seen as an essential feature for inquiry learning.

The Conversational Framework suggests that the guidance provided through inquiry learning activities has to be designed in a way that motivates learners to continue iterating around the teacher practice/modeling cycle – the goal–action–feedback–revision cycle, and the modulate–generate cycle. The point comes up again towards the end of this chapter.

Inquiry Learning as a Distinctive Pedagogy

This discussion of inquiry learning has shown that educational theorists agree that it is a distinctive pedagogy. Consensus on its essential character is harder to find. There is clear agreement that it includes an appropriate task, negotiated with students, using appropriate resources, and guidance on the skills and knowledge they are developing. I have also argued that because of the interdependence of knowledge and skills, and because there is still debate about the nature of the instruction or scaffolding provided, we should recognize the importance of an iterative process that includes feedback on students' practice. The design issues for the teacher to address, therefore, are the *four* features of task, resources, guidance, and iterative feedback:

1. negotiate the task or question that is appropriate for rehearsing students in the ways of thinking and practicing in their field;
2. identify the resources and task environment to be used by students;
3. design scaffolding and fading of guidance in the inquiry process;
4. provide opportunities for learners to test and modulate their developing skills and knowledge.

Some examples of inquiry learning in the literature include collaboration between students. Providing formative feedback can be highly labor intensive for the teacher, who may not have sufficient time for this. So the advantage of peer collaboration is that students receive feedback from other students by having to discuss or defend ideas, and share their attempts at the task, such as their analysis of a document, an interpretation of a rock formation, a graph of data, a problem solution, a collection of images, a summary of a text, etc. Many studies in the literature refer to student collaboration, but are very unclear about what form this takes, and how exactly they are meant to collaborate. There is a lack of detail about all these design tasks for the teacher, as the focus is often on demonstrating students' reactions to the comparative benefits of the approach rather than the design detail (Oliver 2007). This imprecision unfortunately hampers the development of our understanding of how to optimize these methods.

The final section returns to this point as we consider alternative pedagogical patterns for inquiry learning.

Inquiry Learning in the Conversational Framework

The Conversational Framework differentiates between acquisition learning and inquiry learning by representing the latter as covering more transactions, depending on the teacher's role. Figures 7.1(a) and 7.1(b) show how inquiry

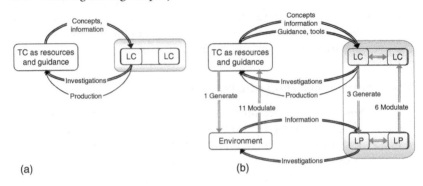

Figure 8.1 (a) Individual independent, and (b) individual supervised inquiry learning
     mapped to the Conversational Framework.

learning is mapped to the Conversational Framework for an individual student
doing independent study, and for individual supervised work.

In Figure 8.1(a) the learner develops their own concepts by investigating
the teacher's concepts presented via books, videos, or other resources.
The learner may consult them many times in different ways to obtain access
to the concepts and information they represent, hence the double lines.
There can be no feedback from this resource environment, only access to
the concepts and information they represent. The learner working on
assembling and interpreting information to produce a report, for example,
cannot know if they are achieving an improving performance. In finding
material for an investigation the learner has to make their own interpretation and evaluation of what they find. The learner's own internal conversation, through reflecting on the ideas, information, and data derived from
the resources, generates further questions with which to go back to the
resources and refine their inquiry and its output. The output is the production of a statement, or a project report or essay, in terms of the task goal.
They may receive feedback from the teacher on this in the form of comments
or grades, but this kind of feedback does not play a role within the inquiry
process itself.

This is the conventional pedagogy the research literature has set out to
replace. The enhanced version of inquiry learning in Figure 8.1(b) adds supervision and coaching from the teacher, who responds to questions, monitors
the student's practice to modulate their guidance and motivate revised investigations, and so assist in scaffolding the process. The teacher's presence here
improves the chance of a productive learning activity because it helps to
modulate the learner's practice, and to motivate further iterations. The effectiveness of inquiry learning is very dependent on the quality of the scaffolding
activities designed for students to work through independently and, as the
above debate in the literature suggests, these activities may sometimes be too
minimalist. There is less risk when the teacher plays an active supervising role
during the inquiry learning, but it is more demanding on their time.

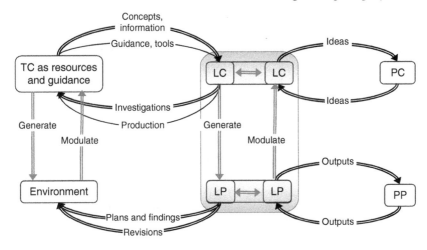

Figure 8.2 Collaborative supervised inquiry learning, showing the additional demands on the learner to share their ideas and output, and the support provided through access to other learners' ideas and outputs.

To reduce the pressure on the teacher, therefore, the literature has advocated collaboration between students, to make demands on the learner to discuss and defend their questions, analysis, and outputs. Figure 8.2 shows how the collaborative form of inquiry learning maps to the Conversational Framework. With the additional impetus of feedback and motivation provided by other learner(s) there is likely to be more iteration around the modulate–generate cycle, prompting further development of understanding and ideas, and lessening the need for teacher guidance and feedback, which is represented here as only one iteration around that loop (see also Chapter 11).

The three representations in the two figures illustrate different ways of offering scaffolding support to students as they work through the inquiry learning process. The prediction is that the more demands from teacher, practice environment, or other learners to generate ideas and actions, and the more information, guidance, feedback, comments, and shared outputs available to them, the more the learner is likely to iterate through the modulate–generate cycle that promotes learning.

By mapping the different forms of inquiry learning to the Conversational Framework we can see the pedagogic value it could have for supporting students in the process of inquiry learning. To what extent can new technologies change and improve the experience of inquiry learning?

How Can Digital Technologies Help?

The effectiveness of inquiry learning depends heavily on the quality of resources, and the "digital revolution" creates an indisputable transformation in the quality and range of resources available to education. There are many ways of building activities around resources in different subject areas and stages of education, but the basic task model is that the learner should be able to follow their own narrative line, navigate their way through, generate and test their ideas, and analyze and synthesize what they find. This is common to all inquiry learning but now the question is how digital technologies can improve this type of learning experience. We look at what they do for both resources and guidance.

With the digital equivalents of libraries, archives, museums, and field trips and their associated learning activities, there are many opportunities for extensive inquiry learning, but what new affordances do they bring for students?

Digital technologies should be valuable for inquiry learning by giving access to informational resources and to guidance, challenge, and support that is present with the learner throughout their study. How well do they do in practice?

Investigating Digital Resources

Digital libraries have been developed in many discipline areas in the form of digitized books, materials, artifacts, documents, data, etc. They provide an extensive resource for students to explore as an expert would, and emulate the physical library for students in remote locations (Koohang 2004). It is exciting for students to come close to the practice of the experts in their field, and teachers are keen to exploit the availability of new kinds of resource this way. In many areas, however, these resources are still innovative, and in the early days of development, so are not always optimally designed for students. One study that based a whole course around using a well-developed digital library found that students were unable to use the specialized library due to its inadequate organization and interface, and instead found their own resources through the higher quality general search engines (Apedoe, Walker, and Reeves 2006). Nonetheless, the evaluation study revealed strong student support for the overall approach, and demonstrated improved inquiry skills:

> Students reported enjoying many of the laboratory activities because the activities allowed them to investigate topics in depth and develop greater understanding of the phenomena under investigation. Students particularly enjoyed the activities in which they were given the opportunity to represent their knowledge in creative ways, such as drawing a pictorial geological timescale.
>
> (Apedoe, Walker, and Reeves 2006: 419)

The study also revealed that the approach covers less of the curriculum than a standard delivery. Does that matter? In this case not, as the experience of the students' responses changed the teacher's attitude, to the extent that she changed her other courses to the same design: "Rather than having students focus on the products of science, the professor began to believe that the process of science was much more important for students to learn" (Apedoe, Walker, and Reeves 2006: 419).

The study is important particularly for the way it contrasts conventional instructional pedagogy with the inquiry approach. The greater curriculum coverage in the original course was achieved through carefully guided work on a larger scientific problem, but it used low-level cognitive activities such as gap-fill, labeling, and memorization activities. None of these activities effectively engage students at the practice level of the Conversational Framework, allowing them simply to realign conceptual descriptions without having to adapt them to any instantiation in practice. There is nothing to motivate the pull-through from theory to practice and *vice versa*. In the revised course these content-oriented activities were dropped in favor of process-oriented activities in which, given the task and data resources, students had to:

- decide on the data to be selected from different sources;
- collect and interpret data;
- develop alternative explanations;
- decide between alternative hypotheses; and
- present evidence to justify their answer.

By introducing the practice level in this way, the teacher elicited the iteration between theory and practice by using the teacher modeling cycle, where learners generate actions to achieve a goal. The redesign makes an important difference, because the students' learning activities are much more challenging. This is the essence of inquiry learning, that the learner develops their knowledge and understanding through activities that are as close as possible to the authentic practice of the discipline. Guessing the nouns missing in a sentence is no part of any professional's authentic practice. Instead, in order to help students develop more authentic skills the teacher modeled the inquiry process through the activities she gave them. This is very different from sending students to the library with a reading list and an essay question.

Digital libraries of collections of online resources provide a wonderful opportunity for the extension of inquiry learning into authentic practice for students in all subjects, but they do not drive the development of learners' skills. That can come only from the scaffolding the teacher sets up to support learners in the process.

Inquiry learning using extensive digital materials on the web, is sometimes referred to as a "webquest" (Kanuka, Rourke, and Laflamme 2007), where an important element of the design is that the teacher selects the websites that are rich enough to be worth exploring, yet constrained enough to focus students' attention on the topic goal, rather than a fruitless general web search. Again, the model is that the learner is conducted through a sequence of activities. One of these studies shows how important it is to make sure that each activity motivates the next (Hassanien 2006). The activities are similar to those above, i.e. given an issue (e.g. philosophies of research):

- propose parameters for investigating the task;
- investigate the topic to decide their own point of view;
- prepare their analysis;
- debate and defend their point of view (Hassanien 2006).

The findings show that students value the sense of personal engagement they experience in the process:

> Students felt that the use of the webquest focused their minds and enhanced their understanding of the competing research paradigms, enabling and empowering them to take a more active role in the debate. Therefore, students were looking forward to participating in the debate to defend their favoured research philosophy and to evaluate their own arguments.
>
> (Hassanien 2006: 45)

The result expresses how the prospect of defending and debating their findings affects the learner's attention to their investigative search activities. The sequence the teacher builds around the resources is a critical aspect of the design, and we should tease out exactly what this needs to be. Making sure that the student is motivated and enabled to work effectively on each activity is an important part of that.

Students exhibit a range of different approaches to information search tasks. A study that focused closely on how students worked on such tasks characterized their approaches in terms of (i) awareness of the task focus, (ii) approach to the task, and (iii) use of reflection. These were defined, in increasing order of capability, as

- "looking for a needle in a haystack", where the focus is the topic but the structure of the environment is not perceived, and planning and reflection are poor;
- "finding a way through a maze", focusing on the process of the information search, an awareness of the search environment, and some planning and reflection;
- "using the search tools as a filter", focusing more on process than content and the structure of the search tool, planning, and looking at quality of information, and reflecting to change practice;
- "panning for gold", where the topic, the structure of the search tool, and the quality of the information resource, planning, and reflection, are all in focus to limit the results to only the highest quality resources by using the most appropriate tools (Edwards and Bruce 2004).

The scaffolding for an inquiry activity therefore has to help learners improve their approach and practice from the lower-level practice to the more accomplished approach of "panning for gold". With this phenomenographic analysis of students' approaches, the teacher was able to critique the course assignments and work out which ones helped students develop a more systematic level of reflection (Edwards and Bruce 2004):

- A *reflective journal* in which they identify their search activity, and evaluate the material they found to determine the validity of their strategy;
- A *client information search*, in which they search a topic for a client, present the relevant results they select with a summary of their contents, and report on their search rationale.

These assignments encouraged better reflection, but because they did not explicitly encourage reflection on how to find and select the highest quality resources, most students did not achieve the "panning for gold" approach. The guidance has to be very explicit. The evaluation showed that students were aware, at least, of the great value of these reflective assignments for the high quality of learning they did achieve.

Studies that build on the different and separate research literature on metacognition and self-regulation (e.g. Corno and Mandinach 1983; Quintana, Zhang, and Krajcik 2005; Winne 1997; Zimmerman 2002) propose similar ways of scaffolding the learners' work online through support environments that help students with task understanding and planning, monitoring and regulation, and reflection. There is the potential, therefore, for a common pedagogical pattern for inquiry learning, as we explore in the next two sections.

Scripted Guidance Through Specialized Resources

Teachers have used technology to enhance inquiry learning by exploiting digital libraries and web resources that give students access to authentic data, information, and tools. The teacher's role here is to constrain the search space for students to some degree (a particular digital repository, or a specific collection of websites), and work out the optimal sequence of activities that helps them develop the high-level skills of planning and reflection.

An alternative approach is for the teacher to design the resources as well, and integrate them with activities that model an authentic experience of the inquiry process. This more scripted approach to designing the learning activities is based on a particular scenario of how an inquiry will progress. This means the teacher-designer cannot trust to the luck of what students may turn up in their own search, and therefore provides the resources they know will afford the experience they intend. The resources developed may be case studies, or tools, or learning objects, but the focus is on developing the skills of a particular kind of inquiry. The technology makes a different kind of contribution here, not just access to the resources, but more importantly, to providing software tools that scaffold the inquiry process itself, emulating the kind of guidance a teacher might offer (Linn 1995; Puntambekar and Hübscher 2005; Schwartz *et al.* 1999).

One example of an extensive implementation of software support for the inquiry process presented an interface with icons for each phase of the inquiry process for meeting a problem challenge:

- Look ahead to preview the topic;
- Generate your own ideas;
- Compare your ideas with the multiple perspectives of experts;
- Develop, assess, and revise your ideas;
- Present your solution to the class;
- Reflect back on what you learned.

Each activity icon in the sequence led to a repository of resources such as videos of interviews, or demonstrations of techniques, and activities such as analyzing video interviews, or practicing the techniques. The sequence is framed by a "Look Ahead and Reflect Back" phase in which students begin by previewing what they expect to learn from the topic, which can then act as a benchmark for them to reflect back on when they have completed the challenge, and compare their progress. The name of this software "Software Technology for Action and Reflection" (STAR) conveys the intention to motivate students to do that all-important reflection through acting to achieve a goal (Schwartz *et al.* 1999). A more recent software tool, the "nQuire toolkit" took a very similar approach by providing icons for support of the phases of inquiry identified as:

- Find my topic;
- Decide my inquiry question or hypothesis;
- Plan my methods, equipment, and actions;
- Collect my evidence;
- Analyze and represent my evidence;
- Respond to my question or hypothesis;
- Share and discuss my inquiry;
- Reflect on my progress.

In this case the topic area was defined, such as "healthy eating" or "pollution," but students developed their own specific challenge problem within the topic. Again, for each phase icon the student could access relevant tools and resources, and guidance on what to do (Scanlon *et al.* 2009). For example, for "Collect my evidence" in a project on healthy eating, students were given a food diary with categories for the data collection, tables in which to record details of food eaten for each meal, and graphs for representing the data collected. The specificity of the tools and activities for such a topic means they must be specially developed – the required tools will not necessarily be found in existing repositories. For "Analyze and represent my evidence" the script for the guidance is more generic. Students are advised as follows:

- During the data analysis, you need to see your data and transform it in order to make sense of it, e.g. through different graphs, charts, etc. to help you understand relationships in data and see trends and patterns.
- During this phase, you may find errors in data, and so think why they occurred (from www.nquire.org.uk).

This more generic advice can be common to all inquiries, which is important if the software tool is to be a tool for teachers to use in their own teaching. A nice feature of both STAR and nQuire is that they have an authoring component. For nQuire, for example, the teacher or educational designer can select, author, and modify the scripts in order to monitor and guide the student activity. If the teacher can generate their own tools and resources to create specific repositories for a topic area, then the toolkit can act as a useful basis for sharing learning designs.

Software tools of this type use a standard sequence of activities, unable to adjust to the learner's own developing ideas and understanding, as a teacher might, so emulation of the good teacher is limited. This is important if they are providing scaffolding to the learner because, as a critique of these tools points out, scaffolding is meant to "fade":

> although the new curricula and software tools now described as scaffolds have provided us with novel techniques to support student learning, the important features of scaffolding such as ongoing diagnosis, calibrated support, and fading are being neglected.
>
> (Puntambekar, 2006; Puntambekar and Hübscher 2005)

The software tools we have discussed here do not provide an ongoing diagnosis because they do not have a computational model of the topic or of the learner in order to make the diagnosis, so they cannot provide calibrated support, and cannot adjust support by "fading" it (or even, potentially, enhancing it). These tools are therefore not providing the kind of practice environment we will be looking at in Chapter 10; they do not have a computational model. However, the teacher can use fading of support. In the STAR Legacy project, for example, the teacher sets challenges of increasing difficulty; in nQuire the teacher can use the authoring tool to monitor the student activity and change the guidance offered. The adaptation to learner needs is done by the teacher, and is enabled by the software.

Digital Tools for Inquiry Learning

Digital resources and tools for inquiry learning provide an exciting range of opportunities for students to explore topics beyond the range of even the best-equipped institutional libraries. The studies discussed here demonstrate several distinct ways in which digital technologies contribute to inquiry learning:

- Digital libraries, digital repositories, websites;
- Tools for recording data;

- Tools for recording reflections;
- Tools for sharing ideas;
- An organized sequence of resources and activities.

The support provided by the types of software tool now being used in education clearly improves on the unsupported private study of conventional pedagogies. It also improves on the kind of unguided online searching targeted in the "minimally guided instruction" technique discussed above. The sequence of activities is designed to motivate the learner at each stage to generate actions to achieve the task goal, act, reflect on what they find, modulate their conceptions and further actions, and then reflect on the process. However, it is important to note the critique that the technology is not scaffolding the learner's development by adapting to their needs: instead it is modeling and guiding them through the desired sequence of activities. What exactly does this mean for the pedagogic force of the approach?

From all these studies the importance of fostering student reflection for inquiry learning has been clear – this is a common finding. But it is interesting that while they exhibit similarities, they also emphasize different activities. Is there a common pattern to guide the teacher-designer in creating the optimal pedagogic design for inquiry learning?

Pedagogical Patterns for Inquiry Learning

We know from the discussion in Chapter 7 that we must enhance the basic forms of learning to make them optimally effective for learners. Learning through acquisition is important, but students need help with making their reading, watching, or listening effective. Similarly, when students use learning through inquiry by conducting their own investigation of what is known in a topic area, they need help with making their inquiry process effective, as this chapter has shown. This will be even more important now that they have digital access to a much wider range of resources than in conventional teaching.

The research on inquiry-based learning and its counterparts in problem-based or project-based learning, has established the fundamental principles of moving beyond the independent study of library resources to providing learners with guidance on the inquiry process itself. Each study outlines its preferred sequence of learner activities, and there is considerable overlap between them, suggesting that we might expect to find a common optimal pedagogical pattern. Table 8.1 combines all the teaching–learning activities from the studies outlined in this chapter. There is overlap, but not complete agreement. The Table presents in the first column the contrasting descriptions of the stages of inquiry learning, based on the main studies discussed in this chapter. In the second column it consolidates these into a common pedagogical pattern, and these are mapped to the learning cycles in the Conversational Framework in the third column.

We can see from Table 8.1 that digital technologies can make a significant contribution in two principal ways: providing access to digital resources, and

Table 8.1 A Consolidated Pedagogical Pattern for Learning Through Inquiry

Teaching-learning activities	Consolidated pedagogical pattern for inquiry learning	Cycles
Decide inquiry question or hypothesis (Sn) Look ahead to preview the topic (Sz)	Learners work individually to preview the resources for the topic and prepare for following group work	TCC1
Decide on data to be selected from different sources (A) Propose parameters for investigating the task (H) Identify search activity (E) Generate own ideas on the topic (Sz) Compare ideas with the multiple perspectives of experts (Sz) Plan methods, equipment and actions (Sn)	Learners work in groups to • generate ideas for investigating the topic • access digital resources of experts presenting and discussing topic • plan search strategy, parameters of data, and use of digital tools for information resources, data collection, and data analysis	PCC2 TCC1 PCC1,2
Collect and interpret information and data (A) Investigate the topic to decide their own point of view (H) Search a topic for most relevant results (E) Collect my evidence (Sn)	Learners work individually to collect and interpret information, and select the most relevant Record and represent information using the digital tools provided	TPC1
Evaluate the material found to determine the validity of the strategy (E) Develop alternative explanations (A) Decide between alternative hypotheses (A)	Learners work in small groups to compare results with peers Learners discuss which results are best and agree how to carry out the analysis	PMC2 PCC1, 2
Prepare analysis (H) Develop, assess and revise ideas (Sz) Analyze and represent the evidence (Sn) Respond to the question or hypothesis (Sn)	Learners individually carry out the analysis and represent their evidence using digital tools provided	TPC1
Present evidence to justify their answer (A) Debate and defend their point of view (H) Present your solution to the class (Sz) Share and discuss my inquiry (Sn)	Learners work in groups to agree a joint presentation	PCC2, 3 TPC1
Reflect on search rationale (E) Reflect back on what you learned (Sz) Reflect on my progress (Sn)	Learners individually write notes in their blog, or e-portfolio to record the lessons they learned from the process	TPC1

Source: Based on studies by Apedoe *et al.* (A), Edwards *et al.* (E), Hassainen *et al.* (H), Scanlon *et al.* (Sn), and Schwartz *et al.* (Sz) mapped to learning cycles.
Note: For codes see Table 6.2.

providing the range of online tools needed to record, represent, analyze and present the information and data collected, to invite reflection, and to support discussion with peers. There is only a practice environment envisaged here, not the kind of modeling environment with intrinsic feedback that we come to in Chapter 10.

Summary: Designing for Learning Through Inquiry

Learning through inquiry is intended as a way for the student to work independently of the teacher, and follow their own pathway to understanding by accessing existing resources that represent the teacher's conceptual knowledge. Figure 8.1(a) depicts this basic form, but learning theory, educational research, and studies of inquiry-based learning, propose more. The teacher's role must be to design the pedagogical patterns that support students through the inquiry process, so that they have a better chance of arriving at the intended understanding of the topic. The term "inquiry" here does not refer to the kind of inquiry that generates new knowledge. This is not expected of learners until doctoral level. It is a term that expresses the value to the learner of being in control of their own knowledge and skills development, in contrast with the teacher-led form of learning through acquisition.

In terms of the Conversational Framework, however, inquiry learning relies primarily on the teacher and other students to assist in motivating the iterative modulate–generate cycles. There is no intrinsic feedback from the resources they access; therefore there is no way the learner can tell if their understanding is improving, and no way that they can tell if their search and inquiry strategy is improving, or even if it is appropriate. That can only come from the teacher's evaluation. Encouraging reflection is important, as all these research studies agree, but it does not in itself ensure that the learner learns what the teacher intends. So the involvement of the teacher in supervision and monitoring, and of other students to provide a check and challenge, becomes a significant part of the pedagogical pattern.

To answer the question posed at the beginning of this chapter: there are ways of augmenting what conventional technologies offer by employing their digital equivalents. We can do more with digital approaches than with conventional approaches alone to improve the coverage of the Conversational Framework, as summarized in Table 8.1. By making use of access to digital resources, online guidance, and software tools for the inquiry process, students are able to develop a more effective approach to learning through inquiry.

9   Learning Through Discussion

Introduction

We know from the emphasis on social constructivism as a critical feature of successful pedagogy, that peer discussion must be an important mechanism for learning. Within conventional teaching methods its role has been recognized in techniques variously called buzz groups, small group sessions, discussion groups, activity groups, tutorials, and seminars. These terms have widely different meanings for different people, however. A tutorial can sometimes approximate to a lecture, being less well prepared by the teacher, perhaps, but still predominantly the teacher talking and students listening. At the other end of the spectrum a tutorial is a carefully prepared presentation by a student, with the teacher and one or two other students questioning, commenting, and challenging the student. The seminar is often this latter style of tutorial, but with a larger group of students, and shorter presentation time. As a teaching method it can also be a group discussion of a shared reading. All these forms involve the students in peer discussion, but they have radically different pedagogic effects. To be sure of eliciting the best learning experience from peer discussion we need to be careful that the underlying reasons for emphasizing its importance are respected in the way we set it up. It is part of the job of this chapter to try and elucidate that rationale.

Learning through discussion is often aligned with learning through collaboration. But there are two different pedagogies here, and it is useful to distinguish them, so collaboration has its own chapter. Collaboration poses a tougher challenge on the discussion: to produce something, a shared something, as the externalized fruit of the negotiated discussion. Charles Crook in his book on computers and the "collaborative experience of learning" phrased it as follows:

> The challenge is to discover how discourse is mobilized in the service of creating joint reference; to see how what is created gets used as a platform for further exploration; and to see how the material conditions of problem-solving can be more or less friendly towards efforts after this mutuality.
>
> (Crook 1996: 225)

So collaboration is about "creating joint reference", something the learners make together, and then use to move on to further exploration. Much of the research that might otherwise appear in this chapter is therefore covered in the chapter on learning through collaboration. While discussion groups may well end with a consensual outcome, the pedagogic focus in this chapter is on the value of the reciprocal critique of ideas, and how this leads to the development of a more elaborated conceptual understanding. It is worth keeping these two approaches to learning distinct.

The digital world has opened up some intriguing opportunities for learning through discussion. We look at both synchronous and asynchronous forms of online discussion, such as discussion environments, conferencing, chat rooms, and forums. As in conventional face-to-face discussions, the teacher can be present, or absent, or occasionally present, with different pedagogic effects, as we will see. The main issue is to look at what theory tells us about the nature of learning through discussion, tracking this through both conventional and digital technologies, and checking the extent to which contrasting forms of discussion learning cover the Conversational Framework.

Learning Through Discussion

The social aspect of learning, identified by Vygotsky from his studies of children learning in school, is frequently cited as the source for the idea that peer discussion plays a significant role in learning, not just in school, but at all levels of education. His observation that "all the higher [psychological] functions originate as actual relations between human individuals" before they can be internalized as cognitive development, demonstrates the importance he attached to communication and dialogue as part of the formal learning process (Vygotsky 1978).

In conventional teaching, peer discussion is used to alleviate the one-way transmission model of learning that survives as the class presentation or lecture. "Discuss among yourselves" is a familiar injunction in large classes, followed by the plenary, to check on what the designated rapporteurs are able to extract from their group. But *peer discussion* as an effective pedagogic technique needs some clarification. It does not just happen; it requires careful planning and support by the teacher if students are really to develop their cognitive understanding.

Vygotsky, like Piaget, saw the role of communication with others in the learner's environment as critical to cognitive development. He argued that the relationship between learning and development is built partly through peer discussion, as we develop our cognitive understanding of concepts, especially those that are taught in education:

> communication produces the need for checking and confirming thoughts, a process that is characteristic of adult thought … learning awakens a variety of internal developmental processes that are able to operate only

when a child is interacting with people in his environment and in coop-
eration with his peers. Once these processes are internalized, they become
part of the child's independent developmental achievement.

(Vygotsky 1978: 90)

For the adult learner, internal developmental processes no longer operate *only*
when the learner is interacting with people, because the experience of their
early years will have developed their capacity to carry out that internal conversation for themselves. Nonetheless, educators have embraced the idea of peer
discussion also for adult learners because that kind of interaction is so powerful for stimulating the productive internal conversation that leads to learning.
Vygotsky did not define precisely the form and nature of the peer discussion
that would produce "the need for checking and confirming thoughts", but to
have the pedagogic value expected of it, clearly the discussion cannot be just
any form of dialogue about a topic. If we want to elevate peer discussion to an
effective pedagogical form, we need to define clearly what makes it valuable,
and to work out what the teacher must do to motivate the type of peer discussion that succeeds in challenging students' thinking in the way that Vygotsky
envisaged.

We cannot expect too much from the literature. An extensive review of
discussion learning points out that empirical research on the pedagogic form
and value of discussion learning is only very recent, but does at least conclude
that "the skillful use of classroom dialogue can help to externalize the rational
processes, socializing students into the new ways of thinking" (Reznitskaya
et al. 2009).

Researchers are agreed that peer discussion must take a particular form to
be effective. Combining the results from a number of studies we can conclude
that students need to:

- take a particular position with respect to a concept or conjecture;
- provide evidence and explanations for their argument or position;
- consider, respond to, or challenge counter-arguments; share and critique
  each others' ideas;
- reflect on their own perspective in relation to those of others;
- work towards an agreed output, negotiating meaning, or collaborating on
  a decision;
- apply what they have learned (Bonk and King1998; Kanuka and Garrison
  2004; Lillejord and Dysthe 2008; Pfister and Oehl 2009; Reznitskaya *et al.*
  2009; Schellens and Valcke 2006; Swann 2007).

The Conversational Framework represents these exchanges as an iterative
series of actions by each learner, in the peer communication cycle, in
Figure 9.1. Of course the effectiveness of discussion as a learning process is
highly dependent on the extent to which those particular types of exchange
actually take place: do learners really challenge each other, and respond to

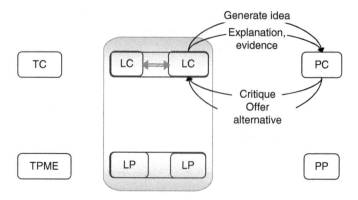

Figure 9.1 Learning through peer discussion.

critiques with evidence and explanations? This is what prompts the internal conversation that is responsible for the further development of the concept. Are they prompted to regenerate their ideas or reconfirm their position? It is important to be sure those are the activities being generated. And what keeps that iterative loop moving?

Figure 9.1 is sparsely populated in terms of the complete framework. The only fuel to drive the engine of idea and challenge, of explanation and critique, of generation and modulation of concepts, is the motivation and intellectual energy of the students themselves. That can be sufficient, of course, but there are many research studies now demonstrating that learning through discussion does not necessarily produce clear learning outcomes, and the conclusion is therefore that we have to work harder to make sure it is productive. This is not a new problem. Learning through discussion has been an important pedagogic technique for some decades, partly due to Vygotsky's influence, and partly to the recognition that the "transmission" method is inadequate on its own. However, the expansion of communicative media offered by digital technologies has led to an explosion of studies of online discussion-based learning, and this is now the major source of our understanding of how best to use the method.

Discussion-Based Methods

Learning through discussion comes in several forms: with or without the teacher present, teacher-led or student-led, small groups or large groups, structured or unstructured, embedded within other methods, or stand-alone. We now also have the choice of face-to-face or online, and synchronous or asynchronous. In this section we look at the broad categories of synchronous, teacher-led, face-to-face discussions (the conventional form). How do they work?

Tutorials, Seminars, and Discussion Groups

The conventional forms of learning through discussion vary principally in the size of the student group, and the degree to which the teacher leads. The classic *tutorial* puts the student at the centre, making a presentation of their point of view, and being challenged by the tutor and one or two other students. Students take turns in making their presentation and in commenting on others' work. The classic *seminar* operates in the same way, but with a larger student group, and less time for each student's presentation over several sessions. The classic *discussion group* is a tutor-led discussion of a specific topic, problem, or case, where students are encouraged to develop their solutions or opinions through interaction with each other, guided by the tutor (Abercrombie 1979). These are the classic ideal forms, each of which fails if the tutor too easily resorts to doing the greater part of the talking (Ramsden 2003).

The principal rationale for student-centered discussion groups is to help students develop critical thinking and autonomy in learning by engaging in spontaneous expression of their ideas, and to clarify and deepen their understanding through dialogue and debate. If the tutor is unpracticed at facilitating such an approach the form collapses, inevitably, into the default form of a lecture (Anderson 1984).

As class sizes continue to increase, discussion groups get larger. The cut and thrust of debate in a "small" group cannot be sustained in discussion groups of 15 and more, and most students only have a vicarious experience of the discussion. This can be valuable, of course, as each student asking a question or making a comment can stand in the place of others, and help to disambiguate a confusion or misconception on behalf of all students. But they are essentially learning through acquisition, not through discussion. The critical form that differentiates discussion from acquisition is the need to find an expression for your own thought, to have it challenged, to place this new idea in relation to your first idea, and through the resolution of that potential discrepancy develop a more elaborated, or better articulated expression of your thought. That "need for checking and confirming thoughts" is fundamental. Listening to others debate and argue, it is often our experience that they have expressed exactly our idea, yet we may not have been able to do it ourselves. Similarly, learners may follow everything the teacher says as they explain it, and yet by trying to regenerate it in practice find they cannot. This is characteristic of learning through acquisition – I can listen, and follow, but that does not mean I have understood it securely as an idea I can generate myself. Being called upon to generate it in discussion enables us either to begin to rehearse that process, or at least to discover that we cannot.

Peer discussion is often not sufficient to secure successful learning. Argument between students about a topic can be an extremely effective way of enabling students to find out what they know, and what they do not know, but does not necessarily lead them to what they are supposed to know. Discussion between students is an excellent *partial* method of learning that often needs to be complemented by further explanation or disambiguation from the teacher, if students are not to flounder in mutually progressive ignorance. We will return to this point repeatedly for the other forms of peer discussion.

How Can Digital Technologies Help?

The digital forms of discussion are either *asynchronous*, where the members take part at any time, or *synchronous*, where they participate during a specific time period, sometimes synchronizing across several time zones if the group is international. In all cases the members go to a specific online space, either public or private, and register to join the group, giving them access to others' messages, to which they can reply, or the means to start a new discussion thread. Different types of discussion space offer different degrees of structure, and this is important for pedagogic purposes, as we shall see.

Asynchronous Online Discussion

As digital access increased during the early 1990s, and email began to be widely used in universities, online communication expanded rapidly, initially in HE and later in colleges and schools. A variety of digital environments were developed to support it. Synchronous methods, where participants wait for each other's messages before they respond, were not feasible for most people, due to the very low connection speeds of the time, but asynchronous methods, where you send your message then wait possibly days for a response, were certainly feasible. It would be another decade before chat rooms and instant messaging could be used. As a result, asynchronous discussion environments have had much longer to develop, and are much more commonly used in education than synchronous environments (Mason 2001).

This is significant, because the simple fact of decoupling a teaching communication from time and place required a much more radical rethink of how we teach, than would have been necessary for a shift to "same time, any place". It is interesting that during this period there were many attempts to exploit satellite technology for exactly this remote but synchronous teaching. They set up "remote classrooms" that could function in much the same way as a normal classroom, but with the teacher at one site and students at another, watching a large screen, and speaking their questions into a microphone. The method enabled teachers to reach a wider group without sacrificing the familiarity of conventional teaching. The expense and technological difficulty of such methods meant that they remained confined to short-term projects, or well-resourced areas such as medical education. Satellite-based synchronous methods have not become mainstream (Bates 2005). In general, educationists had to confront the more radical shift to opening up both time and place to learning that could be offered "anytime, anywhere", which became the mantra for e-learning.

Pedagogically, this shift to asynchronous teaching is important because it recalibrates the way both teachers and students spend their time in a discussion. Analysis of tutor–student messages in a computer conference running during an Open University course showed that the average length of student contribution was 200 words, equivalent to over a minute of continuous speech. Often, tutors make only 10–15% of the contributions in online discussions (Harasim 1987).

The removal of any time constraint in the online tutorial has some important pedagogical effects:

- there is no natural limit to the length or frequency of each individual's contributions;
- students can take their time to reflect on what has been said, and consider carefully how to adapt and phrase their contribution as a result;
- students who hang back from the debate in a tutorial context are released from their inhibitions and become voluble contributors;
- the time it takes to read a message is far less than the time it takes to listen to someone saying it.

These mainly logistical facts change fundamentally the nature of the interaction. The critical difference is that for asynchronous tutorials time is unconstrained. In a one-hour tutorial the tutor is likely to speak for about half the time, which leaves half to be shared among the students for their contributions – about 5% each in a group of ten. The remainder of the time they are listening to other students or the tutor. Compare this measure for the face-to-face tutorial with the asynchronous case, in which there is no time constraint and students can write as much as they wish. If we take the example of the tutor making 10% of the contributions, then 90% is shared between ten students, nearly doubling the proportion contributed by each student. The teacher may not read all the student contributions, so their total teaching time could reduce in comparison with the face-to-face method. Whether they can do this without reducing the pedagogic value of the discussion is something we return to in the section on scaffolding.

Of course, as in face-to-face contexts, peer discussion can take place online with no teacher intervention, requiring all the input to come from the students.

This kind of analysis of how teachers and students spend their time, and how best to optimize it, will be increasingly important as staff–student ratios continue to worsen, so we need to understand how these simple parameters of the different teaching methods work, and how their effects compare in terms of pedagogic effectiveness.

Synchronous Online Discussion

When good connection speeds and personal computing became widespread at the end of the 1990s, synchronous online discussion environments became feasible. It was now possible to replicate the face-to-face tutorial online, and students could engage in peer discussion of a more immediate kind than the asynchronous forums offered. Chat rooms, graphical chat environments, and instant messaging have been successful social environments for synchronous *text-based* communication, but while some students naturally use them for their own study-related discussions, the need for quick reactions and fast typing works against careful thought and reflection. To make the transition to a viable educational medium the teacher needs to set ground-rules for these meetings beyond the classroom (Ingram, Hathorn, and Evans 2000).

By comparison with asynchronous discussions so far these formats seem less interesting for education, especially as the group size needs to be small – up to five participants ideally, even with graphical support for identifying who is talking. They have all the constraints of face-to-face without any obvious gain in pedagogical advantage. Of course the logistical advantage of being able to meet at a distance can be the difference between tutorial and no tutorial, giving the method a distinct pedagogical advantage in that sense.

A more sophisticated form of synchronous discussion is supported by systems that offer a shared *online whiteboard*, with *audio conferencing*, bringing the online experience as close as possible to the small group sitting around a shared object, or physical whiteboard, as in certain kinds of tutorial. The teaching focus here may be on a diagram or other kind of visual, to focus the attention on what the discussion is about. There is no video, so there are no visual cues for facial expression and body language, but the faithful representation of the verbal language in what is now excellent audio online, makes this synchronous format a significant improvement on text-only versions. Whether synchronous communication needs *video-based communication*, rather than audio only, is under-researched in education. One series of experiments on students doing collaborative problem-solving with synchronous audio, with and without video, showed that video changed the pattern of interaction in a way that might facilitate conceptual development, although it did not change performance (Joiner *et al.* 2002). Further studies suggested this was because eye contact facilitates negotiation, and in the context of problem-solving, and perhaps in more general discussion tasks, this improves the quality of the experience and the likelihood of conceptual development (Scanlon *et al.* 2005).

It is important that we understand the contrasting affordances of these different media, and their differential value for learning – instant messaging being good for informal and immediate exchanges, whereas shared-online-audio-whiteboard systems are better for focused tutorials (Weller, Pegler, and Mason 2004). In all forms of synchronous discussion the optimum group size seems to be a maximum of about five, which does affect the staff-student ratio possible for such methods. However, there is still relatively little empirical research in this medium that would tell us about how to support effective discussion, and what studies there are derive from multiple fields of study (de Freitas and Neumann 2009). So far, we know that students like this mode of learning as long as technical problems are minimal, and that it has the potential to support effective discussion.

The Pedagogy of Learning Through Discussion

Peer discussion is important and valuable, as learning theory tells us, but it may not afford high quality learning in either face-to-face or online mode, as practical experience and empirical studies tell us. What they have shown, however, is that if the teacher plays an active role in shaping and structuring the discussion – scaffolding the learning process – then it can deliver the value expected of the social constructivist approach. In this section we look at what this means for conventional and digital environments.

Scaffolding Peer Discussion

The class discussion has always been part of the teacher's pedagogic armory in face-to-face mode, and yet it has not attracted the strong body of empirical research that would enable us to build on the lessons learned as we explore digital discussion environments. For the few valuable face-to-face studies we can draw on, the methods include descriptive case studies and comparisons of different pedagogical approaches. All of them stress the value of the teacher's contribution.

One part of the teacher's role is to design the context within which the discussion sits. The learning design sequence for a typical class discussion session is to:

- provide materials for students to study and analyze;
- advise students to prepare in advance;
- clarify that students will be called on to answer questions ("cold calling") if they do not raise their hands in class;
- grade each student's level of participation.

The value of discussion comes primarily from active participation by the individual student, so the focus on assessment is seen as critical to success:

> to be effective—as well as to guard against inattentive participants or those unwilling or unable to participate fully and contribute equally—instructors need to design discourse where the purpose is clearly articulated with accountability and assessable outcomes.
>
> (Kanuka and Garrison 2004: 9–10)

A second aspect of the teacher's role is the way they conduct the discussion itself, where students value teachers who:

- ensure that ideas are related to real-world experiences, their own and their students';
- facilitate students in structuring, challenging, questioning, and controlling;
- ask critical, leading, open-ended questions;

- create a supportive classroom environment, encouraging, relaxed, creating trust;
- affirm student contributions and provide constructive feedback (Dallimore, Hertenstein, and Platt 2004).

A study comparing alternative approaches to conducting the discussion within class shows that the teacher must not make *too much* contribution. Comparing two contrasting methods: for method A, the teacher questions the students to promote comprehension of a shared reading (the *recitation* method); for method B, the students begin by taking their own position on a "big question" based on a shared reading, and learn the process of dialogic collaborative reasoning (the *collaborative reasoning* method). The former is teacher-led and teacher-focused, isolating students from each other, and engaging only individuals in active response to the question; the latter makes students much more actively engaged contributors, encouraging them to provide reasons and evidence for their positions, to listen to and evaluate each others' reasoning, and to address the issues from multiple perspectives. The study found that the greater degree of engagement in this latter method helps students to rehearse and construct a higher quality of output. If they use collaborative reasoning students engage more, as measured by talking speed, proportion of student talk, and consecutive student turns. This appears to help them also in the qualitative outcomes they achieve on related essays, evaluated in terms of, for example, the number of reasons advanced as evidence for an argument, and the consideration of counter-arguments (Reznitskaya *et al.* 2009). The two pedagogic patterns for class discussion are very different, and in this case led to importantly different learning outcomes.

The teacher's approach has to blend with what the students bring to a class discussion and, as we know from looking at this in Chapter 3, the depth of student engagement with the activity affects the depth of their understanding. This is illustrated in a study of class discussion based on readings, with the focus on understanding concepts and theories rather than their application. The study looked at students' conceptions of learning through discussion, and discerned four ways of seeing it, as either: "challenging", "developing", "acquiring", or "checking" ideas. The first two, "deep approaches" were linked to "cohesive conceptions" of learning through discussion, whereas the second two "surface approaches" were linked to more "fragmented conceptions," and to lower performances in the final assessment (Ellis *et al.* 2006). As in similar studies, there is a holistic relationship between approach and conception and quality of performance (Ellis *et al.* 2004). The authors derive the implications for design as (i) an orientation exercise to model successful approaches to discussion, and (ii) authentic assessment of students' contributions to motivate deeper conceptions of and approaches to peer discussion (Ellis *et al.* 2006).

Students differ, of course, and some will respond better, and become more engaged through the "energy and immediacy" of the face-to-face discussion

(Meyer 2003), while others need time for reflection, and would fare better in the slower pace of online discussion environments. As ever, the optimal approach is for the teacher to offer both – not as options, but as a way of ensuring that all students experience and practice the contrasting advantages of both. Those who are reticent in class will build their confidence through their successes online, and those who are less reflective will have the opportunity to do this online, if, as we see in the next section, the teacher organizes that environment appropriately.

Scaffolding Asynchronous Discussion

Online asynchronous discussion environments have been available and used, especially in higher education, since the 1990s, and the improving technologies over the last decade or so have fuelled much greater interest in this technology in schools and colleges, and therefore much more research. It was also possible for the online discussion forum to acquire additional respectability by being aligned with the learning theory of social constructivism, which was growing in popularity over the same period. But as we saw in the earlier section on "learning through discussion," the pedagogic force of this method is achieved by engaging the students in very active processing of concepts, issues, and ideas, both internally and in their external expression, in a variety of ways. Simply making an online discussion forum available to students is no more or less likely to achieve this than making a meeting room available. Of course they may take advantage of the opportunity, but the teacher's job is to ensure that they maximize the educational benefit of the time spent. So how does this work in the context of the asynchronous text-based form of communication that is so different from anything encountered by Vygotsky? How does the teacher build the foundations students need if they are they are really to be "checking and confirming thoughts?"

In terms of the Conversational Framework, the teacher has to design the peer communication cycle so that it enables each learner to modulate their concept as a result of having to generate articulations, and hear what their peers have to say – which in turn engages their internal conversation to develop their conception.

The framework suggests that the teacher should motivate learners to make links between the theoretical and practical aspects of the concepts being learned by reflecting on their experience, or by thinking through how they might change their practice in the light of the discussion. However, researchers investigating online discussion rarely begin with a methodology for testing the effectiveness of the social constructivist pedagogy; the test is often whether discussion and interaction takes place, not whether something is learned:

> It may not be possible to test what each student actually learns from a particular interaction, but it is possible to analyze aspects of both the interactional patterns and the development of the content, and on the

basis of this make assertions about the learning potential in the particular activity.

(Dysthe 2002)

Web-mediated discussion groups may give students a starting point, and may also help to generate a greater quantity of questions, but the summative effect on final knowledge can remain elusive (Choi, Land, and Turgeo 2005). The attenuated link between pedagogy and final outcome is too great, given the multiplicity of variables involved, to allow clear validation of the pedagogy.

Researchers also argue the benefits of online discussion in terms of the technology-dependent characteristics of online communication: because it is asynchronous and text-based:

> it can support both reflection before responding (Light, Colbourn, and Light 1997; McNeill 1992; Nalley 1995; Steeples, Goodyear, and Mellar 1994; Wilson and Whitelock 1998) *and* on-task recombination of ideas, by providing the text of messages in reviewable and manipulable form (Harasim 1989; Henri 1995; McConnell 1998).

(Tolmie and Boyle 2000: 121)

Many of these studies investigate the ways of generating high quality dialogue, and trust that this will in turn, given the theory of social constructivism, produce learning.

Researchers clearly agree that the most important element of the pedagogy of learning through asynchronous online discussion is to provide students with a structure for their interactions. Engaging students in high-quality forms of exchange and interaction does not just happen as a result of providing the discussion forum (Wu and Hiltz 2004). We know from the studies in the section on learning through peer discussion that the combined conclusions suggest that learners need to: *take a position; explain and defend their position; share and critique each others' ideas; reflect; negotiate an agreed meaning; apply what they have learned.* This is what the teacher has to provide for in the asynchronous context as well.

Researchers have explored several ways in which teachers can structure interactions (De Wever *et al.* 2009; Dillenbourg, Järvelä, and Fischer 2009; Gilbert and Dabbagh 2005; Pfister and Oehl 2009; Salmon 2002; Schellens *et al.* 2009; Weinberger *et al.* 2009). The aim is to scaffold the types of interaction that would count as evidence that social constructivism is taking place, and there seem to be two distinct ways of doing this: (i) to constrain students to select a particular type of intervention as they make it, or (ii) to assign students different roles to play throughout the discussion. Another form of scaffolding is "scripts", but these have been studied most extensively in the research on learning through collaboration, so this is discussed in detail in Chapter 11.

Selecting Types of Intervention

In the "selecting" approach students are given a set of types of intervention from which they select one to describe the type of intervention or contribution they are making, such as:

> Question ... about a definition, function or reason;
> Explanation ... of a concept, a function, a system, or a reason;
> Conjecture ... about an assumption or a prediction;
> Comment ... as a justification, or a commentary;
> Critique ... as a complement, a correction, an alternative.

Some of the studies referenced above set out to test effectiveness, but the empirical evidence remains uncertain. One study, for example, did not manage to establish an unequivocal link with learning outcomes, but did show that students chose to use these techniques when they were made available (Pfister and Oehl 2009).

This approach is also implemented by asking students to "tag" their contributions, with reference to a theoretical classification, such as Garrison's problem-solving stages: *identifying a problem, defining it more clearly, exploring the problem and possible solutions, evaluating their applicability and integrating this understanding with existing knowledge* (Garrison 1992). The digital tool prompts the learner to reflect on the kind of role their contribution is making to the whole process. In one study they were asked to identify their problem-solving contribution in terms of "thinking hats", each one related to one of Garrison's stages, with some interesting results:

> students tagging their contributions by means of the thinking hats, surpassed the control group students significantly in the achieved general depth of critical thinking ... it can be concluded that students who are required to reflect on their type of thinking, in order to tag their contributions, are more prone to engaging in focused and in-depth discussions than their peers in the control condition who are involved in more general online discourse, keeping the topic under discussion open wide. Furthermore, students in the experimental condition are also more likely to introduce new problem-related information and to deal with new discussion ideas, while control group students have a tendency to restating what has been discussed before.
>
> (Schellens *et al.* 2009)

It is a simple device, to get students to reflect on the nature of their contribution simply by tagging it with a formal category, but it can be effective. This is a clear demonstration of the difference between mere discussion, and *learning through* discussion. The latter does not just happen; it has to be deliberately scaffolded by the teacher.

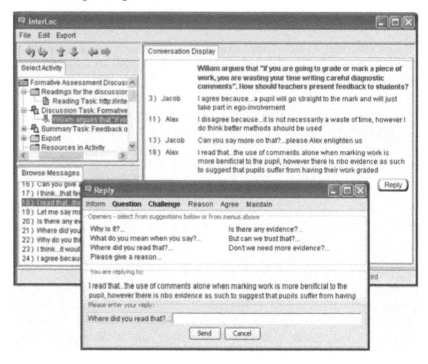

Figure 9.2 InterLoc: A dialogue environment that prompts each student to think about the nature of their contribution before they type their text.

Source: from Ravenscroft 2007.

The classification of contributions to an online discussion can be done by selecting formally defined tags, or types, but it can also be embedded in the format of the online discussion environment (Nussbaum *et al.* 2009). The interactive dialogue tool *InterLoc* is an example, where students can select openers for different types of intervention such as *inform, question, challenge, reason, agree, maintain.* Figure 9.2 shows how the interface enables students to consider the nature and form of their contribution, as they make it.

The claim is that the format facilitates students in making coherent and varied discussions to create constructive conflict with a legitimate argument (Ravenscroft 2007).

Role-play

The role-play approach operates differently, assigning each student a role to play within the discussion. One example is to assign them to the roles of:

- starter
- summarizer

- moderator
- theoretician and
- source searcher.

This study concluded that the roles acted as a valuable structuring tool, especially when they are scaffolded at the beginning and later faded out (De Wever *et al.* 2009).

The idea of assigning roles for discussion is familiar from conventional formats such as class debates. Again, structure is important, and a study that compared different formats for discussion learning: nominal group technique, debate, invited expert, WebQuest, and reflective deliberation, showed that only the "debate" and the "WebQuest" were sufficiently structured formats to be effective (Kanuka, Rourke, and Laflamme 2007). Assigning explicit roles to learners encouraged them to challenge each other's ideas, so these formats were more successful at engaging the students' "cognitive presence", keeping them motivated to iterate around the peer communication cycle.

What does this mean for the teacher's role during the discussion process? In the asynchronous context, as we know from the earlier section, they can expect that students will contribute a much higher proportion of the discussion than is likely in the face-to-face context. The teacher can play an important role as moderator, motivating participation, socializing in the online context, facilitating information exchange, guiding the process, and supporting the development of ideas (Salmon 2003), although several studies have suggested that peer moderation is more effective than teacher moderation (Cifuentes and Murphy 1997; Hara, Bonk, and Angeli 2000; Leh 2002; Poole 2000).

A study of teacher moderation reported the teacher as promoting good discussion by providing student facilitator guidelines (defining their roles and criteria for good postings) and evaluation criteria (number of postings, link to grades), in addition to protocols for postings (limited length of a posting, reference to reading sources). Results showed that directions (protocols for postings) had a more negative impact, while guidelines for student facilitators, and evaluation of student performance both had a positive effect on the amount and quality of student interaction (Gilbert and Dabbagh 2005). Similarly, a study of the effectiveness of peer moderation showed that it improved the quantity and quality of student contributions, in terms of "meaningful interactions", i.e. messages that (a) relate to a discussion topic, (b) respond to a previous statement or invite a comment, and (c) add substance to the discussion (Seo 2007). Student moderators had to perform the following tasks:

1. create a friendly environment;
2. encourage participation by reminding participants of the course expectations;
3. encourage sharing of ideas;

4. start each week's discussion by clarifying the topic and discussion schedule;
5. prompt participants to pursue their ideas; and
6. end each week's discussion by summarizing the shared ideas.

Here students are taking responsibility for the social interaction, which is crucial to effective discussion. This kind of role-play has the benefit of engaging students well, and of enabling them to practice the skills of moderation, and of reducing the need for continual monitoring by the teacher.

The opportunity afforded by online discussion technologies has had the valuable effect of stimulating research and investigation of how best to support this type of learning. We are still in the process of discovering how best to structure the pedagogy, but the guidelines have certainly moved beyond the simplistic belief that discussion is valuable in itself. We now have a better understanding of the importance of structuring this learning process.

Scaffolding Synchronous Discussion

The key difference between synchronous and asynchronous environments is that it is more difficult for the teacher to support and scaffold peer group discussions in the synchronous online environment than in either a face-to-face class, where teacher control and guidance is expected and facilitated by the physical arrangements, or an asynchronous online environment, where the teacher has time to intervene if necessary. The synchronous forum or chat-room is more anarchic, so it is important to create a sense of responsibility for the enabling roles of a moderator in the students themselves. One study took the interesting step of eliciting a set of potential roles from the students, which they were then required to practice. Results showed that they were capable of increasing their adoption of such roles as:

- Exploratory inquiry – asking others to elaborate, explain, or clarify anything that is unclear or not explained in enough depth, or asking for other examples;
- Task management/focus – keeping people focused on the issues to be discussed, encouraging them to move on when necessary and to discuss as many of the issues as possible in the time available;
- Encouraging participation – encouraging those who are not participating to join in whilst encouraging others to make space for them;
- Positive feedback – encouraging contributions by giving positive feedback when someone contributes well;
- Negative feedback – discouraging disruptive off-task behavior, inappropriate social behavior, "shouting" (using capital letters), or non-constructive criticism;
- Content building – responding to requests for suggestions, examples, evidence or explanations.

However, although the adoption of these roles increased during the initial phases, they were not maintained for the full 10-week course (Pilkington and Walker 2003). The conditions of the course could easily account for this – by the later stages students are often more focused on completing assignments than on collaborative learning. But these are valuable ground-rules to set for the medium.

Much easier to manage, from the teacher's point of view, is the online tutorial, usually supported by synchronous audio conferencing, a shared screen for showing slides that are controlled by the teacher, and two-way audio, supplemented by a chat facility. This set-up restores to the teacher the control they have in the face-to-face context, with the immediate downside that students are therefore less active unless the teacher takes steps to reverse this inevitable consequence. As with so many digital technologies, this type of "remote meeting" environment was developed for business, not education. The interactional design supports the chaired meeting, where participants are represented visually with icons, which each individual can change into a "hand-up" icon when they wish to speak. It is not ideal for education. Students linked in from a distance, are often reluctant to make such a move, which can be even more daunting than making a contribution in class. This means that all the techniques discussed for making asynchronous discussion pedagogically effective, such as structured role-play, are just as important in the synchronous context (de Freitas and Neumann 2009). Students need the session to be carefully structured, with the ground-rules laid down in advance, if they are to be actively engaged in learning through discussion.

Pedagogical Patterns for Discussion Learning

There are few studies that have attempted to compare pedagogical patterns for discussion learning in face-to-face and online mode. One study has explicitly compared two contrasting pedagogies (Nicol and Boyle 2003): "peer instruction" (Mazur 1997) and "class-wide discussion" (Dufresne *et al.* 1996). Both were class-based and used audience-response technology to collect data on the frequencies of different responses, though not on the accuracy of responses. The contrasting patterns, based on these two pedagogic forms are shown in Table 9.1. The critical differences are in steps 2 and 5, for individual thinking, and peer instruction.

From interviews, a survey, and a critical incident questionnaire, students judged that both methods provided more active involvement in learning than conventional lectures, and were more motivating. Their preferred sequence was "peer instruction," because (i) it provided initial individual thinking time, which meant they were less passive in the peer discussion groups; (ii) this meant they were more able to engage in dialogue and identify gaps in their thinking; (iii) there was more opportunity for dialogue and debate (Nicol and Boyle 2003). The disadvantage of the "class-wide discussion" was that it was too easy to be confused by a succession of different explanations, some of them

Table 9.1 Alternative Pedagogic Patterns for Class-Based Discussion Learning

Class-wide Discussion	Peer Instruction
1. Concept question posed.	1. Concept question posed.
2. Peer discussion in small groups (3–5 minutes).	2. Individual thinking (1–2 minutes).
3. Students post individual or group responses.	3. Students post individual responses.
4. Students see frequencies of responses as histogram.	4. Students see frequencies of responses as histogram.
5. *Class-wide discussion*, where students give, and listen to, explanations for responses.	5. *Peer instruction*, where each student has to convince a peer that their response is correct.
	Repeat steps 3 and 4.
6. Lecturer summarizes and explains the correct response.	6. Lecturer summarizes and explains the correct response.
Student evaluation: class discussion could be confusing and disorganized; little opportunity to challenge individuals.	*Student evaluation*: provides initial thinking time; more dialogue helps identify gaps in thinking; more opportunity for debate.

misconceived, and with little opportunity to challenge on an individual basis. Mapping the two sequences to the Conversational Framework clarifies the contrasts, as in Figure 9.3.

A clear contrast is apparent in the amount of learning activity generated, not just by the fact that there is an additional response requirement in Figure 9.3(b), but also because of the format of the discussion task:

- The requirement to post a response motivates the learner to generate an articulation of their concept in the "individual thinking" phase;
- The feedback on class responses enables the learner to modulate their concept;
- The requirement to defend their first response motivates each learner to generate, and enables them to hear an articulation;
- The requirement to post a second response, motivates each learner to modulate their concept, enabled by the peer instruction, and generate an articulation of their concept.

In neither case does the teacher provide a "practice environment" for instantiating the concept. And although the study describes the histogram of student responses as "feedback," this is not feedback that is either meaningful or helpful: simply knowing how many other students thought response A was correct tells you precisely nothing about whether it *is* correct. It is probably not entirely pointless; the simple act of making a commitment to an answer,

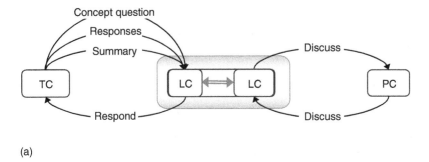

(a)

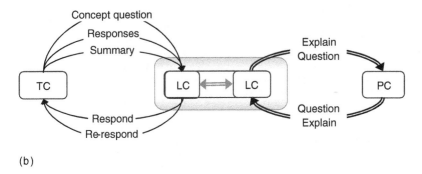

(b)

Figure 9.3 Discussion learning using (a) "class-wide discussion," and (b) "peer instruction."

even if it is anonymous, can be motivating in itself. But the introduction of technology to collect anonymous student responses in a class has very little pedagogic value beyond the value to the teacher of the feedback on their teaching. What this study demonstrates is the value to students of articulating their point of view, because it creates some conflict with their peer in discussion, which in turn enables them to modulate their concept.

The research on learning through online discussion derives originally from studies of learning through face-to-face peer discussion, but the field is seriously under-researched, given its importance and wide usage. There is some overlap in the findings of the characteristics of successful online peer discussion so it is feasible to consider a common optimal pedagogical pattern. Table 9.2 combines all the learner activities from the studies outlined in this chapter to show what they have in common. The Table presents in the first column a family of patterns based on the main studies discussed in this chapter for supporting learning through online discussion. In the second column it consolidates these into a common pedagogical pattern, which is mapped to the learning cycles in the Conversational Framework in the third column. The pattern is for an online discussion group where students are working together

Table 9.2 A Consolidated Pedagogical Pattern for Learning Through Peer Discussion Online

Sequence of activities	Consolidated pedagogical pattern for discussion learning	Cycles
Prepare in advance from materials provided (K, R) Learners take turns to act as "source searcher" (W) Work towards an agreed output, negotiating meaning, or collaborating on a decision (C) Learners take turns to act as "summarizer" (W, Seo)	Learners work individually through resources provided Each learner is assigned a group, a task goal, and a role to find particular types of resource.	TCC1
Each learner is assigned a role (P) Provide evidence and explanations for their argument or position (C) Respond to requests for suggestions, examples, evidence or explanations (P) Take a particular position with respect to a concept or conjecture (C, R) Consider, respond to, or challenge counter-arguments; share and critique each others' ideas (C) Tag the category of contribution they are making (S) Learners take turns to act as moderator and theoretician (W) Encourage participation and sharing of ideas, prompting participants to pursue their ideas (Seo) Ask others to elaborate, explain or clarify; keep people focused on the issues (P)	Learners use a digital intervention selection tool to categorize the type of intervention they are making to prompt them to: • take a position, • share and critique ideas, provide evidence and explanations for their argument or position, and • respond to requests for suggestions, examples, evidence or explanations. Learners take turns each week to act as moderator and theoretician.	PCC2 PCC3 PCC2, 3
Reflect on own views in relation to their peers (C) Create a friendly environment (Seo) Encourage contributions with positive feedback (P) Discourage negative feedback (P) The teacher creates a supportive classroom; affirms student contributions with constructive feedback (D)	The teacher provides guidelines on expectations of the discussion, and how to create a supportive and constructive discussion.	TCC1
The teacher facilitates students in structuring, challenging, questioning, and controlling; relating ideas to real-world experiences, theirs and their students' (D)	Each group provides access to their discussion; teacher provides feedback on how to conduct a productive discussion.	TCC3
Apply what they have learned (C) The teacher grades students' participation (D)	The teacher clarifies how they will grade learners' participation in groups.	TCC1

Note: Letters in parentheses refer to studies by combined researchers (C); Dallimore *et al.* (D), Kanuka *et al.* (K), Reznitskaya *et al.* (R), Schellens *et al.* (S), De Wever *et al.* (W), Seo (Seo), and Pilkington *et al.* (P), mapped to learning cycles. For codes see Table 6.2.

with little teacher intervention, so the peer moderation is important. The teacher's role here is to advise and guide occasionally, but to motivate learners to generate articulations and enable each other to modulate their concepts by providing the guidelines and digital support tools that promote appropriate roles.

Researchers draw different conclusions on what the teacher's role should be: some favor the teacher as moderator; others propose the teacher as facilitator of student moderation. Digital technologies can make a significant contribution by creating an environment in which there is much less time pressure on the student, who can therefore spend a higher proportion of time available in active discussion, and take their time to reflect on their own and peers' contributions. Tagging or identifying the category of contribution they are making is only really feasible online, and this appears to encourage attention to the quality of their contribution.

Summary: Designing for Learning Through Discussion

Learning through discussion has value because it provides the motivation for each participant to articulate their concepts and ideas, defend them, reconsider them in the light of challenge, and use them to mount a challenge to someone else's idea. When it is well structured, the iterative nature of the discussion process provides a powerful engine for conceptual development. But all the research discussed here shows that this demands significant preparation and monitoring by the teacher to make sure it is productive.

10 Learning Through Practice

Introduction

The previous three chapters considered learning through acquisition, inquiry, and discussion. They each take students into the world of the discipline, its theories, concepts, conceptual frameworks, and the types of thinking that are needed to engage with the theory. The access to understanding in each case is primarily through language and forms of representation. The learner is being guided through the formal descriptions of the world (of history, science, business, literature, etc.), and the different ways these are represented in their subject area – through specialized language and concepts, ways of thinking and reasoning about the subject matter, diagrams, classifications, relationships, formalisms, and ways of interpreting and synthesizing. The role of the teacher is to be present, to inform, explain, guide and advise, as well as to design the curriculum and the way of accessing it through documents and other resources.

In this chapter we consider a different way of learning: through practice. It takes place when the teacher has prepared an exercise for the student to apply their understanding of the concepts to achieving a task goal. The focus is mostly on the student working alone, leaving collaboration to Chapter 11. Learning through practice is an essential part of the learning experience, because it invites the learner to adapt their conceptual understanding to the task at hand, and then reflect on what that experience means for how they might modulate their understanding. For some subject areas there are timetabled practical classes, but not for all. In universities and colleges much of this kind of learning takes place in private study; in schools it is carried out as homework. The teacher is not usually present. How do we support that? And how can technologies help?

Learning through practice is a way of enabling the learner to understand and use the knowledge and skills of a discipline. It is sometimes referred to as "learning by doing", or "learning through experience", where the learner adapts their actions to the task goal, and uses the result to improve, without teacher intervention. Neuroscientists refer to it as "learning through prediction", when they account for how every child learns about the world around them through motivation and curiosity, predicting what action is needed to achieve a result, comparing the result of their action with their prediction, and adjusting their next action accordingly (Frith, 2007). This is the goal–action–feedback–revision cycle, the modeling cycle, which is fundamental to the natural learning process.

Traditionally teachers provide homework exercises, worksheets, and problem sheets with model answers, as well as annotated reading lists, study guides, and other means by which the written word can support the lone student engaged in independent learning through practice. With digital technologies other means become available.

Learning Through Practice

As we saw in Chapter 8, inquiry learning helps students engage with the world of descriptions and formal representations, made available through libraries, digital resources and databanks. The nature of the "feedback" on their actions is indirect, as the resource environment does not itself guide them to improve their actions: the feedback from the teacher or other learners is extrinsic to their actions. For inquiry learning of the kind that sends students to study books, resources, data, or information, we cannot expect that the environment could supply any direct feedback; as Socrates pointed out, books "preserve one unvarying meaning".

In Chapter 9 we explored the peer discussion cycle, as a means of powering the internal cycles of generating and modulating ideas and actions when students respond to the suggestions and challenges of their peers. Feedback comes in the form of questions, comments, and guidance from the teacher, and questions, comments, and alternative thinking from other students, all of which provide the occasion to reflect and rethink. For learning through discussion this cycle is taking place at the level of theory, ideas, concepts, examples, evidence, information, but does not in itself require the students to apply their ideas and concepts in practice.

Learning through practice is different because it goes beyond the realm of language and representation. In terms of human evolution, learning from experience long predates learning through language. Learning through language and communication is, of course, a vastly more efficient way of passing on accumulated knowledge and skills, so the teaching professions from earliest times naturally made use of "teaching through telling". Learning through practice in the form of learning through *imitation* has always been part of human, and indeed some animal, society; and learning through apprenticeship, where the imitation is accompanied by communication, is inevitably more efficient. When you learn flint-knapping and find you broke off too large a piece of slate, it saves time to have someone tell you to hit at a different angle when you might have thought you were hitting too hard.

Learning through practice has always been an important part of formal education, from schooling children in the basic skills of reading, writing, and arithmetic, to training adult students in professional skills, but for the conceptual knowledge of formal education, language has always been the key. Around the beginning of the nineteenth century John Dewey was arguing a different line: that learning through experience was just as important for making the curriculum meaningful to learners. That idea has persisted throughout twentieth-century education, with the development of more active forms of learning, using specially designed environments such as labs, field trips, projects, role play simulations, and design activities (Perkins 1991). The aim is to enable students to come to an enriched understanding of the knowledge through practicing the academic skills of experimentation, interpretation, debate, and hypothesis-building. Learning through practice develops our knowledge of the world, as well as the skills needed to develop that knowledge further. The ways of thinking and practicing in a discipline afford each other.

Given that learning through practice is so fundamental to the way we learn in the natural world, it must play an important role in formal learning, and we have to know how to optimize it.

What Counts as Learning Through Practice

Learning through practice is what the child is doing in learning about the world when they are learning through prediction, action and revision. When Seymour Papert asks how babies and toddlers manage to learn so much without teaching, he concludes:

> The answer is obvious. It is because the learning is action-oriented and gets its feedback not from the yes-no of adult authority but from the resistance and the guidance of reality. Some attempted actions do not produce the expected results. Some produce surprising results. The child comes to learn that it is not sufficient to want a result for it to happen. One must act in an "appropriate" way, and "appropriate" means based on understanding.
>
> (Papert 1996: 68)

In an educational context "situated learning" and Papert's "constructionism", discussed in Chapter 4, both situate the learner within a "teacher practice/modeling environment" that provides *goal-oriented action with meaningful feedback and revision*:

- Goal-oriented – because this provides the motivation to generate an action, and defines for the learner what counts as successful action;
- Goal-oriented action – because achieving the goal is what motivates the learner to use their concept to modulate their practice and generate the action;

- Feedback – because this enables the learner to improve their action, by modulating their practice repertoire according to how effective their action was;
- Meaningful feedback – because the learner must be able to interpret the feedback to modulate their practice, and their current concept;
- Revision of action – because this is what motivates the modulate–generate cycle.

This is the essence of learning through practice; and with meaningful *intrinsic* feedback of the kind discussed in Chapter 4 the learner can be self-reliant because they have sufficient means to learn without the teacher's extrinsic feedback.

In the natural world learning through practice is how a child learns to tie their shoelaces; in formal learning it is how the student learns to … what? The high-level cognitive knowledge and skills, the ways of thinking and practicing in formal learning, do not usually connect the action with goal and feedback in such a directly accessible way.

What would this mean, for example, for the arts and humanities student who has to use their discipline's theoretical language to interpret a cultural artifact? They are certainly acting within a practice environment, applying theory to their actions in achieving a goal – i.e. a viable interpretation – but their interpretation does not have a consequence in the real world. Books, poems, paintings, and objects do not themselves provide feedback on an interpretation. As the student checks the coherence of their interpretation by applying it to other key artifacts they may discover the need to adjust it, or make it more general, or create a more sensitive categorization, so a rich diversity of resources to work on would help with that. But the student has to take a lot of responsibility for the process – the environment does not in itself support them. They need the reassurance of extrinsic feedback from the teacher to be sure they are achieving the intended goal.

The next two sections look in detail at the two main theoretical accounts of how to help students learn through practice, in addition to "constructionism", discussed in detail in Chapter 4. Then we can test the digital technologies against these expectations.

Constructionism

The central idea of constructionism, introduced in Chapter 4, is that the learner learns about some aspect of the world not directly from the teacher, but through attempting to build something in it, and in the process of doing so develops an understanding of the underlying concepts. It means that the teacher is not there to give an account of what is known, but has the much more challenging task of working out what form this environment should take, for a given set of concepts or system.

Take, for example, a student developing the idea of meter in a poem by studying particular poems. The teacher has to design the practice/modeling environment to provide *goal-oriented action with meaningful feedback and revision*:

- The collection of poems available must vary in ways that are salient with respect to the concept;
- The learner is given a goal, e.g. to analyze the meter of a poem;
- The goal requires actions that are in or are developing within their current practice repertoire (such as identifying the rhythm of a poem, contrasting the rhythms of different poems); and
- They receive meaningful feedback, which they can interpret to improve their actions.

Extrinsic feedback would be helpful advice and guidance from the teacher, but what form could intrinsic feedback take in such a context? How would the learner elicit helpful information from the context of an action such as marking up a poem? For an action situated in the physical world, such as dividing a pie equally among four people, the learner attempting to do this has both operational and social sources for direct feedback on their attempt (Brown, Collins, and Duguid 1989). The feedback on how good it was comes from their social environment, i.e. whether others are satisfied with their action or not. The learner attempting to find the meter of a poem is not in such a lucky position because their action, i.e. their analysis, elicits no "authentic consequence" of their action that enables them to improve it, and this is common in formal learning. The feedback on how good it was comes from their social environment, in the form of agreement or appreciation, or in the form of an articulated technical evaluation by the teacher, or other students.

The challenge here is for the teacher to create the "microworld" this learner needs – perhaps it would be feedback in the form of a reading of the poem according to the learner's analysis with a contrasting "model" reading using the correct mark-up, enabling the learner to hear the way in which one analysis works better than another, and use the information in what they hear to adjust their marking of the meter. Constructionist learning is often linked to the sciences (Papert and Harel 1991), but is just as important for conceptual learning in the social sciences and humanities (Kafai and Resnick 1996). Whatever the discipline, the tough design challenge here is to work out what form the microworld must take, given the topic and the readiness of the learners.

Authentic and Situated Learning

The interest in authentic learning and situated learning derives from the rise of constructivism in the latter part of the twentieth century, and it has not diminished with time (Brown, Collins, and Duguid 1989; Dede 2005; Duffy and Jonassen 1992; Herrington, Oliver, and Reeves 2006; Jonassen 1999; Lave and Wenger 1991; Mayer 1999; Stein, Isaacs, and Andrews 2004). The two formulations are more or less interchangeable: authentic learning tasks have real-world relevance and utility, and are situated in real or simulated versions of the world, enabling students to anchor their understanding of an abstract concept in its context of use (Herrington *et al* 2007; Karagiorgi and Symeou 2005; Lombardi 2007; Stein, Isaacs, and Andrews 2004). Emphasis on the particular context is fundamental to these approaches:

> constructive instructional designers must situate cognition in real-world contexts. Situated cognition suggests that knowledge and the conditions of its use are inextricably linked ... The context facilitates the application and transfer of knowledge in both heavily ill-structured domains, such as medicine, history, literacy [sic] interpretation, and well-structured domains at advanced levels of study, such as mathematics.
> (Karagiorgi and Symeou 2005: 2)

The importance of situating knowledge in practice was a strong claim in the original article introducing the idea of situated cognition:

> We should abandon once and for all any notion that a concept is some sort of abstract, self-contained substance. Instead, it may be more useful to consider conceptual knowledge as in some ways similar to a set of tools.
> (Brown, Collins, and Duguid 1989: 5)

The reaction against abstraction brought a greater focus on concretizing knowledge in practice (Ackermann 1991). The concept must be understood at a deep level through situated practice and experience in order to be transferred successfully across different contexts.

Authentic learning is important because it situates concepts and subject-specific ways of thinking in a real-world context, providing students with an opportunity to practice the activities of their subject, and reflect on the feedback that context provides. But it creates a design challenge for the teacher. An extensive review of the literature finds broad principles but little precision in how the context, goals, tasks, and feedback must be organized to help students learn how theory relates to practice (Herrington, Oliver, and Reeves 2003; Karagiorgi and Symeou 2005; Lombardi 2007).

"Work-based", "vocational", and "professional" learning all use the ideas of authentic and situated learning, because it is so important to ensure that the curriculum succeeds in linking theory with practice and does not divorce it from its context of use. But the details of the pedagogy of authentic learning are quite unclear. The design principles derived from the literature reviews above leave much of the learning process unspecified, especially the goal–action–feedback–revision cycle. In the next section we consider an approach that pays more attention to the teacher modeling cycle in the Conversational Framework and to the importance of linking this to the peer communication cycle for discussion.

Experiential Learning

The most influential work on experiential learning, since Dewey, has come from David Kolb and colleagues, who developed the "experiential learning cycle" to clarify what is involved (Kolb 1984). He identified a sequence of four stages in the cycle: concrete experience, reflective observation, abstract conceptualization, and active experimentation – leading again to concrete experience to establish a continually iterative cycle, that may begin or end at any point, but which through successive iterations is capable of producing learning and development, as in Figure 10.1(a). This theory of experiential learning was seen as an answer to Dewey's challenge to find a theory of experience. The four stages map directly onto the Conversational Framework, as shown in Figure 10.1(b), to show how these internal and external processes work together.

The Conversational Framework helps to explain why the successive cycles are important: actions and feedback drive the internal modulate–generate cycle that links the learner's conception to their repertoire of actions as practice. It also clarifies the link between the "abstract conceptualization" and how it is turned into "active experimentation", by using reflective observation to modulate the concept in the light of concrete experience (feedback) and generating new actions as active experimentation.

In Kolb's later writing he moves beyond the learning process of the individual learner to focus on giving the learner an environment for their experiential learning that is both challenging and supportive, noting that higher education is good at challenging, less good at being supportive. The claim is that including other students in the experiential learning cycle makes it more effective: "Making space for good conversation as part of the educational process provides the opportunity for reflection on and meaning making about experiences that improve the effectiveness of experiential learning" (Kolb and Kolb 2005: 208).

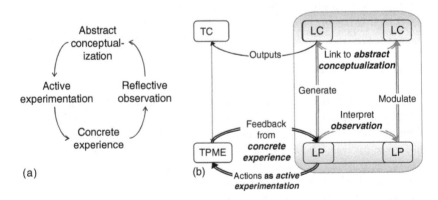

Figure 10.1 (a) Kolb's Experiential Learning Cycle, and (b) The Experiential Learning Cycle (*bold italics*) mapped onto the Conversational Framework.

This means that Kolb's original learning cycle, with its clear emphasis on the iterative relationship between theory and practice should be extended to show how the experiential cycle can be further motivated through engagement with the peer communication cycle (what Kolb and Kolb refer to as "conversational learning"). Figure 10.2 shows how together the "experiential learning" and "conversational learning" cycles cover more of the Conversational Framework.

There is no explicit reference in Kolb's work to learners sharing the products of their action, or submitting their outputs to the teacher, but his studies of team learning based on the experiential learning cycle highlight the importance of the team developing a shared goal:

> it is essential to develop a climate of trust and safety that encourages members to converse openly about their experience on the team, including their personal goals and their perception of the team's purpose (concrete experience). Only then can the team reflect and talk through these issues together (reflective observation), synthesize them into a shared consensus that aligns individual and team goals (abstract conceptualization), and then coordinate action to define and implement specific goals (active experimentation).
>
> (Kayes, Kayes, and Kolb 2005: 342)

So the team of learners here is not learning through sharing products of their separate attempts to achieve a task goal. Instead they are using discussion to

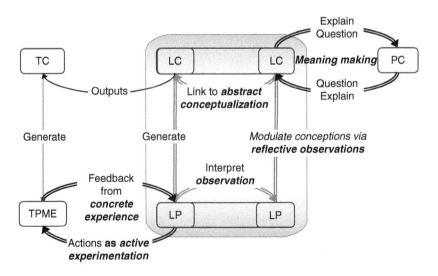

Figure 10.2 Kolb's Experiential Learning Cycle extended to include "Conversational Learning," which affords "meaning making" through reflection on experience.

agree the goal, the actions to achieve it, and the way the feedback should be interpreted and analyzed to modulate a new action from the new conceptualization, and generate the new action. In this way, each individual learner is supported in their internal observation, interpretation, and abstract conceptualization through engaging with the other learners in the discursive meaning-making cycle (or "conversational learning") shown in Figure 10.2. Kolb's experiential learning extended to include conversational learning is very close to the combination of learning through practice and learning through discussion represented in the Conversational Framework.

Learning Through Practice in Formal Education

The aim of this section is to show that the Conversational Framework is powerful enough to discriminate between the more and less successful pedagogies for learning through practice.

Learning through practice should help the learner to link theory to practice, abstractions to instantiations, discussion to experience. The continual iteration between these is represented in the Conversational Framework as follows:

> The teacher modeling cycle:
> → goal → action → feedback → revised action
> drives and is driven by
> the internal cycle of cognition:
> → modulate concept → generate practice → generate new action → use feedback to modulate practice → use modulated practice to modulate concept →

The teacher's design task is to create the practice/modeling environment that provides the feedback the learner needs. As defined in Chapter 6 the *teacher modeling cycle* uses an environment that itself provides intrinsic feedback for the learner to revise their actions without comment from a teacher, while the *teacher practice cycle* requires extrinsic feedback from the teacher.

Intrinsic Feedback

The pedagogic value of learning through practice, with the learner getting feedback on their performance, has been fundamental to every learning theory as we saw in Chapter 4. There we established that students trying to understand an abstracted organization of concepts and ideas need an environment in which their situated actions elicit meaningful *intrinsic* feedback, i.e. a natural or authentic consequence of their action in relation to the intended goal, from which they can work out how to improve it without teacher intervention.

Designing such an environment is not easy, however, as the value of intrinsic feedback to the learner is very dependent on whether they are able to interpret it. Studies of animal cognition provide an arresting example of this. The baby chimpanzee has to learn to crack a nut by watching its mother use one stone as an anvil on which the nut is placed, using a second stone as the hammer. The baby chimp typically takes some time to work out that two stones are needed, and the nut has to be placed correctly, and the hammer has to hit the nut not the stone ... initially the feedback from the environment tells them they have failed to crack the nut, but does not tell them how to improve their action; and there is no help from the mother, who does not teach. Eventually, after some years, they learn, motivated by the goal of being able to crack the nut themselves, to focus their attention on the mother's actions until the feedback is interpretable, and they can tell how to revise their actions to act, as Papert suggests, in an "appropriate" way (Matsuzawa 2003). For intrinsic feedback to work the modeling environment has to be very carefully set up to provide the relationship between task goal, learner action, and feedback that *is interpretable* by the learner, and they have the conceptual organization capable of generating an improved action. The modeling environment must provide support to keep them within their zone of proximal development (ZPD).

The idea of intrinsic feedback is especially valuable when the learner can act on the world and see an effect, as in learning skills, or in science, engineering, programming, design, modern languages, and even the performing arts. But for many topics it is more difficult for the student to "act on the world" to test their concept because it is a formal, abstract description of the world, such as the "meter of a poem," or the concept of "pluralism." Here the modeling environment can provide intrinsic feedback in the form of a model output – traditionally the "model answer" against which the learner can compare their output and interpret what is different and how it can be improved. This technique preserves the distinctive and motivating feature of intrinsic feedback, that the learner can use it to improve their action without teacher intervention.

An intriguing demonstration of the motivational value of this kind of independence comes from a distinctive type of modeling environment, the "teachable agent" (Chase *et al.* 2009). In this study students instruct their teachable agent (TA) in the biology topic they are learning by constructing a concept map. The model for the TA uses the concept map and cause and effect rules to generate answers in a competitive quiz. The intrinsic feedback here is the failure of their agent to generate the correct answer and the contrasting success of other TA's answers. Students improve their agent's performance by going back to their information sources to "re-teach" the concepts. This is very different from scoring a student's answer to the same question because it is the agent that fails:

> By occupying the unique social position of part self, part other, the TA incited motivation to work harder to learn. This type of motivation is unusual in computer environments, because it removes students from the very thing that is motivating them; students leave their TAs to read.
>
> (Chase *et al.* 2009: 349)

The study is a fascinating insight into the importance of engagement and self-efficacy, where the students have a sense of responsibility for the failure of their "protégé" without internalizing the failure. They change the TA's answer constructed from their teaching by putting different articulations of their own concepts into the nodes of the concept map and changing the links between nodes. The environment provides them with the information sources they read to work out how to improve their teaching performance and retest it without teacher intervention.

The form of teachable agent modeling environment is interesting because it could be used for any topic that can be represented adequately in a concept map, where there are complex relationships between concepts. Simply creating a concept map is not sufficient – this is a practice environment that provides no feedback on the quality of what the learner creates. The critical property of intrinsic feedback is to provide knowledge of the result of the action that enables the learner to see how to improve it without extrinsic guidance. The teachable agent format achieves this; the students construct a map of their concepts and then see how well it works.

Learning through practice with appropriate intrinsic feedback is a powerful form of independent learning, which is why learning theorists champion learning through play, situated learning, and constructionism. In the context of complex higher-order cognitive knowledge and skills it is important to find ways of exploiting such a powerful learning mechanism.

Extrinsic Feedback

Education relies heavily on extrinsic feedback, because when well-targeted it is so efficient in terms of teacher and learner time. Good quality extrinsic feedback will emulate intrinsic feedback by making it meaningful in terms of how the learner should adapt their action – rather than saying "very good" or "should try harder" a more helpful comment would be "you have offered good evidence for your arguments here", "you would have achieved a better introduction to this essay by including some historical background to the field", etc. Hounsell *et al.* refer to this kind of feedback as "intrinsic". reserving "extrinsic" for assessment only:

> one of the final-year units ... provided a fascinating instance of intrinsic feedback. Although there was no assessed coursework within that unit (and, thus, no opportunity to get feedback of an extrinsic kind), the ways in which the group problem-solving exercises had been devised meant that the groups' solutions or answers were aired and commented upon in a plenary session led by the lecturer.
>
> (Hounsell *et al.* 2008: 64)

Wiliam similarly emphasizes the importance of feedback being provided during learning, distinguishing it from formative feedback given well after the event (Wiliam 2010: 147).

Feedback on the student's performance has the advantage that it relates their action to the goal, and to how they need to change their action in order to meet the goal. In that sense it is close to the way I have defined intrinsic feedback because it is information about how to improve your action. But consider the pedagogic implications of this. If the teacher interprets the learner's action to provide the feedback on how to improve it, it means that the learner has not had to do that. Figure 10.3 illustrates the difference between the extreme versions of the two forms.

In Figure 10.3(a) the learner using a practice environment is not required to do the work of interpreting the feedback on their action because the teacher does it. It *may* enable them to modulate their concept, but the learner can just obey the instruction without interpreting it in terms of the concept that generated the action. By contrast, in Figure 10.3(b) the learner using a modeling environment has to do their own interpretation of the intrinsic feedback, analyzing it in relation to their action, and modulating their concept, in order to generate a revised action. It is a much richer learning experience, prompting more iteration by the learner. This characterizes the difference between the *teacher practice cycle*, where the learner does not know how well they are doing until the teacher can comment, and the *teacher modeling cycle* which gives the learner intrinsic feedback on their actions. This contrast between intrinsic and extrinsic makes a more powerful pedagogic point, I think, than one that reserves "extrinsic" for assessment.

The importance of feedback in the learning process is well understood, and this is where digital technologies can wield most power: because they are decision-making machines, they can respond conditionally to user input. With digital technology it becomes feasible for learners to engage in learning

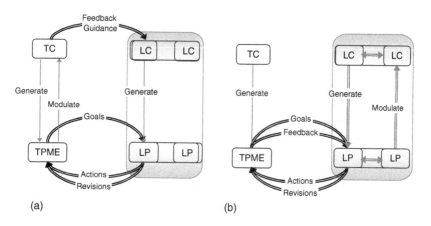

Figure 10.3 (a) How teacher reflection on the learner's actions provides extrinsic feedback, and (b) How the practice/modeling environment provides intrinsic feedback, prompting learner reflection.

through practice in whatever type of environment can be computationally modeled.

The section has shown how we can discriminate between more and less successful pedagogies for learning through practice. The next section puts the Conversational Framework to work to challenge digital technologies on the extent to which they promote the successful pedagogies.

How Can Digital Technologies Help?

The pedagogic requirements for learning through practice, as represented by the Conversational Framework, provide a critique of the extent to which learning technologies are capable of meeting the requirements of good pedagogy. Several types of technology are relevant here: adaptive teaching technologies that can give intrinsic feedback on student action, microworlds and simulations that model some aspect of a system, and games and virtual reality technologies that emulate a real-world experience. The critical feature that separates these technologies from those in other chapters is that they all contain some form of model of a real-world environment or system, which means they can provide intrinsic feedback on the learner's action.

Adaptive Tutoring Programs

The idea of a computer-based tutor is attractive because it uses the decision-making power of an interactive program to respond to learner input, and react to it in a way that emulates the human tutor. It offers personal tuition that can keep the learner within their zone of proximal development, being challenged just enough with each new task, and with guiding feedback on what they do. However, for much of its history, intelligent tutoring systems of this kind have been grounded in a didactic model of learning: they are *instructivist adaptive tutoring programs*. The program sets a series of tasks similar to those used in textbooks, checks the learner's answer, and provides text-based guidance on what to do next, such as hints on the knowledge source they might use, or a more appropriate procedure (Aleven and Koedinger 2002). The clever part is to construct the program so that it can recognize different types of correct and incorrect problem-solutions, and from a learner's input deduce where they need guidance (Lesgold 2009; VanLehn 2006). Such programs have been developed especially for rule-based subject areas such as mathematics and science, and would be less easy to apply to open-ended fields where there could be several different kinds of justification for an argument in a problem solution. So they are not likely to be universal models for learning programs. However, they represent an important aspect of the use of technology in education, because they set out to emulate the instructivist approaches of the one-to-one human tutor, where the aim is to guide the learner towards the correct procedure, using the appropriate knowledge, on a given task.

Microworlds

In intelligent tutoring systems the trick is that the program models the solution procedure, so it can advise on what to do. By contrast, a *constructionist adaptive teaching program* models the task environment itself, so it shows what the learner has done. It is *constructionist* in the sense that it supports the learner in trying to make something (Harel and Papert 1990), and *adaptive* in the sense that the task goal is determined in relation to their current performance – just as a teacher would adapt the goal to the learner's capability, to keep them in the "zone of proximal development".

Papert's constructionism was linked explicitly to his idea of a "microworld": "a computer-based interactive learning environment in which the prerequisites are built into the system and where learners can become the active, constructive architects of their own learning" (Papert 1980: 122).

He wanted to provide learners with an environment that would make complex conceptual learning more intelligible. A "microworld" is a computational model of some aspect of the world, with its own constraints and assumptions, in which a user can experience the target concepts by exploring and manipulating it. They should be able to "engage in tasks of value to them, and in doing so ... come to understand powerful underlying principles" (diSessa 2001). One of the clearest definitions in the literature expresses the formal properties of a microworld as:

1. A set of computational objects that model the mathematical or physical properties of the microworld's domain.
2. Links to the multiple representations of the underlying properties of the model.
3. An ability to combine objects or operations in complex ways, similar to the idea of combining words and sentences in a language.
4. A set of activities or challenges that are inherent or pre-programmed in the microworld; the student is challenged to solve problems, reach goals, etc. (Kalaš 2010).

The most famous example is Papert's "turtle geometry", where the software provides: (i) commands for moving a pointer through distances and angles (the set of computational objects), (ii) drawings made by the learner shown on the screen with the list of commands they used (links to multiple representations), (iii) commands for the learner to select from, put in order, and give values to (an ability to combine objects), and (iv) the goal to "draw a triangle" or "draw a circle" (a set of challenges). In this example, learners experience the world of geometry by attempting to construct geometric shapes. Another example is learning mathematical generalization: in this software the learners can specify a rule to try and generate a particular pattern, and the model in the program produces the pattern corresponding to their rule; from this they can see how close they are and what kind of change they have to make (Noss *et al.* 2009).

In both these examples the learners see intrinsic feedback on their action in the environment, instead of extrinsic feedback as advice and guidance in an instructivist program. It shows them what they made, and how it relates to what they hoped to make. If they can interpret the feedback to modulate their action or the concept that generated it, then they can continue to revise their action as they do in informal, implicit, and unsupervised learning (see Chapter 6). It is what Papert described as "learning without being taught" (diSessa 2001; Papert 1980: 7), which, of course is not at all the same as "learning without a teacher". The teacher puts their teaching into the design of the modeling environment.

Another example comes from programs designed to help learners with dyscalculia who have difficulty in relating the counting sequence to the number of items in a collection. The software sets the goal of finding the right digit to match a number pattern; feedback on a wrong answer shows the pattern that matches their input digit, enabling them to see the contrast with the target pattern. It then counts the dots onto a number line, which they can modify until it matches the number line for the target pattern. The feedback showing the result of their action, and the opportunity to construct the correct representation on the number line, prompts the learner to modulate their concept of the dot pattern. The program is adaptive in the sense that it introduces new number patterns at a rate dependent on the speed and accuracy of the learner's response (Butterworth and Laurillard 2010).

The two contrasting forms of adaptive pedagogy, instructivist and constructionist, are represented in the Conversational Framework in Figure 10.3(a) and (b) respectively. The critical difference expressed in the two figures is that because the tutoring program does the work of modulating their instruction in the light of the learner's actions (Figure 10.3(a)), there is no motivation for the learner's internal modulate–generate cycle to be triggered. In the constructionist account (Figure 10.3(b)) the feedback is intrinsic to the learner's action, so the internal modulate–generate cycle is motivated and enabled by the actions and feedback. This is a very important capability of digital technology. Where we see it working most frequently now is in digital games for mobile apps. It is tragically under-exploited for education.

These are the basic forms for a microworld, but of course it is possible to combine extrinsic advice and guidance from the program with intrinsic feedback from a modeled task environment, and programs offering intelligent support now have a greater focus on supporting tutor-student dialogue, self-explanation, and advice and guidance, to support both the action on the environment and the process being learned (Luckin and du Boulay 1999; Noss *et al.* 2009; Porayska-Pomsta, Mavrikis, and Pain 2008).

Designing the practice/modeling environment to foster the learner's conceptual development is the difficult creative role of the teacher as designer, but this is the critical issue in the pedagogy of learning by doing.

Simulation Environments

Simulation environments used in education are designed to provide a supported and simulated experience of scientific inquiry, deploying existing datasets, visualizations of the data, and problems for the student to solve. The simulation provides an interface to a computational model of a system (which could be anything from an organizational model of a business, to a procedural model of equipment operation, to a scientific model of an eco-system, or an organism, etc.). The interaction with the model usually takes the form of manipulating a selection of parameters to see the result. The full complexity of the underlying model remains hidden, and the instructional focus is to help students see the relationship between the selected parameters. This is much more common than the alternative of requiring the learner to build or discover the model of a system, which is a significantly higher level objective, requiring much more time to teach and support (Alessi 2000; de Jong and van Joolingen 1998).

The aim in using simulation environments is to foster active exploratory learning that enables students to improve their understanding by using the high-level cognitive skills of exploration, analysis, interpretation, and problem-solving, and in doing so to improve those skills as well. These are ambitious programs, but we have to be clear about the learning experience they elicit. For example, the idea of an "adaptive selective simulation" is intended to provide an interactive experience that develops the skills and knowledge of scientific inquiry:

> The adaptive selective simulation technique is innovative. Students are provided with a variety of options before they trigger an event, animation or simulation. Depending on the selection (e.g. selection of a well at a specific geographic location), only a subset scenario (e.g. water level dynamics at the selected well location) is displayed. Students can repeat the selection process to study other scenarios and space–time processes. Adaptive selective simulation stimulates experimental learning through the observation of ecosystem processes using a sequence of events: trigger an event – observe eco-system process – interpretation – assimilation.
>
> (Ramasundaram *et al.* 2005: 26)

The term "adaptive" here refers to the way the system adapts to the student's choice from a menu. The system provides an impressive simulation of the environment, so can act as a good substitute for the field trip itself. But the process of selecting a succession of events is not in itself a learning experience, any more than the real environment would be. The students *may* interpret and assimilate from their observations, but there is nothing in the description of this as a learning design to ensure they do. This is learning through acquisition.

Many of the simulation packages available for computer-based training in engineering systems work in a similar way, providing extensive and rich models of a system, machine, or environment. Their very richness means that there is significant time involved in learning to use such a system (Alessi 2000; Grunwald *et al.* 2007), which is worthwhile if it forms the basis of a substantial part of the student's work on a course. The teacher has to provide guidance on how to use the simulation, therefore, and in so doing is in danger of providing too much of a recipe to follow, with students remaining essentially unchallenged. Figure 10.4(a) shows how we can represent the fact that, in the context of an over-defined set of instructions, students are not motivated to use the feedback on their actions. By following the instructions they are likely to avoid failures. If an action does fail, then their response is more likely to be to return to the instructions than to reflect on how to adjust the action: it was not *their* action, but one defined by the teacher/program. However, if a goal is for the student to achieve through their own actions on the environment, they have no choice but to interpret the feedback if they want to generate a revised action that might succeed. Figure 10.4(b) illustrates the contrasting effect of this more challenging task on the internal learning cycle it is more likely to elicit.

Designing the nature of the task and feedback is critical to the effectiveness of the practice/modeling environment, and this point is well illustrated by a very thorough study that evaluated a simulation design based on the Conversational Framework. The practice environment was a "pregnancy simulator," which gave midwifery students practice in assessing the progress of labor, so "the learning experience is designed as a dynamic combination of the experience of the physical act of palpation (psychomotor skills), together with the interpretive processes of conceptualising, visualising and clinical decision-making" (Milton and Lyons 2003: 301).

Using the Conversational Framework, they set out explicitly to provide "intrinsic feedback whereby the student's action within the world of the

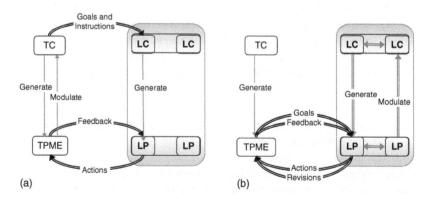

Figure 10.4 (a) An over-defined task for students working on a real or simulated environment, and (b) Goals set for the student to achieve through their own actions on the environment, are more likely to elicit an internal learning cycle.

simulation generates feedback in that world" (ibid.: 302). The evaluation showed that students were anxious about interpreting the feedback and wanted the computer to tell them if they were right or wrong, which is precisely what the designers wanted to avoid. However, the relation between task, action, and feedback has to be carefully interpreted. The practice/modeling environment is a computer-controlled simulation of how a pregnant abdomen feels and behaves, which provided a realistic experience for the student to interpret (using a clever combination of latex and a toy doll wired to the computer). But the task is for the student to interpret what they feel in terms of the formal knowledge of what this means for the way the fetus is lying. The program

> sets a task goal which is in the form of a question, asking the students to palpate and pay attention to an aspect of the simulated world. If the student's hypothesis or rationale displays a known misconception, the question is carefully chosen to bring the student's attention to a contradictory feature of the palpation experience or an aspect which provides vital clues to a more appropriate interpretation.
>
> (ibid.: 306)

This is not the goal–action–feedback–revision loop it appears to be at first glance, because the simulation environment cannot provide feedback on the task of interpreting. That is why the students were asking for more feedback on whether they had got the right interpretation. The simulation does not allow them to "act on the world," but merely to observe it. It is the exact equivalent of the student of art history being asked to interpret an architectural style: the cathedral stands mute and undisturbed by the student's incorrect answer because observation and interpretation is not action. For this kind of learning objective to be achieved through *learning by doing*, the task environment has to be set up in a very different way. Suppose instead the midwifery practice/modeling environment had been designed as follows:

- the task goal is to simulate a particular condition in the simulated abdomen;
- the learner actions are to input parameters to the program controlling the simulated abdomen and to feel the result;
- the feedback is an interpretation by the program of which condition they had actually achieved, together with the way this feels in the simulated abdomen.

This design creates a teacher modeling cycle that provides the intrinsic feedback the students and the designers were looking for. The equivalent for the art history students might be a program that provides a set of architectural features in different styles, which students can assemble with the goal of creating a coherently designed cathedral, with feedback in the form of an interpretation by the program of what style or styles they have actually achieved, together with how it looks.

These examples perhaps help to clarify the complexity of what it takes to design an effective practice/modeling environment for independent learning through practice with intrinsic feedback. It is not necessarily more difficult or time-consuming than creating a model of a complex environment; it just has to be designed with attention to how the teacher modeling cycle relates to the internal learning cycle.

Role-play Simulation

Role-play simulations of authentic practice are especially common in the professional disciplines, such as health, medical, architecture, business, management, and engineering education (Agapiou, Maharg, and Nicol 2010; Kriz 2003). Students use a scenario mapped out by the tutor to explore and interpret a database of resources and information, and use their analysis to produce a report or answer to a defined issue, problem, or question. The resource is a detailed case study taken from or based on real-life experiences of the professionals – a patient in the case of medicine, a project or a client in the case of business or engineering, for example. The key pedagogic idea here is to help students see the link between abstract theoretical concepts and their instantiation in practice, and to engage more directly with the content by playing a role (Agapiou *et al.* 2010).

To do that successfully, the teacher maps out the likely scenario for the professional transactions with a client, or patient, or customer, to conduct the learner through the sequence of events they are likely to encounter. The resources are digital versions of documents found in professional practice, or videos of workplaces, or actors, e.g. staff simulating patients (Nathoo, Goldhoff, and Quattrochi 2005), or charts, pictures, spreadsheets, or whatever is appropriate for the particular discipline context. The resources are usually developed and provided by the teachers themselves, often building on their own professional practice. The burden of development is heavy, therefore, but the resources developed for one course can potentially be used by other universities, colleges and schools, if made widely available – hence the value of the move towards Open Educational Resource repositories (Boyle 2010).

The pedagogic value of this kind of simulation is certainly the exposure to authentic documents and professional practices and procedures, but to what extent does it cover the full sequence for learning through practice as expressed in the Conversational Framework? Here is a generic version of a sequence devised for a very thorough study of this kind (Agapiou, Maharg, and Nicol 2010):

- The student's goal was to conduct a professional process in response to a sequence of tasks simulating a typical professional scenario.
- Students were provided with access to all the documentation they would require to solve a particular task through the use of electronic document libraries.

- The actions taken by students to solve an individual task were recorded online as actions, notes, and communications made in order to resolve a task.
- The class tutor entered feedback in the form of a likely response to the students' actions, notes, or queries, according to the character of the role they were playing.
- Once a task was completed successfully, the tutor released the next scenario.

The evaluation findings of this study were interesting because students did not appreciate the sometimes negative feedback from the tutor's role-play. The researchers concluded:

> What matters is how the students recover from the situation, and what they learn from it. It needs to be made clear to students at the start of the simulation, and almost certainly in any feedback or debrief at the end, that such role-play is a valuable learning opportunity. However, as the students themselves commented, at such points of failure or conflict it is essential to be able to step out of role, and possibly consult with a mentor or other more senior figure as to the possible resolutions of the problem; and this is something that will be reviewed in future iterations of the project.
>
> (Agapiou, Maharg, and Nicol 2010: 49)

A role-play simulation of this kind has the same form as the simulation shown in Figure 10.4(b), where the task environment is the collection of resources, scenarios, and tasks available online, the goal is to conduct the task to a successful conclusion, through actions similar to those of a professional, such as write memos, prepare answers to legal questions, or complete official documentation. The feedback is given in the form of realistic workplace responses to those actions, simulated by the tutor in this case – or it could be an actor simulating a patient in a medical scenario. This is intrinsic feedback, from a kind of microworld, representing an aspect of the real world in such a way that the students are able to engage with the relevant concepts – such as how to write a legally correct letter in a way that does not offend a client. Interestingly, in the evaluation of this scenario students wanted not just the intrinsic feedback but extrinsic guidance from the tutor as well. In fact, rather than have the tutor step out of role to guide them (Figure 10.4(a)) it would be more challenging to the student to give feedback as "model answers" in the form of alternative ways of, for example, writing letters (Figure 10.4(b)).

Serious Games and Immersive Environments

There is a strong argument for the value of games in education because of their affinity with "learning by doing", or even "being" in the context of role-play games (Gee 2003; Squire 2006; Van Eck 2006). By combining "play" with "interactivity" (Roussou 2004), they provide the kind of intensive, motivated concentration of cognitive activity that is precisely what we hope for in learning (Prensky 2003). In the multiplayer game, learning is "... doing, experimenting, discovering for the purposes of action in the world. Players learn in role-playing games for the purposes of acting within an identity" (Squire 2006: 24).

The advocates of "serious games" are right to argue that they have the potential to transform the development of high-level knowledge and skills. The leisure industry is healthy and growing and will continue to be able to invest heavily in the further development of impressively realistic and compu-tationally complex gaming environments. But the driving economic forces never take that industry towards the needs of education, and education is unlikely ever to afford the level of investment needed to emulate these games. There are some corners of the market that have bravely oriented towards game-like immersive environments for educational purposes, but they have not so far engaged very much with the learning theory that should drive their design, nor with the content that would fit well with educational curricula (de Freitas and Oliver 2006).

The massively multiplayer online game (MMOG) is interesting for peda-gogy because of its inherent cognitive and social complexity:

> MMOG game play includes all the traditional characteristics of problem solving—problem representation, conditions, goals, procedures, strate-gies, and metastrategies—as well as shared practices typically found in problem-solving contexts within formal and informal instructional contexts—debriefings, theorizing about the problem space, apprentice-ship, and the valuing of seeking out challenges just beyond the current level of one's ability ... whether you are Level 5 or 55.
>
> (Steinkuehler 2006: 99)

The communities that form around these games act out all the desired charac-teristics of a vibrant academic community of teachers, learners, scholars, experts, and scientists – discovering together and competing together on how to achieve a meaningful goal, albeit in a virtual world.

> Through cognitive (re)construction of mental models, learners change their perception and interpretation patterns of reality. Simultaneously, individuals must deal with the environment in which they live and learn to understand the influence of transformed behavior and communication patterns on that environment ... Simulation games can be defined as the simulation of the effects of decisions made by actors assuming roles that are interrelated with a system of rules and with explicit reference store sources that realistically symbolize the existing infrastructure and availa-ble resources.
>
> (Kriz 2003: 496–97)

This could be a powerful learning environment if the content were educational.

There is an inevitable blurring of the line between immersive virtual games for leisure and serious games for education, because advocates of games in learning would like to see the motivational effects of intense concentration crossing over to the world of education. But games become immersive, not simply because the still primitive graphics look realistic, but because the narrative development of the game has been cleverly designed to set up a continual iteration of expectation of user input, and response to their input, which is what drives the narrative along. Games are highly interactive, and interactivity is important for learning, so the expectation is that game formats should therefore be used for education. But we have to look closely at what kind of pedagogy they actually support.

Games and virtual environments vary in the degree of interactivity they offer, and it is important to distinguish between them for their pedagogic effects. For example, Roussou points out that many VR environments offer interactivity of the form that merely allows the selection of routes through the modeled environment, which is little more than a form of multiple-choice activity. Alternatively, they create the illusion of user influence, although whatever attempts the user makes to modify the world, the outcome is always one of the predefined options, predetermined by the creator. By contrast, "Active participation means placing the user in a central active role with the ability to modify the environment" (Roussou 2004: 9).

This is the design that would fit with the learning theories of constructivism or constructionism, but these virtual worlds are not designed on that basis. Virtual environments created in *Second Life*, for example, often simply give users multiple-choice options of different routes to sources of information, and this is not itself a constructivist learning experience.

A specific example is recounted for a wonderfully complex virtual environment "Active Worlds", used for learning business computing skills, and explicitly grounded in the ideas of constructivism and situated learning. However, for the learner it provides simply a visual metaphor for setting tasks and providing access to information and discussion forums (Dickey 2005). There is no evaluation of this environment, beyond the informal affirmation of students that they enjoyed it more than class, and the attrition rate decreased. But the ambitions of situated and constructivist learning lead us to expect more. Much more was achieved from a second application of the same environment, to teach computer science students about modeling 3D objects. In this case, the object modeling tool was used alongside a chat tool, enabling the teacher to present and illustrate a task that the students could then practice and discuss for themselves (Dickey 2005).

This is proper use of a virtual environment, not as a means to access tasks, information, and discussion, but as the means to interpret concepts as practice, and reflect on the feedback from goal-oriented interactions. Coupled with a chat tool this links the practice to the social dimension, creating a truly rich learning design. Whereas the former case offers little more than learning through acquisition, and basic inquiry learning, this latter application achieves something closer to social constructivism, which supports the learning process more completely.

Exactly this issue has prompted an examination of the role of learning theory for educational games in order to specify the features of game design that will promote learning. A model of experiential gaming design, based on the idea of "flow," or intensive engagement in goal-oriented activity (Csikszentmihalyi 1991), and on constructivist learning theory, has been developed to capture "learning as a cyclic process," with the challenge goals driving the game-player round an "ideation loop" and an "experience loop" (Kiili 2005), i.e. the "internal learning cycle" and "teacher modeling cycle" in the Conversational Framework. Although it explicitly excludes any link to the social dimension, the iterative cycles are seen as developing both concepts and practice:

> After the ideation phase the player tests solutions in the experience loop reflecting greater circulation and observes the outcomes of actions. Game [sic] should be usable and provide clear goals and appropriate feedback to the player in order to facilitate flow experience ... The reflective observation of the feedback may lead to the construction of schemata and enable the discovery of new and better solutions to the problems.
>
> (Csikszentmihalyi 1991; Kiili 2005: 19)

Kiili does not express how the current concept generates the action; reflection using the feedback is explicit, but generating action using the concept is not, and yet this is critical to the process of testing the concept in practice. There is also no reference to the social context of learning, which becomes important for the account of a later application of the model in a business game, where collaboration was found to be one of the most important elements for an effective learning experience (Kiili 2007).

The Conversational Framework can provide a fuller account of learning by doing, as manifested in serious games, but the close relationship between these two models shows that we can represent the learning process in a generic way to support design across a wide range of learning experiences.

Pedagogical Patterns for Learning Through Practice

What would be the form of a "learning through practice" pattern? Table 10.1 shows how a generic pattern motivates the learner to modulate their concept and practice repertoire to generate actions and revised actions. It is mapped to the learning cycles proposed in Chapter 6. An example of this would be the role-play sequence discussed above, where the practice/modeling environment gives intrinsic feedback in the form of the behavior of other participants in the role-play in the teacher modeling cycle. If the designers were to include the

Table 10.1 A Generic Design Pattern for Learning Through Practice, Mapped to the Teacher Modeling Cycle (TMC), Teacher Practice Cycle (TPC), and the Learner's Internal Learning Cycle (ILC) in the Conversational Framework

Mapping to CF	Intended cognition	Sequence of activities	Cycles
Goal		Set a goal for the learner to create or do something that achieves a model output	TMC1
Generate action	The learner uses their current concept to generate an action from their practice repertoire		ILC
Action		The learner generates an action in the modeling environment to achieve the model output	TMC1
Feedback		The modeling environment uses the learner's input to generate the output from their effect on the environment, and compares it with the model output	TMC2
Modulate–generate	The learner interprets the feedback to modulate their concept or practice and generate a revised action		ILC
Revised action		The learner generates a revised action in the modeling environment to achieve the model output	TMC1
Questions Guidance		The learner seeks and receives feedback from the tutor on how to modulate their concept or action	TPC2
Modulate–generate	The learner uses the feedback to (modulate their concept or practice and) generate a revised action		ILC
Revised action		The learner uses their modulated concept or action to generate a revised action in the practice environment to achieve an improved output	TPC1

Note: For codes see Table 6.2.

tutor stepping out of role to give extrinsic feedback instead of intrinsic feedback (represented in the lower part of Table 10.1), then the tutor would be using the teacher practice cycle to monitor the learner's actions and provide guidance on how to improve. However, the learner may use the guidance directly to generate the action without having to modulate their concept or practice. So better than this would be a modeling environment that shows a comparison between the learner's output and a model output, so that they do the interpretation of the feedback for themselves.

A well-designed modeling environment is one that enables the learner to learn unaided, "without being taught". The model can be many things – an architectural form, a condition of pregnancy, a river system, a design tool, the behavior of numbers, the analysis of a poem, a professional procedure – but in all cases the essential pedagogic requirement is to enable the learner to take action to produce an effect on that model or see their own output in comparison with a model output. That is how they get the intrinsic feedback they need. Doing this in the real world can be hazardous and expensive, but it is now feasible in a virtual world.

Summary: Designing for Learning Through Practice

A computational system is the only educational technology that provides intrinsic feedback, other than the real world, which does not typically organize itself to provide feedback on complex formal concepts. If it did, we would not need formal education.

I have spent some time on the issue of intrinsic feedback because it is peculiar to digital technologies. We have scarcely exploited this wonderful capability in education and the examples in this chapter show that when the modeling capability of digital technologies is used it does not always meet the challenge from the Conversational Framework. Education could benefit so much if teacher–designers could develop and share the pedagogical patterns that properly exploit the modeling capability of digital technologies to support learning through practice.

11 Learning Through Collaboration

Introduction

Collaborative learning has attracted a lot of attention from researchers in recent years, although there has been no real consensus on its definition. It has been seen simply as a situation in which two or more people learn or attempt to learn something together (Dillenbourg 1999), or learn in collaborative settings (Jones and Issroff 2005). The recent literature is explicit about distinguishing "collaborative" from "co-operative" learning which was in focus up to the early 1990s (Slavin 1991). Co-operation is seen as implying that individuals play different roles in a team, with each member having a responsibility for part of the whole. By contrast, collaboration works towards building shared public knowledge:

> By the 1990s the idea of knowledge building as the collaborative creation of public knowledge had assumed ascendancy, with individual learning as an important and demonstrable by-product.
>
> (Scardamalia and Bereiter 2006: 106)

> Collaboration is a coordinated synchronous activity that is the result of a continued attempt to construct and maintain a shared conception of a problem.
>
> (Roschelle and Teasley 1995: 70)

Learning through collaboration is separable from learning through acquisition, inquiry, or discussion, because although it builds on inquiry and uses discussion it is about taking part in the process of knowledge building itself (Scardamalia and Bereiter 2006), through participation not acquisition (Sfard 1988). It is separate from learning through practice because although it builds something this is necessarily done through participation and negotiation with peers.

The definition above from Roschelle and Teasley neatly characterizes why collaboration is thought to be pedagogically valuable: *coordination* helps to manage the process to its conclusion, the *continued attempt* suggests iteration, *to construct* means the learners are developing their ideas, and a *shared conception* means they have to agree, which is what drives the iteration.

The output could be a simple text – the joint communiqué – or one of many media: a diagram, animation, video, program, model, performance, design ... and this is where digital technologies make a difference: they provide a variety of design tools for creating the output.

But while the output is important as a principal driver of the learning cycle, the process is what makes the learning happen. So to understand how best to support learning through collaboration we have to look at what pedagogical features promote good collaboration. The environment could be the conventional classroom or lab, with small groups of students working together under the guidance of the teacher to make something to show at the end of the session. That captures all the characteristics identified by Roschelle and Teasley. Is that enough? And when we take collaboration online, what are the design features of that environment that promote those desirable characteristics?

Learning Through Collaboration

In studies of cooperative learning the focus is on the individual constructing their learning in the context of the group, while for collaborative learning the focus is the social and cultural description of how the group constructs a shared outcome. I have used the term "collaboration" for this chapter, but most of the studies in cooperative and collaborative learning agree that both are distinctive because they focus on students producing a shared output, which is what takes it beyond just learning through discussion.

> Why should cooperative or collaborative learning be effective for learners, who are, after all, exchanging only imperfect understandings of the content, if the teacher is not present to advise or correct them? Slavin's comprehensive review of research on cooperative learning suggests that, once the appropriate conditions for the cooperative learning task have been attended to, it works because it elicits three valuable learning activities from the students: Provision of group goals based on the individual learning of all group members might affect cognitive processes directly by motivating students to engage in peer modeling, cognitive elaboration, and/or practice with one another.
>
> (Slavin 2004: 287)

The shared goal motivates the three learning activities:

- Engaging in "peer modeling" means each learner can learn from how the others work, what they say and how they address the topic.
- Each learns by "cognitive elaboration" through the reciprocal process of articulating and critiquing their points of view (Boud, Cohen, and Sampson 1999).

- Being motivated to "practice with one another", to spend time on generating their explanations and ideas, is more likely to happen as part of the group, than in individual learning.

The first two points are versions of the "peer modeling cycle" and the "peer communication cycle" in the Conversational Framework; the final point explains how the group motivates those cycles. The learning activities identified as important by Slavin are very similar to those in reviews of "peer learning," which also stress the importance of the skills involved in the peer communication cycle: "listening, explaining, questioning, summarizing, speculating, and hypothesizing" (Boud, Cohen, and Sampson 1999; Topping 2005).

In a critical review of key papers in collaborative learning Schwarz emphasizes the importance of "productive agency" because the individual, as a contributor to the group, must have the intention to learn, choose to collaborate, and be seen by the others as having that intention (Schwartz 1999). This analysis acknowledges the social value of the peer group as the means for motivating and enabling the processes of negotiation, learning, and a shared output. For the individual learner it is important that the group cognition being developed is available to them beyond the immediate group context, so they can transfer it to other situations. The learner has to construct and produce that knowledge:

> One of the reasons that production is so important to collaborative learning is that learning itself is productive. People construct their knowledge through generative mental and physical activities. They do not simply assimilate someone else's knowledge or practices; they actively produce their understanding. The constructive nature of learning has implications for how people learn, how they come to understand one another, and what they are likely to learn in groups.
>
> (Schwartz 1999)

The group is valuable to each of its members because it makes demands on them to produce a contribution to the group goal. In the process of doing so the learner has to construct an idea, explanation, or description. This idea is then available to the others to challenge or modify, and for the originator to defend or redevelop. Each member of the group reciprocates the demands and contributions of the others.

This analysis clarifies why collaborative learning should have pedagogic value. Two aspects are particularly salient:

(a) Peer modeling:

> a critical component of collaboration involves the representations that individuals have of one another's thoughts ... this may be at the heart of understanding collaboration ... The "deep secret" of collaborative

learning seems to lie in the cognitive processes through which humans progressively build a shared understanding.

(Weiss and Dillenbourg 1999)

learning seems more likely to occur to the extent that agents expend greater cognitive effort towards mutual understanding than that which would be minimally required for communication.

(Baker *et al.* 1999)

Collaborative learning takes agency and productive effort precisely because people must develop shared meaning across the differences in their roles and knowledge.

(ibid.: 202)

(b) Constructing something together:

it is the effort after shared meaning that helps explain why we learn when we collaborate.

(ibid.: 203)

[In a study of 7th grade science students] collaboration among the pair members led them to generate something new [abstract visualizations] that was not found in otherwise similar individuals.

(ibid.: 210)

Without production, there is no feedback ... People contribute and they look forward to the responses. This is one way that we come to learn, by creating ourselves and reappropriating the feedback from our creation.

(ibid.: 207)

The importance of peer feedback also emerges in a more recent study that shows very clearly how the use of peer review can act as a valuable form of collaboration. Each student has to produce an output (in this case draft pages of an assignment), which is shared with two others for them to comment. The act of creating an output in order to share it plays a role in motivating the student's practice, but being encouraged to engage in peer review of each other's work establishes an iterative cycle of:

- seeing an alternative solution in the output of a peer;
- generating feedback for their peer;
- using the feedback from others to modulate their concept; and
- generating a new output as a result, which enables modulation of their practice.

The peer review activity, which neatly exemplifies the combination of the *peer communication and modeling cycles*, was evaluated as useful by 84% of the students (Kear 2004).

These studies have all helped to clarify why collaborative learning is important and valuable. However, empirical studies are also very clear that students have low expectations of collaboration, do not necessarily collaborate just because they are put in a group, and do not necessarily collaborate well, even when they try to (Amhag and Jakobsson 2009; Dillenbourg 2002; Kollar, Fischer, and Hesse 2006; Lillejord and Dysthe 2008; Valaitis *et al.* 2005). This is not surprising. It is the most complex form of learning we have looked at in these chapters. This is evident in its representation in the Conversational Framework. Figure 11.1 shows how student collaboration, without teacher intervention, still touches all parts of the framework, precisely because it combines learning through practice – constructing something as a production – with learning through inquiry, discussion, and sharing.

As in Chapter 9, the discussion process is not simply the exchange of ideas, it is also a debate and dialogue, involving conflict and challenge, support and scaffolding, but with the shared product as the focus. Outputs are continually shared, having been informed by investigating the teaching resources, and constructed in the practice environment. Studies of collaborative learning do not usually include a practice environment that gives feedback on the constructs learners produce. The expectation seems to be that the learners

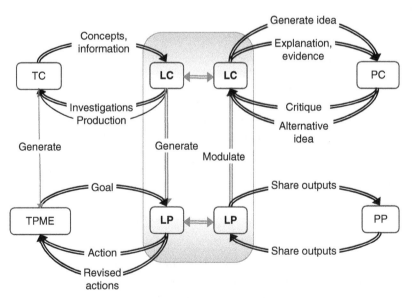

Figure 11.1 Learning through collaboration as a combination of learning through discussion and sharing of the outputs from practice and inquiry.

themselves will provide sufficient challenge to keep improving their output until it is ready for submission to the teacher. The only alternative is for the formative feedback to come from the teacher during the collaboration process. Most of these studies make the assumption that learners are not genuinely contributing new knowledge but are making their own constructions of the existing knowledge specified in the learning outcomes. If there is no other model for them to test it against, the validation of what they construct must come from the teacher.

The Teacher's Role in Collaborative Learning

Confirming this central role for the teacher, a recent study explicitly focused on the teacher's role (Urhahne *et al.* 2010). They developed five principles for supporting collaborative learning, derived from the literature and from the researchers' experience of this teaching method:

- Envision the lesson: create an image of the lesson, plan and organize student tasks.
- Enable collaboration: arrange small groups or pairs so that one can learn from the other.
- Encourage students: support learners and provide guidance during knowledge acquisition.
- Ensure learning: monitor learning processes and check learning outcomes.
- Evaluate achievement: choose suitable means to assess processes and products of learning.

These principles were used to categorize the activities of teachers helping their students to collaborate in their use of computer-based learning environments: some teachers succeeded in motivating students, while others failed. This level of description was not sufficient to differentiate successful from unsuccessful groups, leading them to conclude that "learning environments and the teacher have only limited influence on collaboration between peers" (Urhahne *et al.* 2010), even though their main point is to demonstrate that a collaborative learning environment does not diminish the role of the teacher, who is meant to be actively monitoring and guiding at each of the five stages of the process outlined above.

A similar lack of clarity about the teacher's role was identified in a critical review of the area:

> At present, the design of computer-supported group-based learning (CSGBL) is often based on subjective decisions regarding tasks, pedagogy and technology, or concepts such as "cooperative learning" and "collaborative learning". Critical review reveals these concepts as insufficiently substantial to serve as a basis for CSGBL design. Furthermore, the

relationship between outcome and group interaction is rarely specified a priori.

(Strijbos, Martens, and Jochems 2004: 403)

The authors argue for a more systematic approach that identifies how to elicit the type of student interaction that will lead to productive learning. The framework they propose outlines the design elements that are appropriate for any teaching design: to decide on learning objectives, expected student interaction, task type, amount of pre-structuring, group size, and computer support. This is constructed as a checklist of questions that map out the kinds of decisions there are to be made. To determine the expected interaction the teacher must decide whether the focus will be on

- feedback (e.g. commenting draft/final version)?
- exchanging (or creating) ideas (or findings)?
- discussion, argumentation of multiple alternatives/opinions? (ibid.: 418.)

… and whether the interaction requires co-ordination of activities whilst solving a complex problem, or a collaboratively written report representing shared understanding. This is essentially a description of the different properties an interaction can have; while it may be useful for suggesting possibilities, it does not itself provide guidance on how to elicit the types of student interaction needed. For selecting the task type the teacher is asked to consider "Will they have to solve a complex and ambiguous problem with no clear solution?" – but is offered no help on the consequences of their decision, or how to make it. To determine the type of pre-structuring needed the teacher is asked to consider, for example, whether students are

- each assigned to a portion of the material?
- each assigned individual responsibilities for interaction and group performance? (ibid.: 418)

These may be important questions to decide, but on what basis should the teacher decide them? Do they have to decide between them? As the review suggests, the literature on collaborative learning may be too immature as yet to provide clear guidelines on many of these issues. But we can be a little more ambitious, I think, in trying to offer more principled support.

What must the teacher do to ensure that learning does take place in a collaborative group? What are the "appropriate conditions" that drive or enable the productive learning activities to take place? To summarize the collective conclusions from these reviews in the literature, the students need:

- Construction of a shared output to motivate the need to share meaning, produce ideas, elicit feedback, and promote abstraction, and to motivate peer modeling, cognitive elaboration, and practice with one another;

- peer modeling to provide competent performance and enthusiasm;
- cognitive elaboration through conflict and challenge, articulating and critiquing points of view, support and scaffolding;
- practice with one another, involving listening, explaining, questioning, summarizing, speculating, and hypothesizing.

This is not yet the definitive list of requirements for successful collaborative learning. Learners are expected also to be able to refer to authoritative resources to help them construct their ideas, or solutions, depending on the nature of the task set, so this requirement should also be included. It gets very little attention in the literature on collaborative learning, even though it seems to be an assumption that students will be consulting existing resources to develop their ideas. And many studies have established that we cannot expect students to perform this complex set of skills unsupported; we must provide feedback and guidance on what they produce. A more complete set of requirements for collaborative learning, therefore, would be the full analysis of what it takes to learn, represented in the Conversational Framework. In addition to what is covered in Figure 11.1 this would include the teacher's roles in guidance and extrinsic feedback if they do not provide a practice/modeling environment that gives intrinsic feedback.

So the teacher's role is to create and promote these conditions, but collaborative learning is an unfamiliar pedagogy for teachers too. Might digital technologies help? Can they take any of the load of supporting the information provision, guidance on inquiry and discussion processes, and on the practice and sharing environments that learners need?

How Can Digital Technologies Help?

The perceived value of collaborative learning coincided with the rise of communication technologies, and together they have generated a significant new area of research and development in learning technology usually referred to as Computer Supported Collaborative Learning (CSCL). The principal requirements of collaborative learning – the construction of a shared output, negotiated through dialogue and debate – are very well suited to being implemented through digital technologies. Since the 1990s there have been many studies designed to demonstrate, discover, or generate the value of CSCL as a form of learning that suits both the demands of education and the affordances of the technology. The technology can support communication between participants and the construction of representations, so we must expect that it has something important to contribute to a form of learning that requires both.

The fundamental question for CSCL was articulated by Stahl, Koschmann, and Suthers: "In order to design technology to support collaborative learning and knowledge building, we must understand in more detail how small groups of learners construct shared meaning using various artifacts and media" (Stahl, Koschmann, and Suthers 2006: 10).

Their concern was to leverage the unique opportunities provided by technology, rather than simply replicate what can be done face-to-face. They identified three properties of digital technology that "mediate and encourage social acts that constitute group learning and lead to individual learning":

- Computational media are reconfigurable – so it is easy to construct and reconstruct representations of knowledge and ideas.
- Computer-mediated communication environments keep a record of activity and product – so there is potential for the persistent record of interaction and collaboration to act as a resource for inter-subjective learning.
- Computational media can analyze interaction – so there is potential for adaptive media to prompt, analyze, and selectively respond to the communication (ibid.: 12).

Combining these and the requirements for collaborative learning defined so far, Table 11.1 summarizes what the technology can offer.

In the following sections we look at three different types of technology. All have been identified as forms of computer supported collaborative learning – wikis, discussion environments, and design environments, and each offers at least some of the required properties.

The Wiki as a Collaborative Learning Environment

A wiki is a collective website, available either on the internet or on a local server; it contains text-based content, and enables its users to debate and change its content online. The wiki therefore fulfils requirements 3, 5, and 6 in Table 11.1 for collaborative learning, which is why it is seen as a new opportunity for computer-supported collaborative learning (Cress and Kimmerle 2008). The shared goal is the website itself – the text-based document being developed by the users. The format provides the means for users to construct their representations as contributions to the shared final document. The availability on a website or local server provides the means to share their representations. The wiki is not set up as a discussion environment, but contributions can be arguments in defense of a change, questions, or challenges to a change, so it can act as a discussion environment alongside the development of the output itself.

The critical characteristic of the wiki is that, being in essence a collaboratively built encyclopedia, it takes a "neutral point of view", which means that the students collaborating to produce the public document must first negotiate the content. This shared goal motivates the cut and thrust of argumentation, providing the drive for the peer communication and peer modeling cycles in the Conversational Framework. This marks it out from the authorial essay or blog, where the student is expected to provide a coherent critique from their own point of view, and from the online discussion forum, which has no such

Table 11.1 A Summary of how Digital Technologies can Support the Requirements of Collaborative Learning

Requirements	What technology can offer
1. A shared task goal.	Nothing – for the teacher to specify.
2. Resources relevant to the task.	Websites, digital libraries, Open Education Resource repositories.
3. The means to discuss the task.	Online discussion environment, both synchronous and asynchronous, recording all discussions.
4. Guidance on managing the discussion-solution process.	Roles, scripts, worksheets, teacher intervention.
5. The means to construct and revise representations of the task goal.	Applications for visual representation design, user-generated content.
6. The means to share representations of the task goal.	Design environment, file exchange, file management.
7. The means to test ideas and solutions to meet the task goal.	A modeling environment that gives intrinsic feedback on the learner's solution.

imperative to negotiate and agree on a shared output. The wiki therefore supports the kind of engagement with concepts that will be sustained in work and life post-education: "it reflects more authentically the conditions of workplaces, where conflict resolution, compromise and consensus building are often required in order to carry out the work" (Bruns and Humphreys 2005: 28).

However, the potential of any technology is not realized simply by making it available, and the promise of fostering student collaboration depends very much, as always, on the teacher's role, who must ensure that students are clear about the goals of each group, the rules of negotiation and consensus, the level and amount of contribution expected from individuals and groups, and how these are to be tracked and used for assessment (Bruns and Humphreys 2005).

> Wikis present themselves as an interesting tool for enhancing social constructivist learning environments. As non-linear, evolving, complex and networked texts with multiple authors, they can provide a great opportunity for student collaboration, co-production of texts, argument, and interaction.
>
> (Bruns and Humphreys 2005: 27)

But wiki technology only provides a structure for creating a page of text, publishing it to a group, and enabling others to edit that page and publish the result (which is what makes it a tool for collaboration, unlike a blog, which cannot be changed by others). There are ground rules for a public wiki, such as Wikipedia. These could be emulated by a teacher to encourage, for example, the proper sourcing of content, objectivity, and politeness in debates over conflicting entries.

But there is nothing essentially new in wiki technology that goes beyond a collaborative class project to create, say, a wall-poster to give an account of a topic researched by the class. For pedagogic purposes a wiki can even be quite ineffective, if students only read their own wiki pages, or feel inhibited from changing what others have written, or only contribute during class hours, and do not feel ownership of the product (Bruns and Humphreys 2005; Wheeler, Yeomans, and Wheeler 2008).

The large-scale communicative power of digital technology transforms this type of collaborative activity into something special that can use the wisdom of the crowds to build a better consolidation of knowledge than any one individual or group can do. Wiki technology in this more global sense is exciting and stimulating. But its use within courses is not for such a public purpose; it is rather to encourage students to engage in negotiating ideas, challenging each other to clearer and better representations of a topic. The goal of producing a negotiated and shared output may be the essence of a wiki, but students do not necessarily embrace that ideal. So the teacher plays a critical role in designing the task to guide and encourage students to debate and exchange their outputs. Simply making the technology available would be the equivalent of giving the class a large piece of paper and sets of post-it notes in the expectation they could produce a viable presentation of a topic. Again the researchers in this relatively new area of online collaboration emphasize the important role of the teacher in making it work (Bruns and Humphreys 2005).

Collaborative Discussion Environments

Chapter 9 looked at online discussion environments as a means of supporting learning through discussion. Collaboration learning is distinctive because of the intention to produce a shared output. In the collaborative learning literature the term "CSCL" sometimes refers to using an online discussion environment where the pedagogic design requires collaboration (Lillejord and Dysthe 2008; Schellens and Valcke 2006; Valaitis *et al.* 2005). These studies define a clearly stated shared goal, and look at how the student interaction progresses. The issue is how best to support students in managing the discussion–solution process to get the intended value from the social construction of the output. Effective pedagogic design is difficult. What research demonstrates is that learners do not easily offer diverse viewpoints or contribute interactions of the kind the researchers expect (Kirschner *et al.* 2004; Puntambekar 2006), just as we found in the literature on discussion learning.

One study set rules for student contributions to foster good quality interaction:

- contributions had to be based on clear argumentation;
- the argumentation had to be derived from the knowledge base presented during the weekly face-to-face sessions;

- they could refer to a chapter or paragraph of the course reader;
- contributions and responses to others students had to reflect the theoretical framework, the terminology and the propositions of the course reader.

The students' contributions were evaluated in terms of the following qualitative categories, derived from a transcript analysis tool (Fahy *et al.* 2000):

- Closed questions – with a specific correct answer.
- Open questions – with no one right answer.
- Statements – supplying facts, resources, or information.
- Reflections – argumentations, negotiations, thoughts, opinions, judgments, doubts, beliefs and transfer of personal information.
- Scaffolding – learners acknowledge one another, encourage, recognize contributions, thank, and greet.

The study found high percentages of "statements" and "reflection", but low levels of "scaffolding" to foster the collaborative process, possibly because feedback on contributions was explicitly supplied by the teacher (Schellens and Valcke 2006). They were able to prove the hypothesis that this CSCL environment produced a high proportion of task-oriented communication. Unfortunately, this methodology does not tell us what aspect of the design achieved the good result. They surmise that it was the very operational guidelines to direct learner discussion behavior; this was not tested, although this is what teachers really need to know.

The transcript analysis has a useful set of categories, but Murphy's analysis of the nature of the discussion needed for collaborative learning, derived from the literature on communities of inquiry and collaboration, provides a fuller set:

- Social presence.
- Articulating individual perspectives.
- Accommodating or reflecting the perspectives of others.
- Co-constructing shared perspectives and meanings phases.
- Building shared goals and purposes.
- Producing shared artifacts.

This set of categories makes more explicit reference to the range of contributions students should be making, and covers all those proposed above by Fahy. As a means of evaluating the extent to which students are engaging in collaborative learning, this set of categories gives a more complete analysis, but does not explicitly cover the requirements to challenge, debate, and argue. The tagging tools for discussion in Chapter 9, for example, made explicit the need for students to *inform, question, challenge, reason, agree, maintain,* which are part of the process of "co-constructing". We still have a rather incomplete set of categories for describing what it takes to manage a successful discussion–solution process.

In all these cases the researchers are demonstrating that the teacher has an important role to play in setting up the initial task, creating the expectations in students of what their contributions should be, and guiding them as they work through the process. The technology enables, it does not drive, or ensure success.

There is often confusion in this literature between what the technology enables and what students do with it. An argument for the value of mobile technologies is that they can "scaffold" the mutual support and coordination for participants by providing a network available from any location (Zurita and Nussbaum 2007). But they "can" does not mean they will: the internet enables communication and mobile technologies enable access, but the two technologies do not motivate or scaffold communication, and in particular do not help to ensure that learners coordinate their work and support each other, or drive the communication process. What students do depends on the teacher's design.

In a comparison of two learning designs for collaboration on producing a shared output from a field trip, such as a visit to an art gallery, I showed how mobile learning can enhance a conventional learning design, but also showed how the mobile-supported version is very dependent on the teacher making use of the affordances of the technology, and providing clear guidance on the communication to be carried out between students without the teacher being present (Laurillard 2007). In this case the instructions for students making use of their mobile phones as digital support were to:

> identify features in particular paintings, upload their answers and check against the teacher's model answer, set quiz questions to challenge other pairs, answer challenges from other pairs, record these and their observations on each painting, uploading these to a shared website.
>
> (Laurillard 2007: 165)

In this design the teacher embeds their guidance in the design of the practice environment: the technology enables the learners to motivate each other's contributions to the class observations on the trip. It is scaffolding a productive interaction in the form of a peer communication and practice cycle, releasing the teacher from the need to be constantly present. It does not evaluate how well they do it, or provide model answers, or offer responsive guidance and extrinsic feedback, in the way a teacher could, but the role of the technology in limited scaffolding at least is explicit.

One scaffolding technique is unique to technology: the tagging feature that invites or requires students to categorize their own contribution as they make it. This is how the technology elicits the appropriate "discourse pragmatics" for collaboration (Schwartz 1999). In one such study two groups of learners collaborating online asynchronously on a complex economic problem were compared. One group was given a tool to use for indicating the nature of their message as (i) a new contribution, (ii) a verification, (iii) a clarification, or (iv) an elaboration. The messages of both groups were coded for these instances. Interestingly, the tool afforded a much longer discussion, a third as much again, mainly because it elicited more contributions categorized by the students as verification and clarification (Kirschner *et al.* 2004). So it is possible to promote these instances of "reflections" or "co-constructions," i.e. high level forms of knowledge-building interaction.

Similar tools, "InterLoc" and AcademicTalk, are discussed in Chapter 9, where students had to select "openers" as a way of categorizing the type of contribution they were making to a tutorial dialogue, such as *inform, question, challenge, reason, agree, maintain.* The tools help students make constructive challenges and arguments, and so develop better conceptual constructs in the science topics being tested (Ravenscroft 2007). This is one of the most promising ways in which digital technologies can scaffold students' work to improve the quality of contributions they make and so modulate their conceptions as they plan their contribution:

> with AcademicTalk students addressed previous contributions more clearly and directly and more arguments were examined and challenged compared with students using a Chat client. Students were able to engage in more thoughtful and relevant contributions using this tool, and felt able to challenge others with direct questioning, which rarely occurred in similar Chat discussions on the same topics and with the same preparations. This was shown in the strength and frequency of rebuttals in discussions, which was not replicated in the Chat discussions.
>
> (Ravenscroft 2007: 8)

Intriguingly, an important difference from the Chat discussions was that students challenged and questioned the ideas being discussed, rather than the person proposing them. But the research study also concluded that we need a greater emphasis on designing for effective argumentation, going beyond a "prepare–interact–summarize" sequence to engaging more closely with students' interests. Again, the conclusion is that the teacher must provide.

Collaborative Construction Environments

This section looks at how digital technologies can help with constructing the shared output in collaborative learning. The shared output is usually a text-based document, perhaps with diagrams, or a set of slides, perhaps with animations. It may not be possible to represent it within the collaborative discussion environment, and then it is shared as files. *Collaborative construction environments* often focus on supporting the construction of the shared output, not the collaborative discussion, which takes place in the class, face-to-face, although this could be online.

An interesting early example of this was Roschelle and Teasley's "envisioning machine". This modeling environment set a complex mechanics problem as the problem solving task, and asked students to work in pairs to model motion by adjusting parameters in the model, and then compare the resulting motion with an animation of the real-world motion they were trying to match (Roschelle and Teasley 1995). This is a good example of a microworld, where the students are using a modeling tool to create a representation of complex motion, and the mismatch between the motion they create and the target motion provides intrinsic feedback to help them modulate their action. The computer model plays several roles in supporting the collaboration:

- It disambiguates language by providing precise objects and behaviour both learners can refer to, e.g. "make it more" has a precise meaning in terms of what happens on the computer screen.
- Feedback from trial actions resolves conflicts over what would work.
- Experiments with the interface helped to generate new ideas.
- Because the model is constrained to behave according to the theory its behavior constrains possible interpretations.

In a non-digital environment, where students are working on a shared problem with paper none of these features are available, so this type of digital environment makes a valuable contribution to the collaboration by making the output explicit and testable. Without the intrinsic feedback on their actions the learners are unsupported and unable to be sure their actions are on the right lines. This feature marks out the modeling environments from constructionist environments like drawing programs or website construction tools, where a learner can represent their idea but the technology cannot evaluate it. The learner can test their input against the machine's model of how the mechanical system behaves. Among educational technologies this is unique to digital technologies, and among digital technologies unique to computational models, like microworlds. The real world can do it too, but only for aspects of the world that students can test.

This type of practice environment helps to drive the modulate–generate learning cycle for each individual, as it motivates the *peer communication cycle* through the need to share interpretations of results, as well as the *peer modeling cycle* when learners generate successive attempts to solve the challenge as the product of their collaboration.

The observation of students using the envisioning environment revealed the characteristics of student work that are important if collaborative learning is to take place:

> In periods of successful collaborative activity, students' conversational turns build upon each other and the content contributes to the joint problem solving activity.
>
> (ibid.: 76)

collaborative problem solving includes periods in which partners are not fully engaged ... [they] withdraw from active interaction ... to work on ideas that are too ill-formed or complicated to be introduced into the shared work ... usually followed by periods of intense interaction ... to incorporate the individual insight into the shared problem solving knowledge.

(ibid.: 77)

the attempts to reduce conflict by resolving misunderstandings ... take the form of "repairs" ... a major means for the achievement and consolidation of understanding.

(ibid.: 78)

Narration informs one's partner of the intentions corresponding to actions. This enhances the partners' opportunities to recognize differences in the shared understanding.

(ibid: 78)

both partners agreed their solution was perfect. The challenge closed on this note of mutual satisfaction.

(ibid: 94)

This detailed account of the learning activity shows how Roschelle and Teasley have been able to address many of the requirements of collaborative learning by creating an environment that supports the construction and representation of the students' developing knowledge. The collaborative discussion takes place in class, however, not online.

Online Collaborative Construction Environments

It is possible to achieve collaborative constructive discussion online. One of the most extensively researched and widely used collaborative online discussion environments is CSILE (Computer Supported Intentional Learning Environments). It is designed to support inquiry, information search, and creative work with ideas, among learners of any age, collaborating to build knowledge (Scardamalia 2004). It addresses the main requirements for collaborative learning in the following ways:

- a multimedia community knowledge space – the means to discuss and share;
- participants contribute theories, working models, plans, evidence, reference material, as text-based notes, diagrams, graphs or concept maps – the means to construct and revise representations;
- knowledge building supports, for the creation of notes and for the ways they are displayed, linked, and made objects of further work – visualizations and discourse pragmatics;

- revisions, elaborations, and reorganizations over time provide a record of group advances – affordances to support the discussion–solution process.

The "knowledge building supports" serve the purpose of scaffolding the contributions students make by using the tagging technique, i.e. selecting terms to categorize a contribution, such as refining theory, providing constructive criticism. The student can then edit the term into their contribution, which "helps students embed these forms of discourse in their everyday work" (ibid: 188). Using tagging tools such as this, digital technology does seem to be able to make a difference by enabling students to generate articulations at the higher level forms of knowledge building that make collaborative learning worthwhile. How is the knowledge construction validated? Again, the teacher is responsible, because "ascertaining that knowledge building has taken place requires digging into the content of Knowledge Forum databases and recordings of class interactions" (Scardamalia and Bereiter 2006). This is labor intensive work.

Constructing knowledge is seen as being different from inquiring into existing knowledge, so the two areas do not cross-refer very much, but inquiry learning is also described as a form of computer-supported collaborative learning. An example of CSCL for inquiry learning is the Web-based Inquiry Science Environment (WISE), which defines the problems to be investigated and the resources needed to solve them, such as web pages, online activities, electronic notebooks, and interactive simulations. Students represent their answers as documents submitted to the server. The activities provide some guidance on how to develop solutions to the problems, therefore, but teachers play a key role in classroom support of the inquiry process. WISE inquiry projects are so intensively researched that much is known about the teacher's role (Linn and Hsi 2000). Experience has shown that teachers differ considerably in their interactions with students when teaching with WISE (Slotta 2004). Researchers therefore spend many months mentoring teachers to ensure they develop appropriate teaching strategies for making good use of this online inquiry environment. Again, the teacher is the focus of making the technology work effectively.

Similar environments focusing on investigating challenges and constructing solutions provide not just the means to represent shared outputs, but the means to test them as well, by providing an interactive model or simulation (Buckley *et al.* 2004; Urhahne *et al.* 2010; van Joolingen *et al.* 2005). The modeling environment should be able to take some of the load off the teacher by providing the intrinsic feedback that supports independent learning.

A distinctive example is the work on Co-Lab, which provides the means for learners to collaborate on producing a solution, and test their understanding in a model:

Learners express their initial understanding of scientific phenomena in a model sketch, which is then used to predict and explain what will occur in the phenomena being modeled. By testing these hypotheses with the simulation or the remote lab, learners gain knowledge they can use to refine or extend their model.

(van Joolingen *et al.* 2005: 674)

Guidance is offered in the form of procedural advice:

Each goal statement comes with a description stating what learners should do to accomplish that goal, and one or more hints that answer frequently asked questions ... As learners' self-regulatory skills are expected to improve, planning support can be gradually faded. In keeping with the building metaphor, the Process Coordinator contains fewer and less explicit directions on higher floors. Fading may occur by removing the subgoals, the descriptions, and the hints in any preferred order.

(ibid: 677)

A synchronous online discussion environment takes the form of a chat tool for pairs of students working together, although the environment is more often used in face-to-face classes.

This is a serious attempt, therefore, to cover all the requirements for collaborative learning. It creates a very complex environment, difficult for students to learn to use, and difficult for teachers to implement with confidence. Those who do use it contribute extensive preparation and student guidance (Urhahne *et al.* 2010), so the work has continued in the form of providing more resources for collaborative work, and intelligent guidance intended to emulate how a teacher supported students as they used the model (Bravo, van Joolingen, and de Jong 2009). The development load for such environments is high, and research funding is too restricted and short-term typically to take promising developments such as this to full implementation. Instead Co-Lab stands as an exemplar of what CSCL could be like if it were possible to exploit digital technologies fully for education.

The conclusion we have to draw, again, is that the teacher's role is critical for making a success of these technological opportunities. CSCL is still a developing field; its contributions and results are promising but teachers need more help with embracing it. It is not enough to urge the importance of it, due to its basis in theory, and it is not enough to describe its essential components. Teachers need to know the principles of pedagogical design they should be adopting for collaborative learning, and how best to use technology to support it. The Conversational Framework can help by going beyond a description of the components of a collaborative process, to an account of how the components of the pedagogic design combine to motivate the learner to modulate and generate their concepts and actions. The question is, how can teachers engage with that, and embrace the still developing systems for CSCL?

Pedagogical Patterns for Collaborative Learning

Recognizing the difficulty of ensuring that learners interact appropriately, so that collaborative learning works as it should, researchers have looked at supporting students by offering "scripts" (e.g. Ertl *et al.* 2007; King 2007; Rummel and Spada 2007; Weinberger *et al.* 2007). A script is a form of pedagogical pattern:

> A collaboration script is a set of instructions prescribing how students should form groups, how they should interact and collaborate and how they should solve the problem. In computer-supported collaborative learning (CSCL), the script is reified in the interface of the learning environment.
>
> (Dillenbourg 2002: 61)

Dillenbourg defines five properties of a script, while an alternative definition defines a more elaborated subset of some of these (Kollar, Fischer, and Hesse 2006), so I have combined them make a superset of properties:

- learning objectives;
- task definition;
- group size and composition;
- sequence of learning activities;
- distribution of roles;
- type of representation;
- mode of interaction (whether online or face-to-face, tutor-supported or not); and
- timing (duration and scheduling).

These are similar to the properties of a pedagogical pattern defined in Chapter 6, although "roles" and "representation" are specific to collaborative learning, and the "sequence of learning activities" begs the question of what form this should take.

The research studies show that both face-to-face and CSCL teaching practice can be described in these terms, not surprisingly. But the problem is that the research studies only describe what collaborative learning needs to do, without being prescriptive enough to provide a test of whether it succeeds. There is insufficient challenge to the pedagogy being practiced.

Without a clear representation of what it takes to achieve effective collaborative learning, CSCL risks being unable to leverage the unique opportunities provided by technology. The Conversational Framework sets out to challenge the technology to provide a particular kind of goal, activity, and form of feedback, and by proposing a generic theory-derived set of *requirements* can test the extent to which collaborative learning environments addresses them.

In a recent analysis of this approach I looked at Dillenbourg's "Argue-Graph" script (Jermann and Dillenbourg 2003; Kobbe *et al.* 2007), in terms of the extent to which it covers the Conversational Framework requirements (Laurillard 2009), and found that it met more of the requirements than a "social script," which operates simply at the level of exchanging ideas (Weinberger *et al.* 2005) and maps directly onto the representation of learning through discussion in Figure 6.5(a). The social script does not ask learners to construct a shared argument, but simply to offer comments on each other's analysis.

By contrast, the "Argue-Graph" script (Jermann and Dillenbourg 2003), requires more:

> Students first individually argue for or against items on a questionnaire. Their opinion is plotted onto a two-dimensional graph. Students with highly conflicting opinions (point distance in the graph) are grouped together in pairs and receive another copy of the questionnaire to fill out. Students discuss what arguments to write for each item. The teacher collects the questionnaires and helps each small group in turn to elaborate on and revise their arguments. The teacher then groups all arguments by item. Finally, each student is assigned one item for which to write a synthesis of all arguments.
>
> (Kobbe *et al.* 2007: 215)

The design of the Argue-Graph script requires more than an exchange of ideas: it motivates the construction of a shared representation of the learners' arguments in defense of their conception of the topic. The external practice environment does not give intrinsic feedback, as a lab, or an audience, or a simulation, could. It simply motivates the learner to generate their answers to the questions, and gives extrinsic feedback on how they compare with those of their peers. The goal to generate a shared set of arguments is what motivates them to modulate their concept. The Argue-Graph script as a pedagogic design works in a similar way to the tool-mediated construction activity reported by Hmelo-Silver (Hmelo-Silver 2003), and the sequence of collaborative activities recorded by Luckin (Luckin 2003).

Even in the Argue-Graph script the role of the technology is quite minimal, as it does not itself provide the intrinsic feedback, or promote or support the collaboration, which is done primarily by the teacher. A script, or pedagogical pattern for collaborative learning should go beyond this to demonstrate how to make the best use of technology.

This is the challenge I want to confront. From all the ideas offered from the literature we should be able to develop a script that covers the essentials of what makes collaborative learning different from other kinds of learning, and that also shows what the technology can do to help. Table 11.2 is an example of such a pattern, designed to meet the requirements specified in the literature and to elicit the successive cycles in the Conversational Framework, the teacher

Table 11.2 A Generic Pedagogical Pattern for Collaborative Learning Designed to Elicit the Successive Cycles in the Conversational Framework

Sequence of activities	Cycles
Teacher generates (1) the modeling environment to set a task goal (2), and to provide an analysis of learners' actions as feedback on the extent to which their actions met the goal.	TMC1
Learner uses their concept to generate (3) draft actions (4) from their practice repertoire.	TMC1
Model feeds back (5) an analysis to each learner of the extent to which their actions met the goal.	TMC2
Learner uses the feedback to modulate (6) their concept in order to generate (3) a revised action (7).	TMC1
Learners each generate for peers their draft actions and the results from the model to share outputs (8).	PMC1 PMC2
Learners each use peer outputs and results to modulate their respective concepts (6) and generate explanations, questions, critiques, and defenses of their respective outputs (9), and to generate (3) and test revised actions (7).	PCC1 PCC2 TMC1
That cycle repeats until they are ready to negotiate an agreed output (10).	PMC PCC TMC
The teacher reflects on the output (10) and their performance on the model (11).	TMC1
The teacher presents their summary of the learners' output and commentary as extrinsic feedback on how well their output meets the task goal, in the light of theory (12).	TCC3

Note: Numbers refer to the labels in Figure 11.2. For codes see Table 6.2.

communication cycle (TCC), teacher modeling cycle (TMC), peer communication cycle (PCC), and peer modeling cycle (PMC).

The sequence of teaching and learning activities summarized in Table 11.2 addresses the main requirements that have come from education and from CSCL studies of collaborative learning. These are mapped onto the Conversational Framework in Figure 11.2.

It is difficult to represent dynamic cycles in static diagrams, but what the table and figure both show is the repetition of the modulate–generate learning cycle. How does the technology help?

- The iteration round the modulate–generate learning cycle is being driven partly by the technology contributing the model to provide feedback on learner actions, which prompts the need to consider how to generate better actions.

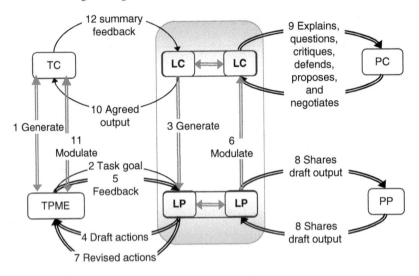

Figure 11.2 The pedagogical pattern for collaborative learning mapped onto the Conversational Framework, showing the succession of teaching–learning activities planned into the design outlined in Table 11.2.

- The technology enables the representation and sharing of outputs, while the requirement to produce a shared output drives this process.
- The technology enables a higher quality discussion by providing a discussion scaffolding tool where learners select the type of contribution they have to make to the discussion.

Without the modeling environment, learners receive no help in deciding how good their actions are, so it assists the teacher by providing feedback while the students are working, and motivates their quest for better actions. Insofar as the discussion contribution tools work, they assist the teacher by stimulating higher-level student discussion. This means that the teacher contribution can be the single interventions shown in Figure 11.2, without too great a loss of learner benefit.

Summary: Designing for Learning Through Collaboration

Collaborative learning has been recognized for some time as a valuable pedagogic technique. It combines at its most complex all the other forms of learning discussed in this book. I have described it as a combination of learning through practice and discussion, with the added imperative that students share their outputs and use these to create an agreed output to meet the goal. The value of this form of learning is immediately apparent from its representation in the Conversational Framework, because it has such good coverage. But the question is how well does it drive the moderate–generate learning cycle? That depends on the design, as we have seen, and the extent to which the design exploits the technology (a) to provide a model that gives learners intrinsic feedback to drive their revised actions, and (b) to promote the higher level forms of learner interaction.

12 Teaching as Developing Pedagogical Patterns

Introduction

Did the technology come good in the end? Chapter 1 posed the question and chapters 7–11 answered it in the light of the research on teaching and learning covered in the earlier chapters. The truth is, the story of digital learning technologies has hardly begun, and there will be no end until they have become so fully embedded in education that we will not even ask the question. My favorite analogy is with the story of paper in education. Its role is now so completely embedded, and it is so diverse in its benefits, and potential for even further benefits, that no-one begins to ask how "effective" it is. And yet paper is extremely limited as a technology in comparison with digital technologies. So 30 years after the first program for computers in schools we are still investigating the potential of technology. Understanding and fully exploiting its potential will take a lot longer (Laurillard 2010).

The task of doing that has to lie with the teaching profession. That is tough, because the technology industry innovates fast, and not for education. Teachers could potentially innovate by experimenting and discovering, because they are close to students every day, and able to test innovative ideas about the roles technology could play. Researchers in the field deploy the tiny funding opportunities to chase down each new technology to explore its potential. This is how the field has been able to build its knowledge and practice so far. But there is not the capacity in the system to maintain its everyday business and keep pace with technological innovation, so what work there is makes little impact on the main policy drivers in education (Laurillard 2008d). Investment has not been directed at changing the system, only at acquiring the technology.

One approach to this dilemma is to argue that investment in education to exploit technology would deliver a significant return. There are two simple reasons why digital technology has the capacity to do this: it can improve costs by operating at scale, and improve benefits by supporting independent active learning (Laurillard 2011).

While we wait for the investment there is another approach that is equally necessary: to harness the work of every teacher, working with their students to discover what they can do with technology. Even with a well-designed investment program education would still need a teaching profession able to innovate and build its knowledge about teaching and learning with technology. This is equally true of educational innovations in areas outside the use of technology. Often it is the technology-related work where the most interesting or even the only research on pedagogy is being done, but innovative practice in pedagogy is taking place all day every day in our educational institutions.

This final chapter pulls together the conclusions from the previous chapters to propose a way of harnessing and consolidating this knowledge and practice by looking at what it means to treat teaching as a design science.

Requirements for a Design Science

Chapter 1 proposed that teachers acting as design scientists would observe four basic precepts, to

1. keep improving their practice,
2. have a principled way of designing and testing improvements in practice,
3. build on the work of others,
4. represent and share their pedagogic practice, the outcomes they achieved, and how these related to the elements of their design.

These principles of professional conduct are free of any mention of technology because they should be neutral with respect to how the practice operates, so the methodology should work just as well for conventional teaching. Any test of effective and improving practice should be able to test all forms of teaching to discover what is optimal for different contexts and settings.

The first requirement is straightforward because teachers already work to improve their practice as part of their professional role. In many countries teachers in all educational sectors are required to do it, although with differing degrees of accountability. It causes difficulty when teachers have too high a workload to be able to spend time on improving their practice, but this is a cultural and organizational issue for the institution, not a characteristic of the professional culture itself.

The second point requires a shared set of criteria for making the design as effective as possible – as developed in the Conversational Framework. The criteria could come from any frameworks or theories as long as they can be clearly related to the learning outcomes and elements of the design.

The third point, building on the work of others, requires a way for teachers to find each other's designs, and adopt and adapt them for their own context, and that means being able to represent them in a formal way, hence the fourth point.

The fourth point means that the teacher must be able to represent their design in a way that is findable, understandable, and adaptable by others. A formal representation that has clear context descriptors will make it findable.

To be understandable it must be possible for the originator to describe its essence briefly and clearly, and that is covered in the section below on representing designs.

The four points above are familiar in the academic world as (1) the scholarly endeavor that sets out to advance knowledge, (2) the methodology of the field, (3) scholarship itself, and (4) the scholarly publishing on which this depends, the form of exchange of ideas and findings.

The next section builds on the ideas in Chapters 7–11 of how we might capture and represent teachers' effective pedagogic ideas in the form of pedagogical patterns. The basic design principle they aim for, introduced in Chapter 6, is "to motivate or enable the learner to generate their articulations and actions that modulate their concepts and practice" and the elements of the Conversational Framework have been defined to formalize that aim.

Representing Patterns for Learning

The history of patterns for use in teaching has generated many categories for defining what it takes to provide good teaching. These can be found in the reports of several different types of project, to represent and transfer good pedagogic ideas (Bergin 2002; Conole and Weller 2007; Goodyear 2005; Goodyear and Yang 2009; Green *et al.* 2006; Herrington, Oliver, and Reeves 2003; McAndrew and Goodyear 2007; Oliver and Conole 2002), to find ways of formalizing teaching designs for computational manipulation (Laurillard and Ljubojevic 2011; Mor *et al.* 2006; Oliver *et al.* 2002; Paquette *et al.* 2005; Sharp, Manns, and Eckstein 2003), or to build and evaluate the design tools that represent patterns (Dalziel 2003; Laurillard and Masterman 2009; Masterman and Vogel 2007; McAndrew and Weller 2005; Neumann and Oberhuemer 2009; San Diego *et al.* 2008). A valuable recent overview of the field lists the categories researchers have developed for describing ways of teaching (Derntl, Neumann, and Oberhuemer 2009). This resulted in the development and evaluation of a "Teaching Method Template" as part of the iCOPER project, which describes a teaching design in terms of:

- general categories, such as Summary, Rationale, Learning outcomes, Duration, Group size, Learner characteristics, and Setting;
- detailed teaching information, such as Sequence of activities, Roles, Assessment method, Resources, References; and
- comment sections, such as Teacher reflection, Student feedback, and Peer review.

As the most comprehensive analysis of formal descriptors for teaching this is useful as a way of describing a teaching design, but such a set of categories does not itself provide criteria for analyzing the design, or for understanding how it should work. The most interesting part of a teaching design that other teachers might want to build on is buried within the single category of "Sequence of activities" (Laurillard and Ljubojevic 2011). If we want to capture good pedagogy we need a representation that displays it, not one that buries its creative detail (Laurillard 2008c). Following Derntl, Neumann, and Oberhuemer (2009), it is certainly valuable to divide the categories of description into general, pedagogic, and evaluative, but we can say more about the pedagogy.

The general descriptors are those that enable other teachers to find the patterns relevant to their context, linked to their pedagogic design principles. The pedagogic descriptors are those that pass on the lessons of the knowledge and practice of teaching and learning with technology. The evaluative descriptors help the knowledge to build by proposing how the pattern might be improved. The general descriptors are defined here as "context descriptors," using the categories proposed above and augmented by those discussed in Chapter 6. These are the givens the teaching design has to work to.

Context Descriptors

- Origin (the original source and later contributors).
- Summary (brief description of what is being taught and how).
- Topics (keywords that will help other teachers decide the relevance to them).
- Learning outcome (what the learner will know or be able to do by the end).
- Rationale (the learning approach or pedagogic design principle).
- Duration (total learning hours, not necessarily continuous).
- Learner characteristics (educational pre-requisites, experience, interests).
- Setting (face-to-face, blended, or online).
- Group size (the range of minimum to any maximum).

The origin or provenance of a pedagogical pattern is as important as citations are in research. Teachers considering adopting a new pattern need to know its origin, and should be able to track the way it has developed into alternative versions. Equally, originators and contributors will want their work acknowledged. This category is the means by which intellectual property rights can remain intact.

Stating the intended learning outcome for a pattern is the most contentious descriptor. There will often be many. Knowledge and skills are so closely interrelated that it is difficult to improve on one without improving on the other, so it is tempting to list all the outcomes that are achieved in a session – a category of "additional learning outcomes" would allow this. But a single primary outcome helps to clarify how the pattern achieves it, and focuses the teaching design on making sure at least that is achieved.

These descriptors define the context: what the pattern covers, whom it is for, and what it tries to do. The pedagogy descriptors must capture what it does, and how and why it works.

Pedagogy Descriptors

The pedagogy descriptors include both "teaching information" and "comments." Since effective pedagogy depends on the internal relationship between the learning outcome, the activity sequence, and how it assesses whether the learner has achieved the learning outcome, all these categories are relevant to the pedagogy. The learner's experience also depends on the size of the group they are working in – discussing in a group of three is very different from a group of ten – so group size for each activity is important. The duration of each activity inevitably affects what is learned – using a simulation program for half an hour in class is very different from using it for several hours over several weeks – so duration should be included.

There should also be an account of the evidence that the pattern has worked, which can be given in "Teacher's reflection" and the "Student feedback" sections of the evaluative comments. This is important, and enables teaching knowledge to build on a secure foundation, but *that* it worked does not always tell us *why* it worked.

Why a design should work, the design rationale, has to come from theory, even though this may need to change after evaluation of the design in practice. The rationale for the way the pedagogy is designed may link it to a learning approach such as social constructivism, or situated cognition, but the detail of the sequence of teaching–learning activities can also be linked to design criteria.

Table 7.1 showed how a pattern could demonstrate its comparative pedagogic power by mapping it to the learning cycles in the Conversational Framework that will "motivate or enable the learner to generate their articulations and actions that modulate their concepts and practice." The formal categories for the teaching–learning design criteria are defined as the teacher/peer communication, practice and modeling cycles, and were introduced in Table 6.5. These can be used to clarify the extent to which the sequence of teaching–learning activities in a pattern covers the range of learning cycles in the Conversational Framework. Previous chapters showed how generic pedagogical patterns for acquisition (Table 7.1), inquiry (Table 8.1), discussion (Table 9.2), practice (Table 10.1), and collaboration (Table 11.2) can be mapped to the learning cycles in the Conversational Framework.

Whether the pattern is implemented face-to-face or online, and the tools and resources used by learners make an important difference to the learning experience (as illustrated in Figures 10.3 and 10.4 for example). The pattern description must therefore show how the conventional or digital technologies are being used. The pedagogic design criteria make explicit demands on the technologies to be used, so Table 12.1 collects together all the types of digital tools and resources discussed in previous chapters, to show where they can meet those demands.

The full pedagogic description of a pattern must therefore include the design criteria, the properties of the teaching–learning activities, and the capabilities of the conventional and digital tools and technologies being used.

The context descriptors together with the pedagogy descriptors should give the teacher (i) a principled way of designing and testing the improvements in their practice (ii) a way of representing and sharing their pedagogic practice, and (iii) a way of relating outcomes to the rationale and elements of their design. These are the requirements for being able to contribute to a design science.

Format for a Pedagogical Pattern

The context and pedagogy descriptors combine in the complete format for a pedagogical pattern, capable of enabling teachers to share their pedagogic ideas in a principled way appropriate for a design science. Table 12.2 brings them together in a proposed format. It is completed for a particular pattern relevant to a dentistry course where the aim is to give students practice in a skill (San Diego *et al.*, in press). The categories of description cover all those found in the literature, but the pedagogy descriptors are organized to make the sequence of activities prominent, as this is where the creative power of the teacher's pedagogy lies. To reflect how it achieves what it does, this section of the format categorizes each activity in terms of the size of the group the learner is working in, and the duration of the activity, since both have significant effects on the learning experience. The activities are also categorized in terms of the type of learning cycle they support. Although the acronyms are not self-explanatory, this should be one of the clearest and simplest ways of accounting for the value of a design pattern.

The set of principles enshrined as a framework like the Conversational Framework cannot carry the infinite variety of detail that makes good teaching. The detail is preserved in the text of a pattern, which links the topic to the learning outcome and the tools and resources being used. In Table 12.2 the topic-specific parts are in italics; the rest is the detail of the pedagogy being mapped to the learning cycles. This enables the teacher to record the detail of their creative pedagogic idea, but also provides a formal account of what they have designed and why. Categorizing the teaching–learning activities in terms of the principles in a pedagogic framework helps to clarify why they work, how to improve them, and where the design might benefit from the use of technologies, given the way they are categorized in Table 12.1.

What this book aims to contribute to the process of teaching design is a formal description of why a design should work at the planning stage, and the means to express this at the publication stage. The format of a pedagogical pattern is intended to provide such a formal description.

Exploring the Idea of Pedagogical Patterns

If the teaching community broadly comes to accept the idea of structured formats for pedagogical patterns, a number of interesting avenues of further development begin to open up. This section explores the main ideas still in development.

Table 12.1 How Digital Technologies Contribute to the Pedagogic Design Criteria

Design criteria	Digital tools and resources that can make a difference to pedagogical patterns
Access to the teacher's conception and means of production (TCC1, 2)	Partially completed slides for the learner to complete using access to digital resources and presentations. Multimodal presentations, digital libraries or repositories of documents and resources, animations, podcasts, videos.
Extrinsic feedback or information from the teacher (TPC1, 2)	Clicker technologies in class improve teacher-student dialogue. Provide model answers to learner activities and FAQs, available for access after a certain time, or on condition of learner input. Webquest activities to support information searches. Reflective journal to report and share search strategies. Online guidance on how to select high quality online sources. Icons to link to advice and guidance on steps in the inquiry process. Authoring tool for teacher to adjust guidance and tasks. Tools for recording data, reflections and ideas. Teacher access to selected student online discussions to monitor and guide their process.
Intrinsic feedback on actions from the model in a practice environment (TMC1, 2)	An adaptive teaching program can adjust difficulty of the task depending on how it analyzes learner input. A model of the inquiry or problem process can give extrinsic advice and guidance depending on how it analyzes learner input (Chapter 10). A microworld or simulation gives intrinsic feedback that can help a learner work out how to improve their action by showing the output from their input in relation to the goal or model or intended output. Role-play simulations provide scenarios of alternative actions in response to problems, challenges or questions, depending on how the simulation analyzes learner input. User-design tools show how the learner's representation of a system or idea compares with an expert model or real-world data.
Access to peers' conceptions and extrinsic feedback from peers (PCC1, 2, 3)	Asynchronous online discussion environments enable time for reflection and a higher proportion of learner discussion time than face-to-face groups. Synchronous meeting environments with online whiteboard, audio and chat tools with someone in a chairing role to ensure good discussion. Online guidance in the form of defined roles, scripts. Selection tools for tagging contributions. Websites, blogs, e-portfolios for posting ideas and suggestions for others. Clicker tools for posting answers to questions for follow-up in groups.

Continued

Table 12.1 How Digital Technologies Contribute to the Pedagogic Design Criteria (*Continued*)

Design criteria	Digital tools and resources that can make a difference to pedagogical patterns
Sharing output of practice and using feedback from their peer's output (PMC1, 2)	In addition to 3 and 4, a shared modeling environment assists the collaborative progress to an agreed output. Wiki environments for collaborating to produce a shared output with ground rules for optimal negotiation and outputs (Chapter 11). Digital project tools assist the collaborative negotiation of the output through file sharing, manipulating and managing successive documents and designs.

Note: For codes see Table 6.2.

Pattern Languages

One of the intriguing ideas in the design patterns world is the idea of a "pattern language." A pattern has the simple basic form of "context–problem–solution," and the pedagogical pattern format has exactly that basic structure, where the context descriptors set out the context, the learning outcome is the problem, and the sequence of activities describes the solution. The specific pattern in Table 12.2 and all the generic patterns in earlier chapters are designed to address a particular learning outcome.

I have not discussed other kinds of design patterns, to solve problems such as "how to help students get to know each other" (ice-breakers), "how to get students to ask questions in class" (small group role-play). These teaching techniques are targeted on solving a teaching problem, not on achieving a learning outcome, but they could be part of a pedagogical pattern. So patterns can be made up from other patterns, or could strongly resemble each other with small variations, making up families of patterns. The appropriate ways of combining patterns to make other well-formed patterns suggests there could be rules – rather like grammatical rules for the structure of language (Avgeriou *et al.* 2003; Goodyear 2005): "The hope is that the patterns will build towards a pattern language, potentially giving educators an alternative way of understanding the intention behind pedagogical source materials, alongside the instantiation intended for the learner" (McAndrew and Goodyear 2007: 99).

The format of the "sequence of activities" as a collection of teaching design patterns building towards an elaborated solution in the pedagogical pattern could help to do exactly this.

Whether a pattern language for pedagogy will develop is hard to say at this stage, and in any case it will depend on much more extensive engagement with the idea of patterns among the teaching community. It is an intriguing vision.

Table 12.2 Format for a Pedagogical Pattern

Title	*Drilling a decayed tooth*		

Origins	School of Dentistry		
Summary	Students are introduced to the goal of *a well-prepared tooth*, heuristic principles of how to achieve it, then practice the skill of *drilling a decayed tooth* using *the drill* and *plastic teeth*, and revise their approach in the light of feedback.		
Topics	*Drilling a decayed tooth*		
Learning outcome	To be practiced in the skill of *drilling a decayed tooth*, and able to improve their own performance in achieving the goal of *a well-prepared tooth*.		
Rationale	Experiential learning; learning through practice.		
Duration	3 hours.		
Learners	Science A-levels; first year dentistry…		
Setting	Face-to-face, Lab.		
Resources and tools	*Handouts* with detailed instructions on the practice of *drilling a decayed tooth*; the tool (*drill*) and resources (*plastic teeth*), questionnaire.		
Learning cycles	*Sequence of teaching–learning activities*	*Group size*	*Time mins*
TCC1	The tutor introduces students to the principles and practice of *drilling a decayed tooth*. Talks through the *Handouts* giving instructions on how to achieve the best result. Explains how they will be advised and evaluated.	70	20
TPC1	Students individually practice drilling a decayed tooth using the drill and plastic teeth, and *Handouts*.	1	60
TPC2	The tutor checks what the student is doing, and advises on how to improve.	1	(2.5)
TPC1	Students individually have a second try at the skill of *drilling a decayed tooth* using the *drill* and *plastic teeth*, and *Handouts*. Students hand in their completed work.	1	60
TPC2	The tutor checks and evaluates the student's performance against the goal of *a well-prepared tooth*.	1	(2.5)
PCC1, 2, 3	The tutor chairs a class discussion, asking for reflections on experiences, and consolidating the lessons learned.	70	30
TCC2	Students complete a questionnaire assessing what they have learned.	1	10
Designer's reflection	The two one-hour sessions in the conventional classroom require a lot of tutor time (3 tutors for 70 students) for rather little guidance for each student. Tutor guidance is estimated at 2.5 minutes per student for each hour in class.		

Note: For codes see Table 6.2.

Conventional to Digital Pedagogical Patterns

If teachers were able to treat teaching as a design science, using pedagogical patterns as the means of exchanging ideas and demonstrating the principle of why they work, then as a community they would be better armed to take a critical approach to using digital technologies. One reason for categorizing the sequence of activities in a design is that the categories tell us something about why it works and how it can be improved. They also show where different kinds of technologies can make a difference because of what they contribute to the teaching–learning process. We saw examples of this in Tables 6.4 and 11.1. Here is a worked example, using Table 12.2 as a starting point. The pattern documented a design for a face-to-face teaching lab for developing students' practical skills. The research project that set out to turn this into a technology-enhanced design used the same basic pedagogical structure but replaced the physical resources and tools with digital ones – in this case a "virtual drill microworld", i.e. a virtual drill using haptic technology, a 3D representation of the mouth, and 3D glasses, for students to experience the same feel of the drill, but to get better quality feedback from the software than the physical tools could give. Table 12.3 shows the new pattern, with the same pedagogy but replacing the original resources and tools with the virtual drill. The new pattern represents the change in the categories of learning cycles from TPC to TMC in the new design – replacing the teacher's occasional extrinsic feedback with the model's continual intrinsic feedback, enabling unsupervised supported learning for the students, independent of the tutors' presence.

This is a clear representation of the value of the digital version. The total time is the same, but the learner experience is very different: instead of receiving extrinsic teacher feedback for a few minutes, each learner has continual intrinsic feedback on their actions. They can also replay what they did with the virtual tooth, and destroy far more virtual teeth than there are plastic teeth (and even be more ecologically sound by not using plastic). The format of the pedagogical pattern enables this kind of distinction to be articulated in comparing conventional and digital patterns – and of course it can go both ways, demonstrating in some cases the greater value of the conventional.

Generic Patterns and Specific Instances

There is another interesting benefit of the pattern format. Having a well-structured way of describing an instantiated pattern means it can be abstracted (Laurillard 2008c; Laurillard and McAndrew 2003):

- the topic content can be removed from the specific instance of a pattern to create a generic form;
- the generic form of the pattern can be turned into a different specific instance of the pattern by inserting new topic content.

A project setting out to experiment with this idea is showing some promise that it could be a way of enabling patterns to travel across subject areas (Laurillard and Ljubojevic 2011). The best teaching ideas are most likely to be developed in very specific subject matter contexts. They have even been referred to as the "signature pedagogies" of a discipline (Shulman 2005). But why should the best ideas be confined to their original discipline? If good pedagogic ideas are to migrate from one teacher to another, and one discipline to another, what transfers is not the content knowledge, but the "pedagogic content knowledge" (Shulman 2005) and the "technological pedagogic content knowledge" (Mishra and Koehler 2006). Can content and pedagogy be disentangled? We need to develop good ideas about the use of technology, so it is important to ask if technological pedagogy can be disentangled to travel across discipline boundaries. It is too early to be sure, as we have only just begun to ask the question and develop suitable patterns, but it is an important and promising area of development. As Chapter 2 demonstrated, the intended learning outcomes across very different subject areas have a lot in common, so collaboration across discipline boundaries is feasible.

To see how it might work, we look at an example of how patterns might evolve from the specific to the generic and back. The pattern in Table 12.3 highlights its specific topic content to separate it from the pedagogy. This can be replaced with entirely new topic content to generate the same pattern in a different subject area. The pedagogy is designed to help students achieve the learning outcome specified, but this can be defined more generically by removing the highlighted content-specific parts to leave the generic form: "To be practiced in the skill of [X], and able to improve their own performance in achieving the goal of [Y]." This is a common learning outcome, and if there is a good way of teaching it, teachers in many other areas would be interested to try it. Replacing the "content variables" with content terms from another topic area, for example, for learning the universally difficult skill of "bay parking", gives a new specific form: "To be practiced in the skill of [bay parking], and able to improve their own performance in achieving the goal of [accurate alignment]." If we replace these content terms throughout the pattern, and use a "virtual car microworld" instead of a "virtual drill microworld", the new instance of the pattern fits the new learning outcome, as Table 12.4 illustrates.

The most difficult design issue is to develop the microworld, but if one existed in the Open Education Resource repository then the pattern would show how to use it more productively than simply giving learners access to it.

The evolution of a pattern from one setting to another – from conventional to digital, and from one discipline to another – would be a way of generating families of patterns for particular kinds of learning outcome. As they migrate from one context to another it is likely they would pick up valuable modifications that could be shared with others. It is hard to say now if this will be a reality for education, but it is an intriguing vision of what might be. Steps towards formal definitions of pedagogical patterns are part of that process.

Table 12.3 A Pedagogical Pattern to Substitute Physical Resources and Tools with Digital Equivalents

Title	*Drilling a decayed tooth*		
Origins	School of Dentistry.		
Summary	Students are introduced to the goal of *a well-prepared tooth*, heuristic principles of how to achieve it, then practice the skill of *drilling a decayed tooth* using a *virtual drill microworld*, and revise their approach in the light of feedback.		
Learning outcome	To be practiced in the skill of *drilling a decayed tooth*, and able to improve their own performance in achieving the goal of *a well-prepared tooth*.		
Rationale	*Constructionism*; learning through practice.		
Learners	Students of dentistry.		
Setting	*Classroom or IT Lab.*		
Resources and tools	*Handouts* with detailed instructions on the practice of *drilling a decayed tooth*; the *virtual drill microworld*, questionnaire.		
Learning cycles	*Sequence of teaching–learning activities*	*Group size*	*Time mins*
TCC1	The tutor introduces students to the principles and practice of *drilling a decayed tooth*. Talks through the *Handouts* giving instructions on how to achieve the best result. Explains how they will be advised and evaluated.	70	20
TMC1, 2	Students individually practice *drilling a decayed tooth* using the *virtual drill microworld*, and *Handouts*.	1	120
PCC1, 2, 3	The tutor chairs a class discussion, asking for reflections on experiences, and consolidating the lessons learned.	1	30
TCC2	Students complete *a questionnaire* assessing what they have learned.	1	10
Designer's reflection	*The first and second tries in the two one-hour sessions in the Lab have been replaced with the virtual drill microworld that offers independent practice with intrinsic feedback over two-hours.*		

Note: For codes see Table 6.2.

Learning Design Tools and Resources

The pedagogical pattern format is a good way of circulating the currency of ideas, but the teaching design community will also need the means of exchange that sustains an infrastructure around the patterns. This will be a mix of tools for generating designs, and repositories to store, organize, and provide search and access mechanisms for the resources being created.

There have been several recent research and development projects focusing on digital support for teachers (Britain 2007), taking the form of digital design tools, such as a learning activity management system (LAMS), a toolkit (Conole and Fill 2005), online learning design toolkits such as iCOPER (Derntl, Neumann, and Oberhuemer 2009) and CloudWorks,[1] interactive design tools (Boyle 2008; San Diego *et al.* 2008), a customizable inquiry learning platform (Anastopoulou *et al.* 2009; Schwartz *et al.* 1999), and collections of resources, such as a learning object repository (Boyle 2006; Littlejohn and Margaryan 2006), a patterns collection (Agostinho 2006; Derntl, Neumann, and Oberhuemer 2009; Mor and Winters 2007), an elicited commentary on practice (Donald *et al.* 2009), and a wiki for learning design ideas, approaches and research findings (Masterman and Manton 2011). Digital technologies can play many valuable support roles, and given the complexity of the learning design process, all these methods are likely to be components of a fully supportive infrastructure for teachers.

One of these projects (the Learning Design Support Environment project)[2] uses the implications of the Conversational Framework to inform the pedagogic principles underlying an interactive online tool to support teachers in designing teaching and learning for individual sessions or for whole courses and modules. We have drawn on the ideas of microworlds, adaptive systems (i.e. an ontology of the user's teaching and learning concepts that adjusts its definitions according to what the user does), online advice and guidance in the form of a community wiki, and collaborative learning, to build the "Learning Designer" support tool (Charlton and Magoulas 2010a; ibid. 2010b; Laurillard *et al.*, in press; Laurillard and Masterman 2009). The project is ongoing but responses from the initial evaluation studies show that teachers in universities and colleges welcome the idea of interactive intelligent support of this kind to help them develop their teaching ideas (Laurillard *et al.* in press).

Teachers given the opportunity enjoy innovation. Every type of new commercial digital tool has been recruited for teaching and learning, even though none, with the honorable exception of institutional virtual learning environments, have been developed for education. Historically, tools have provided the major engine of human development, because they improve the efficiency of human effort (Wolpert 2003). Teachers, as much as any other profession, need custom-built digital tools to help them with their ever more complex working environment. They deserve better support from digital technology. And it could make the critical difference to changing what they are able to do with their students.

Collaborative Learning for Teachers

A common conclusion from the studies covered in the last five chapters has been to put a heavy design responsibility onto teachers using technology. To make it work effectively we have seen many examples where there is an additional load of advice, guidance, activity design, monitoring, and resource organization to be done. The learning technology community, especially its commercial arm, has always been keen to emphasize the important role of the

Table 12.4 A Pedagogical Pattern Adapted for a Different Topic Area

Title	*[Bay parking]*		
Origins	School of Dentistry: drilling a decayed tooth.		
Summary	Students are introduced to the goal of *[accurate alignment]*, heuristic principles of how to achieve it, then practice the skill of *[bay parking]* using a *virtual car microworld*, and revise their approach in the light of feedback.		
Learning outcome	To be practiced in the skill of *[bay parking]*, and able to improve their own performance in achieving the goal of *[accurate alignment]*.		
Rationale	Constructionism; learning through practice.		
Learners	Adults learning to drive.		
Setting	Online.		
Resources and tools	*Handouts* with detailed instructions on the practice of *[bay parking]*, the *virtual car microworld*, *questionnaire*.		
Learning cycles	*Sequence of teaching–learning activities*	*Group size*	*Time mins*
TCC1	The tutor introduces students to the principles and practice of *[bay parking]*. Talks through the handouts giving instructions on how to achieve the best result. Explains how they will be advised and evaluated.	??	20
TMC1, 2	Students individually practice *[bay parking]* using the *virtual car microworld*, and a *Handout*.	1	120
PCC1, 2, 3	The tutor chairs a class discussion, asking for reflections on experiences, and consolidating the lessons learned.	1	30
TCC2	Students complete a *questionnaire* assessing what they have learned.	1	10
Designer's reflection	??		

Note: For codes see Table 6.2.

teacher, and the supplementary role of the technology. Commercial software suppliers are sensitive to the anxiety among some teachers that technology could be used to replace them. This is now fading as technology shows no sign at all of doing this, and also perhaps as workloads increase. But as a result of the collusion between the various interested parties that technology should not be used to replace teachers in any way, it has not been developed to do so. It has been developed to replace physical libraries, meeting rooms, notice-boards, paper communication, and whole buildings, but not teaching activities.

This creates a difficulty because technology can only therefore add to teaching responsibilities, by demanding familiarity with continual technical innovations, and then more design and organization. We have to confront this dilemma if the teaching community is to harness technology to exploit fully what it can do in education. One solution is to shift to an explicit intention that technology should make the teacher's work more efficient, in the sense of creating greater benefit for students for the design work they put in – a kind of power tool for teachers. A second solution is to spread the design workload through collaboration. We need both.

In Chapter 6 the comparison in Table 6.3 showed that there are digital versions of all the conventional technologies, and in each of the succeeding chapters there were examples of how digital technologies can enhance different types of learning. While technology is still used to emulate traditional forms of teacher–student interaction we make no progress on exploiting its potential, but we have also seen ways in which it can make a new kind of difference – microworlds, intervention tagging, adaptive advice and guidance – these are examples of technology giving the learner effective support in the absence of the teacher. There could be many more examples if teachers as a design community were driving the development of learning technologies in this direction.

Operating as a design community would imply collaboration. The teaching community has not gone very far in this direction as yet. One way of spreading the design workload is to use the Open Educational Resource (OER) repositories, such as JORUM in the UK (www.jorum.ac.uk), and MERLOT in North America (www.merlot.org), but they are still underused by the great majority of teachers. We have not yet developed a strong culture of building on the work of others in designing teaching.

Teaching is often a very personal activity. Teachers love their subject and have a vocation to help others love it too, so the idea that we should use materials and resources that embody someone else's pedagogy runs counter to our instinct that nothing should come between the teacher and their relationship with their students. The pedagogical patterns approach avoids that problem. The approach enables the teacher to adopt, but also adapt teaching designs – to build on and improve the work of others – which many OERs do not allow. Collaboration between teachers would be to exchange and contribute pedagogic ideas, sharing the design responsibilities that are necessary to use the technology well.

As Chapter 11 showed, there is a strong move now towards computer supported collaborative learning for students. Why not for teachers as learners? The argument in Chapter 1 for teaching as a design science was based on the imperative for teachers to be able to harness the power of digital technologies, rather than be driven by them. The teaching community has to be able to learn and adapt to the continually changing technological environment as part of its professional capability. Teachers as learners need to operate in the most effective way possible. The analysis of collaborative learning in relation to the Conversational Framework shows how valuable it can be.

The framework can be applied equally well to teachers learning, so it can also represent collaborative learning for "the teacher learning about teaching and learning" (Laurillard 2008b). Figure 12.1 shows how each element of the framework can be reinterpreted for teachers' collaborative learning. The "teacher's concept" becomes the collective knowledge of the teaching community residing in repositories of theories, resources, and pedagogical pattern collections. Each teacher uses the practice environment of their learners learning to achieve the goal of meeting learner needs through generating and modulating their practice and ideas in the light of the feedback from their learners' performance. Working collaboratively with their peers they exchange comments and explanations about their teaching, and share their pedagogical patterns as models of their practice.

The approach has been instantiated, for example, in an innovative project to improve the pedagogies in developmental education (Mellow, Woolis, and Laurillard 2011), where the college supported teachers' collaboration by providing a "Web Library" to store the teachers' developing collective knowledge, an online "Pedagogy Circle" for the discussion environment, and an "ePorfolio" and "Pathfinder tool" for sharing and finding pedagogical patterns the teachers were developing and testing in their classes. As a result, teachers are learning from each other, building on each other's work, and acting as a collaborative design community on developing their knowledge of pedagogy.

Concluding Points

Teaching is a design science. Like the professions of engineering, architecture, computer science, and medicine, it is not only trying to understand the world but to make the world a better place. Unlike these professions, however, it has

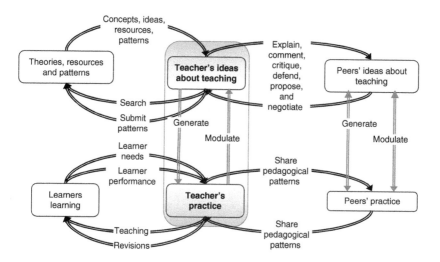

Figure 12.1 The Conversational Framework for teachers' learning collaboratively about teaching and learning.

not, traditionally, been treated as if teaching is meant to be anything other than a craft-amateur enterprise, where every teacher works alone with their students to do the best they can, given their initial training. Professional development programmes provide occasional updates, but this does not embed in the teacher's everyday role the idea that they are in a position to discover something that could be of benefit to other teachers. Could this culture change?

The difference that marks out the early years of the twenty-first century from any previous period in education is that digital technologies not only enable a change to treating teaching as a design science, they also require it. The ambitions of education are vast, and on any scale, local, national or global, cannot be met by our current educational systems. The UNESCO Millennium goal of *Education for All* exemplifies the gap between ambition and reality. The teaching profession cannot bridge the gap without the support of national governments, but it does have the responsibility to work out how it might be done, and to press for what it needs. Teachers need the professional capacity to learn through collaboration, to build the knowledge of what it takes to teach. A step towards this would be to create the tools and the culture that enable teaching to be a design science.

Notes

1 http://cloudworks.ac.uk/cloudscape/view/1882)
2 https://sites.google.com/a/lkl.ac.uk/ldse/

References

Abercrombie, M. L. J. (1979). *The anatomy of judgment*. London: Penguin.

Ackermann, E. (1991). Perspective-taking and object constriction: Two keys to learning. In Y. Kafai & M. Resnick (Eds.), *Constructionism in practice: Designing, thinking, and learning in a digital world* (pp. 25–36). Mahwah, NJ: Lawrence Erlbaum Associates.

Agapiou, A., Maharg, P., & Nicol, E. (2010). Construction and constructivism: Learning contract management and administration via simulated transactions. *CEBE Transactions, 7*(2), 37–54.

Agostinho, S. (2006). The use of a visual learning design representation to document and communicate teaching ideas. Paper presented at the 23rd annual Ascilite Conference.

Ainsworth, S. (2006). DeFT: A conceptual framework for considering learning with multiple representations. *Learning and Instruction, 16*(3), 183–198.

Alessi, S. (2000). Designing educational support in system-dynamics-based interactive learning environments. *Simulation & Gaming, 31*(2), 178–196.

Aleven, V. A. W. M. M., & Koedinger, K. R. (2002). An effective metacognitive strategy: Learning by doing and explaining with a computer-based Cognitive Tutor. *Cognitive Science, 26*, 147–179.

Alexander, S. (2004). Learners creating the learning environment. In M. Selnger (Ed.), *Connected schools: Essays from international thought leaders in education* (pp. 26–33). London: Premium Publishing.

Amhag, L., & Jakobsson, A. (2009). Collaborative learning as a collective competence when students use the potential of meaning in asynchronous dialogues. *Computers & Education, 52*, 656–667.

Anastopoulou, S., Sharples, M., Ainsworth, S., & Crook, C. (2009). Personal Inquiry: linking the cultures of home and school with technology mediated science inquiry. In N. Pachler & J. Seipold (Eds.), *Mobile learning cultures across education, work and leisure; Proceedings of the 3rd WLE Mobile Learning Symposium*: Work-Based Learning for Education Centre.

Anderson, C. (1984). Enabling and shaping understanding through tutorials. In F. Marton, D. Entwistle & D. Hounsell (Eds.), *The experience of learning*. Edinburgh: Scottish Academic Press.

Apedoe, X. S., & Reeves, T. C. (2006). Inquiry-based learning and digital libraries in undergraduate science education. *Journal of Science Education and Technology, 15*(5), 321–330.

Apedoe, X. S., Walker, S. E., & Reeves, T. C. (2006). Integrating inquiry-based learning into undergraduate geology. *Journal of Geoscience Education, 54*(3), 414–421.

Ausubel, D. P. (1980). Schemata, cognitive structure, and advance organizers: A reply to Anderson, Spiro, and Anderson. *American Educational Research Journal, 17*(3), 400–404.

Ausubel, D. P. (2000). *The acquisition and retention of knowledge.* Dordrecht: Kluwer.

Avgeriou, P., Papasalouros, A., Retalis, S., & Skordalakis, M. (2003). Towards a pattern language for learning management systems. *Educational Technology and Society, 6*(2), 11–24.

Baker, M., Hansen, T., Joiner, R., & Traum, D. (1999). The role of grounding in collaborative learning tasks. In P. Dillenbourg (Ed.) *Collaborative learning: Cognitive and computational approaches.* New York: Elsevier Science.

Bandura, A. (2006). Toward a psychology of human agency. *Perspectives on Psychological Science, 1*(2), 164–180.

Barnett, R., & Coate, K. (2005). *Engaging the curriculum in higher education.* Maidenhead, UK.: Open University Press, McGraw-Hill Education.

Bates, A. W. (2005). *Technology, e-learning and distance education,* 2nd edition. London: Routledge.

Beaty, E., Gibbs, G., & Morgan, A. (1997). Learning orientations and study contracts. In F. Marton, D. J. Hounsell, & N. J. Entwistle (Eds.), *The experience of learning,* 2nd edition (pp. 72–88). Edinburgh: Scottish Academic Press (now only available at www.tla.ed.ac.uk/resources/EoL.html).

Becta (2006). *The Becta Review 2006: Evidence on the progress of ICT in education.* Coventry, UK: British Educational Communications and Technology Agency.

Becta (2008). *Harnessing Technology Review 2008: The role of technology and its impact on education.* Coventry, UK: British Educational Communications and Technology Agency.

Beetham, H., & Sharpe, R. (Eds.). (2007). *Rethinking pedagogy for the digital age.* London: Routledge.

Bergin, J. (2002). Fourteen pedagogical patterns. Pedagogical Patterns Project. http://csis.pace.edu/~bergin.

Beynon, M., & Roe, C. (2004) *Computer support for constructionism in context.* Fourth IEEE International Conference on Advanced Learning Technologies (ICALT'04).

Biggs, J. (1993). From theory to practice: A cognitive systems approach. *Higher Education Research and Development, 12*(1), 73–85.

Biggs, J. (2003). *Teaching for quality learning at university.* Buckingham: SRHE/OUP.

Bodemer, D., Ploetzner, R., Feuerlein, I., & Spada, H. (2004). The active integration of information during learning with dynamic and interactive visualisations. *Learning and Instruction, 14,* 325–341.

Bok, D. C. (2006). *Our under-achieving colleges: A candid look at how much students learn and why they should be learning more.* Princeton, N. J.: Princeton University Press.

Bonk, C. J., & King, K. S. (Eds.). (1998). *Electronic collaborators: Learner-centered technologies for literacy, apprenticeship, and discourse.* Mahwah, NJ: Lawrence Erlbaum.

Boud, D., & Falchikov, N. (2006). Aligning assessment with long-term learning. *Assessment & Evaluation in Higher Education, 31*(4), 399–413.

Boud, D., & Solomon, N. (2000). *Work as the curriculum: Pedagogical and identity implications.* Sydney, Australia: UTS Research Centre Vocational Education & Training.

Boud, D., & Solomon, N. (Eds.). (2001). *Work-based learning: A new higher education?* Buckingham: Open University Press/SRHE.

Boud, D., Cohen, R., & Sampson, J. (1999). Peer learning and assessment. *Assessment and Evaluation in Higher Education, 24*(4), 413–426.

Boyle, T. (2006). The design and development of second generation learning objects. In E. Pearson & P. Bohman (Eds.), *Proceedings of Ed-Media 2006, world conference on educational multimedia, hypermedia & telecommunications.* Orlando, Florida.

Boyle, T. (2008). The design of learning objects for pedagogical impact. In L. Lockyer, S. Bennett, S. Agostinho, & B. Harper (Eds.), *The handbook of research on learning design and learning objects: Issues, applications and technologies.* Hershey: Information Science Reference.

Boyle, T. (2010). Introduction to JIME special issue on Open Educational Resources (OER). *Journal of Interactive Media in Education* (http://jime.open.ac.uk/issue/ 2010-OER).

Bransford, J. A., Brown, A. L., & Cocking, R. R. (Eds.). (2003). *How people learn: Brain, mind, experience and school.* Washington D.C.: National Academy Press.

Bransford, J., Stevens, R., Schwartz, D., Meltzoff, A., Pea, R., Roschelle, J., Vye, N., Kuhl, P., Bell, P., Barron, B., Reeves, B., & Sabelli, N. (2006). Learning theories and education: Toward a decade of synergy. In P. Alexander & P. Winne (Eds.), *Handbook of educational psychology,* 2nd Edition. Mahwah, NJ: Lawrence Erlbaum Associates.

Bravo, C., van Joolingen, W., & de Jong, T. (2009). Using Co-Lab to build System Dynamics models: Students' actions and on-line tutorial advice. *Computers & Education, 53,* 243–251.

Brennan, J., & Little, B. (1996). *A review of work based learning in higher education.* Sheffield: Department for Education and Employment.

Britain, S. (2007). Learning design systems: Current and future developments. In H. Beetham & R. Sharpe (Eds.), *Rethinking pedagogy for a digital age* (pp. 103–115). New York: Routledge.

Brown, D. (1992). Using examples to remediate misconceptions in physics: Factors influencing conceptual change. *Journal of Research in Science Teaching, 29,* 17–34.

Brown, J. S., Collins, A., & Duguid, P. (1989). Situated cognition and the culture of learning. *Educational Researcher, 18*(1), 32–42.

Bruner, J. (1961). The act of discovery. *Harvard Educational Review, 31,* 21–32.

Bruns, A., & Humphreys, S. (2005). *Wikis in teaching and assessment: The M/Cyclopedia Project.* Paper presented at the Proceedings International Wiki Symposium, San Diego.

Buckley, B. C., Gobert, J. D., Kindfield, A. C. H., Horwitz, P., Tinker, R. F., & Gerlits, B. (2004). Model-based teaching and learning with BioLogica: What do they learn? How do they learn? How do we know? *Journal of Science Education and Technology, 13,* 23–41.

Butcher, C., Davies, C., & Highton, M. (2006). *Designing learning: From module outline to effective teaching.* London: Routledge.

Butterworth, B., & Laurillard, D. (2010). Low numeracy and dyscalculia: Identification and intervention. *ZDM Mathematics Education Special issue on Cognitive neuroscience and mathematics learning, 42*(6), 527–539.

CEC. (2006). Delivering on the modernisation agenda for universities. Education, research and innovation. Brussels: Commission of the European Communities.

Charlton, P., & Magoulas, G. (2010a). *Self-configurable framework for enabling context-aware learning design.* Paper presented at the IEEE International Conference on Intelligent Systems, London.

Charlton, P., & Magoulas, G. D. (2010b). *Autonomic computing and ontologies to enable context-aware learning design.* Paper presented at the Proceedings of the 22nd International Conference on Tools with Artificial Intelligence, Arras, France.

Chase, C. C., Chin, D. B., Oppezzo, M. A., & Schwartz, D. L. (2009). Teachable agents and the protégé effect: Increasing the effort towards learning. *Journal of Science Education and Technology, 18,* 334–352.

Chi, M., T, H, & Roscoe, R. D. (2002). The processes and challenges of conceptual change. In M. Limon & M. L. (Eds.), *Reconsidering conceptual change: Issues in theory and practice.* Dordrecht, Netherlands: Kluwer.

Choi, I., Land, S. M., & Turgeo, A. J. (2005). Scaffolding peer-questioning strategies to facilitate metacognition during online small group discussion. *Instructional science, 33,* 483–511.

Cifuentes, L., and K. L. Murphy. (1997). Design considerations for computer conferences. *Journal of Research on Computing in Education, 30,* 177–202.

Clement, J. (1993). Using bridging analogies and anchoring intuitions to deal with students' preconceptions in physics. *Journal of Research in Science Teaching, 30*(10), 1241–1257.

Cobb, P., Confrey, J., diSessa, A., Lehrer, R., & Schauble, L. (2003). Design experiments in educational research. *Educational Researcher, 32*(1), 9–13.

Coll, R. K., & Zegwaard, K. E. (2006). Perceptions of desirable graduate competencies for science and technology new graduates. *Research in Science & Technological Education, 24*(1), 29–58.

Collins, A. (1999). The changing infrastructure of education research. In E. Lagemann & L. S. Shulman (Eds.), *Issues in education research* (pp. 289–298). San Francisco: Jossey-Bass.

Collins, A., Joseph, D., & Bielaczyc, K. (2004). Design research: Theoretical and methodological issues. *The Journal of the Learning Sciences, 13*(1), 15–42.

Conole, G., & Fill, K. (2005). A learning design toolkit to create pedagogically effective learning activities. *Journal of Interactive Media in Education* (http://jime.open.ac.uk/2005/08).

Conole, G., & Weller, M. (2007). The Open University Learning Design Project. In L. Cameron, A. Voerman & J. Dalziel (Eds.), *Proceedings of the 2007 European LAMS Conference: Designing the future of learning* (pp. 65–72). Greenwich: LAMS Foundation.

Conole, G., Dyke, M., Oliver, M., & Seale, J. (2004). Mapping pedagogy and tools for effective learning design. *Computers and Education, 43*(1–2), 17–33.

Conole, G., Scanlon, E., Kerawalla, L., Mulholland, P., Anastopoulou, S., & Blake, C. (2008). *From design to narrative: The development of inquiry-based learning models.* Paper presented at the World Conference on Educational Multimedia, Hypermedia and Telecommunications. Chesapeake, VA.

Cook, J., Bradley, C., Lance, J., Smith, C., & Haynes, R. (2007). Generating learning contexts with mobile devices. In N. Pachler (Ed.), *Mobile learning: Towards a research agenda. Occasional Papers in Work-based Learning 1* (pp. 25–38). London: WLE Centre for Excellence.

Coombs, G., & Elden, M. (2004). Introduction to the special issue: Problem-based learning as social inquiry–PBL and management. *Journal of Management Education, 28*, 523–535.

Copley, J. (2007). Audio and video podcasts of lectures for campus-based students: production and evaluation of student use. *Innovations in Education and Teaching International 44*(4), 387–399.

Corno, L., & Mandinach, E. B. (1983). The role of cognitive engagement in classroom learning and motivation. *Educational Psychologist 18*, 88–108.

Crebert, G., Bates, M., Bell, B., Patrick, C.-J., & Cragnolini, V. (2004). Developing generic skills at university, during work placement and in employment: Graduates' perceptions. *Higher Education Research and Development, 23*(2), 147–165.

Cress, U., & Kimmerle, J. (2008). A systemic and cognitive view on collaborative knowledge building with wikis. *Computer Supported Collaborative Learning, 3*(2), 105–122.

Crook, C. (1996). *Computers and the collaborative experience of learning: A psychological perspective*. London: Routledge.

Cross, N. (2001). Designerly ways of knowing: Design discipline versus design science. *Design Issues, 17*(3), 49–55.

Csikszentmihalyi, M. (1991). *Flow: The psychology of optimal experience*. New York: Harper Perennial.

Cuban, L. (2001). *Oversold and underused: Computers in the classroom*. Cambridge: Harvard University Press.

Cutts, Q., Kennedy, G., Mitchell, C., & Draper, S. (2004). *Maximising dialogue in lectures using group response systems*. Paper presented at the IASTED International Conference on Computers and Advanced Technology, Hawaii.

Dallimore, E., Hertenstein, H., & Platt, M. (2004). Classroom participation and discussion effectiveness: Student-generated strategies. *Communication Education, 53*(1).

Dalsgaard, C., & Godsk, M. (2007). Transforming traditional lectures into problem-based blended learning: Challenges and experiences. *Open Learning, 22*(1), 29–42.

Dalziel, J. R. (2003). *Implementing learning design: The Learning Activity Management System (LAMS)*. Paper presented at the ASCILITE, Adelaide, Australia.

Dayan, P., & Abbott, L. (2001). Classical conditioning and reinforcement learning. In P. Dayan & L. Abbott (Eds.), *Theoretical neuroscience* (pp. 331–358). Cambridge, MA: MIT Press.

de Freitas, S., & Neumann, T. (2009). Pedagogic strategies supporting the use of Synchronous Audiographic Conferencing: A review of the literature. *British Journal of Educational Technology, 40*(6), 980–998.

de Freitas, S., & Oliver, M. (2006). How can exploratory learning with games and simulations within the curriculum be most effectively evaluated? *Computers & Education, 46*, 249–264.

de Jong, T., & van Joolingen, W. R. (1998). Scientific discovery learning with computer simulations of conceptual domains. *Review of Educational Research, 68*(2), 179–201.

De Wever, B., Van Keer, H., Schellens, T., & Valcke, M. (2009). Structuring asynchronous discussion groups: The impact of role assignment and self-assessment on students' levels of knowledge construction through social negotiation. *Journal of Computer Assisted Learning, 25*, 177–188.

Dede, C. (2005). Planning for "neomillennial" learning styles: Implications for investments in technology and faculty. In J. Oblinger & D. Oblinger (Eds.), *Educating the net generation* (pp. 226–247). Boulder, CO: EDUCAUSE Publishers.

Derntl, M., Neumann, S., & Oberhuemer, P. (2009). Report on the standardized description of instructional models. *ECP 2007 EDU 417007*.

Dewey, J. (1938). *Experience and education*. New York: Kappa Delta Pi.

Dewey, J. (2001). *Democracy and education*. Hazleton, PA: The Pennsylvania State University.

Dickey, M. D. (2005). Three-dimensional virtual worlds and distance learning: Two case studies of Active Worlds as a medium for distance education. *British Journal of Educational Technology, 36*(3), 439–451.

Dillenbourg, P. (1999). What do you mean by "collaborative learning"? In P. Dillenbourg (Ed.), *Collaborative learning: Computational and cognitive approaches*. Oxford: Elsevier.

Dillenbourg, P. (2002). Over-scripting CSCL: The risks of blending collaborative learning with instructional design. In Kirschner, P. A. (Ed.), *Inaugural address, Three Worlds of CSCL: Can we support CSCL?* (pp. 61–91). Open University of the Netherlands.

Dillenbourg, P., & Traum, D. (2006). Sharing solutions: Persistence and grounding in multimodal collaborative problem solving. *Journal of the Learning Sciences, 15*(1), 121–151.

Dillenbourg, P., Järvelä, S., & Fischer, F. (2009). The evolution of research on computer-supported collaborative learning: From design to orchestration. In N. Balacheff, S. Ludvigsen, T. de Jong, A. Lazonder & L. Montandon (Eds.), *Technology-enhanced learning. Principles and products*. Berlin: Springer.

diSessa, A. A. (2001). *Changing minds: Computers, learning and literacy*. Cambridge, MA.: MIT Press.

diSessa, A., & Cobb, P. (2004). Ontological innovation and the role of theory in design experiments. *The Journal of the Learning Sciences, 13*(1), 77–103.

Donald, C., Blake, A., Girault, I., Datt, A., & Ramsey, E. (2009). Approaches to learning design: Past the head and the hands to the HEART of the matter. *Distance Education, 30*(2), 179–199.

Duffy, P. (2008). Engaging the YouTube Google-eyed generation: Strategies for using web 2.0 in teaching and learning. *The Electronic Journal of e-Learning, 6*(2), 119–130.

Duffy, T. M., & Jonassen, D. (Eds.). (1992). *Constructivism and the technology of instruction: A conversation*. Mahwah, New Jersey: Lawrence Erlbaum Associates.

Duffy, T. M., & Kirkley, J. R. (Eds.). (2004). *Learner-centered theory and practice in distance education*. Mahwah, New Jersey: Lawrence Erlbaum Associates.

Dufresne, R. J., Gerace, W. J., Leonard, W. J., Mestre, J. P., & Wenk, L. (1996). Classtalk: A classroom communication system for active learning. *Journal of Computing in Higher Education, 7*, 3–47.

Durbridge, N. (1984). Using audio-vision to teach mathematics. In E. Henderson & N. Nathenson (Eds.), *Independent learning in higher education*. Inglewood Cliffs, New Jersey: Educational Technology Publications.

Dysthe, O. (2002). The learning potential of a web-mediated discussion in a university course. *Studies in Higher Education, 27*(3), 339–352.

Edwards, S. L., & Bruce, C. S. (2004). The assignment that triggered change: Assessment and the relational learning model for generic capabilities. *Assessment & Evaluation in Higher Education, 29*(2), 141–157.

Ellis, R. A., Calvo, R., Levy, D., & Tan, K. (2004). Learning through discussions. *Higher Education Research and Development, 23*(1), 73–93.

Ellis, R. A., Goodyear, P., Prosser, M., & Hara, A. (2006). How and what university students learn through online and face-to-face discussion: Conceptions, intentions and approaches. *Journal of Computer Assisted Learning 22*, 244–256.

Ellis, R. A., Goodyear, P., Hara, A., & Prosser, M. (2007). The university student experience of face-to-face and online discussions: Coherence, reflection and meaning. *ALT-J Research in Learning Technology, 15*(1), 83–97.

Entwistle, N. (2005). Learning outcomes and ways of thinking across contrasting disciplines and settings in higher education. *Curriculum Journal*, 16(1), 67–82.

Entwistle, N., & Smith, C. (2002). Personal understanding and target understanding: Mapping influences on the outcomes of learning. *British Journal of Educational Psychology, 72*(3), 321–342.

Entwistle, N., & McCune, V. (2004). The conceptual bases of study strategy inventories. *Educational Psychology Review, 16*(4), 325–36345.

Entwistle, N., & Peterson, E. R. (2004). Conceptions of learning and knowledge in higher education: Relationships with study behaviour and influences of learning environments. *International Journal of Educational Research, 41*, 407–428.

Entwistle, N., McCune, V., & Hounsell, J. (2003). Investigating ways of enhancing university teaching-learning enviroments: Measuring students' approaches to studying and perceptions of teaching. In E. de Corte, L. BVerschaffel, N. Entwistle, & J. van Merrienboer (Eds.), *Powerful learning environments: Unravelling basic components and dimensions*. Oxford, UK: Elsevier Science Ltd.

Eraut, M. (2004). Informal learning in the workplace. *Studies in Continuing Education, 26*(2), 247–273.

Ertl, B., Kopp B., & Mandel H. (2007). Supporting collaborative learning in video-conferencing using collaboration scripts and content schemes. *Scripting Computer-Supported Collaborative Learning 6*(3): 213–23.

Evans, C. (2008). The effectiveness of m-learning in the form of podcast revision lectures in higher education. *Computers & Education 50*, 491–498.

Fahy, P. J., Crawford, G., Ally, M., Cookson, P., Keller, V., & Prosser, F. (2000). The development and testing of a tool for analysis of computer mediated conferencing transcripts. *Alberta Journal of Educational Research, 46*(1), 85–88.

Felder, R., & Brent, R. (2005). Understanding student differences. *Journal of Engineering Education, 94*(1), 57–72.

Foucault, M., Kritzman, L. D., & Sheridan, A. (1990). *Politics, philosophy, culture: Interviews and other writings, 1977–1984*. New York, NY: Routledge.

Frederickson, N., Reed, P., & Clifford, V. (2005). Evaluating web-supported learning versus lecture-based teaching: Quantitative and qualitative perspectives. *Higher Education Research and Development, 50*, 645–664.

Frith, C. D. (2007). *Making up the mind: How the brain creates our mental world*. Oxford: Blackwell Publishing.

Frith, U. (2011). *Neuroscience: Implications for education and lifelong learning*. London: Royal Society Working Group.

Fry, H. (2009). A *handbook for teaching and learning in higher education: Enhancing academic practice*. London: Taylor & Francis.

Fry, H., Ketteridge, S., & Marshall, S. (Eds.). (2003). *A handbook for teaching and learning in higher education: Enhancing academic practice*. London: Kogan Page.

Fung, Y. Y. H. (2005). Teachers' views on and use of printed materials in a distance learning teacher education course. *Open Learning, 20*(2), 175–183.

Garrison, D. R. (1992). Critical thinking and self-directed learning in adult education: An analysis of responsibility and control issues. *Adult Education Quarterly, 42*, 136–148.

Gee, J. (2003). *What video games have to teach us about learning and literacy.* New York: Palgrave Macmillan.

Gibbons, M., Limoges, C., Nowotny, H., Schwartzman, S., Scott, P., & Trow, M. (1994). *The new production of knowledge: The dynamics of science and research in contemporary societies.* London: Sage Publications.

Gibbs, G. (2010). *Dimensions of quality.* York, UK: The Higher Education Academy.

Gilbert, P. K., & Dabbagh, N. (2005). How to structure online discussions for meaningful discourse: a case study. *British Journal of Educational Technology, 36*(1), 5–18.

Gonzalez, J., & Wagenaar, R. (2005). *Tuning educational structures in Europe II: Universities' contribution to the bologna process.* Bilbao, Spain: University of Deusto.

Goodyear, P. (2005). Educational design and networked learning: Patterns, pattern languages and design practice. *Australasian Journal of Educational Technology, 21*(1), 82–101.

Goodyear, P., & Yang, D. F. (2009). Patterns and pattern languages in educational design. In L. Lockyer, S. Bennett, S. Agostinho & B. Harper (Eds.), *Handbook of research on learning design and learning objects: Issues, applications and technologies, Vol 1* (pp. 167–187). Hershey, PA: Information Science Reference.

Green, S., Jones, R., Pearson, E., & Gkatzidou, S. (2006). Accessibility and adaptability of learning objects: Responding to metadata, learning patterns and profiles of needs and preferences. *ALT-J, 14*(1), 117–129.

Grunwald, S., Ramasundaram, V., Bruland, G. L., & Jesseman, D. K. (2007). Expanding distance education in the spatial sciences through virtual learning entities and a virtual GIS computer laboratory. *Journal of Distance Education Technologies, 5*(1), 54–69.

Haggis, T. (2004). Meaning, identity and 'motivation': Expanding what matters in understanding learning in higher education? *Studies in Higher Education, 29*(3), 335–352.

Haggis, T., & Pouget, M. (2002). Trying to be motivated: Perspectives on learning from younger students accessing higher education. *Teaching in Higher Education, 7*(3), 323–336.

Hague, D. (1991). *Beyond universities: A new republic of the intellect.* London: Institute of Economic Affairs.

Hannon, P., Umble, K. E., Alexander, L., Francisco, D., Steckler, A., Tudor, G., et al. (2002). Gagne and Laurillard's models of instruction applied to distance education: A theoretically driven evaluation of an online curriculum in public health. *International Review of Research in Open and Distance Learning, 3*(2), 1–16.

Hara, N., Bonk, C. J., & Angeli, C. (2000). Content analysis of online discussion in an applied educational psychology course. *Instructional Science, 28*, 115–152.

Harasim, L. (1987). Teaching and learning on-line: Issues in computer-mediated graduate courses. *Canadian Journal of Educational Communication, 16*(2), 117–135.

Harasim, L. (1989). Online education: A new domain. In R. Mason and A. Kaye (Eds.) *Mindweave: Communication, computers and distance education.* Oxford: Pergamon.

Harel, I., & Papert, S. (1990). Software design as a learning environment. *Interactive Learning Environments, 1*(1), 1–32.

Hassanien, A. (2006). Using Webquest to support learning with technology in higher education. *Journal of Hospitality, Leisure, Sport and Tourism Education*, 5(1), 41–49.

Henri, F. (1995). Distance learning and computer-mediated communication: Interactive, quasi-interactive or monologue? In C. O'Malley(Ed.) *Computer supported collaborative learning*. Berlin: Springer-Verlag.

Herrington, J., Oliver, R., & Reeves, C. T. (2003). Patterns of engagement in authentic online learning environments. *Australian Journal of Educational Technology, 19*(1), 59–71.

Herrington, J., Oliver, R., & Reeves, C. T. (2006). Authentic tasks online: A synergy among learner, task and technology. *Distance Education, 27*(2), 233–248.

Herrington, J., Reeves, C. T., Oliver, R., & Woo, Y. (2007). Designing authentic activities in web-based courses. *Journal of Computing in Higher Education, 16*(1), 3–29.

Hevner, A. R. (2007). A three cycle view of design science research. *Scandinavian Journal of Information Systems*, 19(2), 87–92.

Hevner, A. R. (2009). Interview with Alan R. Hevner on "Design Science". *Business & Information Systems Engineering*, 1, 126–129.

Hmelo-Silver, C. E. (2003). Analyzing collaborative knowledge construction: Multiple methods for integrated understanding. *Computers & Education, 41*, 397–420.

Hmelo-Silver, C. E. (2004). Problem-based learning: What and how do students learn? *Educational Psychology Review, 16*, 235–266.

Hmelo-Silver, C. E., Duncan, R. G., & Chinn, C. A. (2006). Scaffolding and achievement in problem-based and inquiry learning: A response to Kirschner, Sweller, and Clark (2006). *Educational Psychologist, 42*(2), 99–107.

Honkimäki, S., Tynjl, P., & Valkonen, S. (2004). University students' study orientations, learning experiences and study success in innovative courses. *Studies in Higher Education, 29*(4), 431–449.

Horgan, J. (2003). In H. Fry, S. Ketteridge & S. Marshall (Eds.), *A handbook for teaching and learning in higher education: Enhancing academic practice* (pp. 75–90). London: Kogan Page.

Hounsell, D., & Entwistle, N. (2005) Enhancing teaching and learning environments in undergraduate courses. Final Report to the Economic and Social Research Council on TLRP Project L139251099. www.ed.ac.uk/etl/

Hounsell, D., McCune, V., Hounsell, J., & Litjens, J. (2008). The quality of guidance and feedback to students. *Higher Education Research and Development, 27*(1), 55–67.

Illich, I. (1973). *Tools for conviviality*. New York, NY: Harper and Row.

Ingram, A. L., Hathorn, L. G., & Evans, A. (2000). Beyond chat on the internet. *Computers & Education, 35*, 21–35.

Jermann, P., & Dillenbourg, P. (2003). Elaborating new arguments through a CSCL script. In J. Andriessen, M. Baker & D. Suthers (Eds.), *Arguing to learn: Confronting cognitions in computer-supported collaborative learning environments*. (pp. 205–226). Dordrecht: Kluwer.

Jewitt, C. (2005). Multimodality, "reading", and "writing" for the 21st century'. *Discourse: Studies in the Cultural Politics of Education*, 26(3), 315–331.

Jewitt, C. (2008). *The visual in learning and creativity: A review of the literature*. London: Arts Council.

Jonassen, D. H. (1999). Designing constructivist learning environments. In C. M. Reigeluth (Ed.), *Instructional-design theories and models, Vol. II* (pp. 215–239). New Jersey: Lawrence Erlbaum Associates.

Jones, A., & Issroff, K. (2005). Learning technologies: Affective and social issues in computer-supported collaborative learning. *Computers & Education, 44*, 395–408.

Jones, R. H. (2009). Technology and sites of display. In C. Jewitt (Ed.), *The Routledge handbook of Multimodal Analysis*. London: Routledge.

Kafai, Y., & Resnik, M. (1996). *Constructionism in practice: Designing, thinking and learning in a digital world*. Mahwah, N.J.: Lawrence Erlbaum Associates.

Kalaš, I. (2010). *Recognizing the potential of ICT in early childhood education: Analytical survey*. Moscow: UNESCO Institute for Information Technologies in Education.

Kanuka, H., & Garrison, D. R. (2004). Cognitive presence in online learning. *Journal of Computing in Higher Education, 15*(2), 30–49.

Kanuka, H., Rourke, L., & Laflamme E. (2007). The influence of instructional methods on the quality of online discussion. *British Journal of Educational Technology, 38*(2), 260–271.

Karagiorgi, Y., & Symeou, L. (2005). Translating constructivism into instructional design: Potential and limitations. *Educational Technology & Society, 8*(1), 17–27.

Kayes, B. A., Kayes, C. D., & Kolb, A. D. (2005). Experiential learning in teams. *Simulation and Gaming, 36*(3), 330–354.

Kear, K. (2004). Peer learning using asynchronous discussion systems in distance education. *Open Learning, 19*(2), 151–164.

Kember, D., & Leung, D. Y. P. (2006). Characterising a teaching and learning environment conducive to making demands on students while not making their workload excessive. *Studies in Higher Education, 31*(2), 185–198.

Kiili, K. (2005). Digital game-based learning: Towards an experiential gaming model. *The Internet and Higher Education, 8*(1), 13–24.

Kiili, K. (2007). Foundation for problem-based gaming. *British Journal of Educational Technology, 38*(3), 394–404.

Kinchin, I. (2006). Developing PowerPoint handouts to support meaningful learning. *British Journal of Educational Technology, 37*(4), 647–650.

King, A. (2007). Structuring peer interaction to promote higher-order thinking and complex learning in cooperating groups. *Scripting Computer-Supported Collaborative Learning 6*(1): 13–37.

Kirschner, P. A., Sweller, J., & Clark, R. E. (2006). Why minimal guidance during instruction does not work: An analysis of the failure of constructivist, discovery, problem-based, experiential, and inquiry-based teaching. *Educational Psychologist, 41*(2), 75–86.

Kirschner, P., Strijbos, J. W., Kreijns, K., & Beers, P. J. (2004). Designing electronic collaborative learning environments. *Educational Technology Research and Development, 52*(3), 1042–1629.

Kobbe, L., Weinberger, A., Dillenbourg, P., Harrer, A., Hämäläinen, R., Häkkinen, P., & Fischer, F. (2007). Specifying computer-supported collaboration scripts. *International Journal of Computer-Supported Collaborative Learning, 2*(2), 211–224.

Kolb, A. Y., & Kolb, D. A. (2005). Learning styles and learning spaces: Enhancing experiential learning in higher education. *Academy of Management Learning & Education, 4*(2), 193–212.

Kolb, D. A. (1984). *Experiential learning: Experience as the source of learning and development*. Englewood Cliffs, New Jersey: Prentice-Hall.

Kolb, D. A., Boyatzis, R. E., & Mainemelis, C. (2000). Experiential learning theory: Previous research and new directions. In R. J. Sternberg & L. F. Zhang (Eds.), *Perspectives on cognitive, learning, and thinking styles*. Mahwah, NJ: Lawrence Erlbaum Associates.

Kollar, I., Fischer, F., & Hesse, W., F. (2006). Collaboration scripts – A conceptual analysis. *Educational Psychology Review 18*, 159–185.

Koohang, A. (2004). Students' perceptions toward the use of the digital library in weekly web-based distance learning assignments portion of a hybrid programme. *British Journal of Educational Technology, 35*(5), 617–626.

Kriz, C. W. (2003). Creating effective learning environments and learning organizations through gaming simulation design. *Simulation and Gaming, 34*(4), 495–511.

Lajoie, S. P., & Azevedo, R. (2006). Teaching and learning in technology-rich environments. In P. Alexander & P. Winne (Eds.), *Handbook of Educational Psychology*, (2nd Edition). Mahwah, NJ: Lawrence Erlbaum Associates.

LAMS. Learning Activity Management System. (http://lamsfoundation.org/

Laurillard, D. (1987). The different forms of learning in psychology and education. In J. Richardson, M. Eysenck & D. Warren-Piper (Eds.), *Student learning*. Guidlford, Surrey: SRHE.

Laurillard, D. (1991). Mediating the message: Television programme design and students' understanding. *Instructional Science, 20*(1), 3–23.

Laurillard, D. (2002). *Rethinking university teaching: A conversational framework for the effective use of learning technologies*, 2nd edition. London: RoutledgeFalmer.

Laurillard, D. (2007). Pedagogical forms of moblie learning: Framing research questions. In N. Pachler (Ed.), *Mobile learning: Towards a research agenda* (Vol. 1). Occasional papers in Work-based Learning. London:WLE Centre, Institute of Education.

Laurillard, D. (2008). Open teaching: The key to sustainable and effective open education. In T. Iiyoshi & M. S. Vijay Kumar (Eds.), *Opening up education: The collective advancement of education through open technology, open content, and open knowledge*. Boston: MIT Press.

Laurillard, D. (2008a). *Digital technologies and their role in achieving our ambitions for education*. London: Institute of Education.

Laurillard, D. (2008b). Open teaching: The key to sustainable and effective open education. In T. Iiyoshi & M. S. Vijay Kumar (Eds.), *Opening up education: The collective advancement of education through open technology, open content, and open knowledge*. Boston: MIT Press.

Laurillard, D. (2008c). Technology enhanced learning as a tool for pedagogical innovation. *Journal of the Philosophy of Education. New Philosophies of Learning: Special Issue 42*(3–4): 521–533.

Laurillard, D. (2008d). The teacher as action researcher: Using technology to capture pedagogic form. *Studies in Higher Education, 33*(2), 139–154.

Laurillard, D. (2009). The pedagogical challenges to collaborative technologies. *International Journal of Computer-Supported Collaborative Learning, 4*(1), 5–20.

Laurillard, D. (2010). Effective use of technology in teaching and learning in HE. In Peterson, Baker & McGaw (Eds.), *International encyclopedia of education*. Oxford: Elsevier. 4: 419–426.

Laurillard, D. (2011). *Cost-benefit modelling for open learning*. Moscow: UNESCO Institute for Information Technologies in Education.

Laurillard, D., & Ljubojevic, D. (2011). Evaluating learning designs through the formal representation of pedagogical patterns. In C. Kohls & J. W. Wedekind (Eds.), *Investigations of e-learning patterns: Context factors, problems and solutions* (pp. 86–105). Hershey, PA: IGI Global.

Laurillard, D., & Masterman, E. (2009). TPD as online collaborative learning for innovation in teaching. In O. Lindberg & A. D. Olofsson (Eds.), *Online learning communities and teaching professional development: Methods for improved educational delivery*. Berlin: Springer: 230–246.

Laurillard, D., & McAndrew, P. (2003). Reusable educational software: A basis for generic learning activities. In A. Littlejohn (Ed.), *Reusing online eesources: A sustainable approach to e-learning*. London: Kogan Page.

Laurillard, D., Stratfold, M., Luckin, R., Plowman, L., & Taylor, J. (2000). Affordances for learning in a non-linear narrative medium. *Journal of Interactive Media in Education*, 2 (www-jime.open.ac.uk/00/2/laurillard-00-2-t.html).

Laurillard, D., Charlton, P., Craft, B., Dimakopoulos, D., Ljubojevic, D., Magoulas, G., Whittlestone, K. (in press). A constructionist learning environment for teachers to model learning designs. *Journal of Computer Assisted Learning*, (Accepted).

Lave, J., & Wenger, E. (1991). *Situated learning: Legitimate peripheral participation*. Cambridge: Cambridge University Press.

Lazzari, M. (2009). Creative use of podcasting in higher education and its effect on competitive agency. *Computers & Education 52*, 27–34.

Leh, A. (2002). Action research on hybrid courses and their online communities. *Educational Media International, 39*, 31–38.

Leitch, S. (2006). Prosperity for all in the global economy–world class skills: Final Report. London: HM Treasury.

Lesgold, A. (2009). *Better schools for the 21st Century*. Pittsburgh, PA: School of Education.

Levasseur, D., & Sawyer, K. K. (2006). Pedagogy meets PowerPoint: A research review of the effects of computer-generated slides in the classroom. *Review of Communication, 6*(1&2), 101–123.

Light, P., Colbourn C., & Light, C (1997). Computer-mediated tutorial support for conventional university courses. *Journal of Computer Assisted Learning 13*, 228–235.

Lillejord, S., & Dysthe, O. (2008). Productive learning practice–a theoretical discussion based on two cases. *Journal of Education and Work, 21*(1), 75–89.

Linn, M. C. (1995). Designing computer learning environments for engineering and computer science: The scaffolded knowledge integration framework. *Journal of Science Education and Technology*, 4, 103–126.

Linn, M. C., & Hsi S. (2000). *Computers, teachers, peers*. Hillsdale, NJ: Lawrence Erlbaum Associates.

Linnenbrink, E., & Pintrich, P. (2003). The role of self-efficacy beliefs in student engagement and learning in the classroom. *Reading and Writing Quarterly, 19*(2), 119–137.

Littlejohn, A., & Margaryan, A. (2006). Cultural issues in the sharing and reuse of resources for learning. *Research and Practice in Technology Enhanced Learning, 1*(3), 269–284.

Lo, M. L., Marton F., Pang, M. F., & Pong, W. Y. (2004). Toward a pedagogy of learning. In F. Marton & A. B. M. Tsui (Eds.), *Classroom discourse and the space of learning*. Mahwah, NJ: Lawrence Erlbaum Associates.

Lockwood, F. (1992). *Activities in self-instructional texts*. London: Kogan Page.

Lombardi, M. M. (2007). Authentic learning for the 21st century: An overview. *EDUCAUSE Learning Initiative, ELI Paper 1*.

Lowyck, J., Elen, J., & Clarebout, G. (2004). Instructional conceptions: Analysis from an instructional design perspective. *International Journal of Educational Research, 41*, 429–444.

Lowyck, J., Lehtinen, E., & Elen, J. (2004). Students' perspectives on learning environments. *International Journal of Educational Research, 41*, 401–406.

Luckin, R. (2003). Between the lines: Documenting the multiple dimensions of computer-supported collaborations. *Computers & Education, 41*, 379–396.

Luckin, R., & du Boulay, B. (1999). Ecolab: The development and evaluation of a Vygotskian design framework. *International Journal of Artificial Intelligence in Education, 10*, 198–220.

Luckin, R., Plowman, L., Laurillard, D., Stratfold, M., Taylor, J., & Corben, S. (2001). Narrative evolution: Learning from students' talk about species variation. *International Journal of Artificial Intelligence in Education, 12*, 100–123.

Manguel, A. (1997). *A history of reading*. London: Flamingo.

Marginson, S., & van der Wende, M. (2007). Globalisation and higher education. OECD Education Working Papers, No. 8. OECD Publishing.

Marra, R., & Palmer, B. (2004). Encouraging intellectual growth: Senior college student profiles. *Journal of Adult Development, 11*(2), 111–122.

Marsick, V. (2006). Informal strategic learning in the workplace. *Work-Related learning, 1*, 51–69.

Martin, P. W. (2003). Key aspects of teaching and learning in arts, humanities and social sciences. In H. Fry, S. Ketteridge & S. Marshall (Eds.), *A handbook for teaching and learning in higher education: Enhancing academic practice*. London: Kogan Page.

Marton, F. (1981). Phenomenography–describing conceptions of the world around us. *Instructional Science, 10*, 177–200.

Marton, F., & Booth, S. (1997). *Learning and awareness*. Marwah, New Jersey: Lawrence Erlbaum Associates.

Marton, F., & Pang, M. F. (2006). On some necessary conditions of learning. *Journal of the Learning Sciences, 15*(2), 193–220.

Marton, F., & Pong, W. Y. (2007). On the unit of description in phenomenography. *Higher Education Research and Development, 24*(4), 335–348.

Marton, F., & Säljö, R. (1976a). On qualitative differences in learning I: Outcome and process. *British Journal of Educational Psychology, 46*, 4–11.

Marton, F., & Säljö, R. (1976b). On qualitative differences in learning II: Outcome as a function of the learner's conception of the task. *British Journal of Educational Psychology, 46*, 115–127.

Marton, F., & Tsui, A. B. M. (2004). *Classroom discourse and the space of learning*. Mahwah, NJ: Lawrence Erlbaum Associates.

Marton, F., & Wenestam, C.-G. (1979). Qualitative differences in the understanding and retention of the main point in some texts based on the principle-example structure. In M. M. Gruneberg, P. E. Morris & R. N. Sykes (Eds.), *Practical aspects of memory*. London: Academic Press.

Marton, F., Hounsell, D., & Entwistle, D. (1997). *The experience of learning*, 2nd edition. Edinburgh: Scottish Academic Press (now only available at www.tla.ed.ac.uk/resources/EoL.html).

Mason, R. (2001). Effective facilitation of online learning: The Open University experience. In J. Stephenson (Ed.), *Teaching and Learning Online* (pp. 67–75). London: Routledge.

Mason, R. (2004). *Learning and technology*. Association for Learning Technology, Oxford Brookes University.

Masterman, E., & Manton, M. (2011). Teachers' perspectives on digital tools for pedagogic planning and design. *Technology, Pedagogy and Education, 2*(2), (in press).

Masterman, L., & Vogel, M. (2007). Practices and processes of design for learning. In H. Beetham & R. Sharpe (Eds.), *Rethinking pedagogy for the digital age* (pp. 52–63). London: Routledge.

Matsuzawa, T. (2003). The Ai project: Historical and ecological contexts. *Animal Cognition, 6*, 199–211.

Mayer, R. E. (1999). Designing instruction for constructivist learning. In C. M. Reigeluth (Ed.), *Instructional-design theories and models: A new paradigm of instructional theory* (Vol. II). Mahwah, NJ: Lawrence Erlbaum Associates.

Mazur, E. (1997). *Peer instruction: A user's manual*. Englewood Cliffs, NJ: Prentice Hall.

McAndrew, P., & Goodyear, P. (2007). Representing practitioner experiences through learning design and patterns. In H. Beetham & R. Sharpe (Eds.), *Rethinking pedagogy for a digital age: Designing and delivering e-learning* (pp. 92–102). London: Routledge.

McAndrew, P., & Weller, M. (2005). Applying learning design to supported open learning. In R. Koper & C. Tattersall (Eds.), *Learning design: A handbook on modelling and delivering networked education and training*. New York: Springer.

McAndrew, P., Goodyear, P., & Dalziel, J. (2006). Patterns, designs and activities: Unifying descriptions of learning structures. *International Journal of Learning Technology, 2*(2-3), 216–242.

McConnell, D. (1998). Group communications via computer conferencing: The educational potential. In D. Smith (Ed.), *New technologies and professional communications in education*. London: National Council for Educational Technology.

McNeill, D. P. (1992). Computer conferencing: the causes for delay. In M. D. Waggoner (Ed.) *Empowering networks: Computer conferencing in education*. Englewood Cliffs, NJ: Educational Technology Publications.

Mellow, G. O., Woolis, D. D., & Laurillard, D. (2011). Teaching developmental education: In search of a new pedagogy. *Change Magazine*.

Meyer, J. H. F. and R. Land (2005). Threshold concepts and troublesome knowledge (2): Epistemological considerations and a conceptual framework for teaching and learning. *Higher Education* 49: 373–388.

Meyer, K. A. (2003). Face-to-face versus threaded discussions: The role of time and higher-order thinking. *Journal of Asynchronous Learning Networks, 7*(3), 55–65.

Milton, J., & Lyons, J. (2003). Evaluate to improve learning: Reflecting on the role of teaching and learning models. *Higher Education Research and Development, 22*(3), 297–312.

Mishra, P., & Koehler, M. J. (2006). Technological pedagogical content knowledge: A framework for teacher knowledge. *Teachers College Record, 108*(6), 1017–1054.

Mor, Y., & Winters, N. (2007). Design approaches in technology-enhanced learning. *Interactive Learning Environments, 15*(1), 61–75.

Mor, Y., Winters, N., Cerulli, M., & Bjork, S. (2006). *Learning patterns for the design and deployment of mathematical games: Literature review*. Kaleidoscope Project, London Knowedge Lab, Institute of Education.

Nalley, R. (1995). Designing computer-mediated conferencing into instruction. In Z. L. Berge and M. P. Collins (Eds.), *Computer mediated communication and the online classroom, Volume II: Higher education*. Cresskill, NJ: Hampton Press.

Nathoo, A. N., Goldhoff, P., & Quattrochi, J. J. (2005). Evaluation of an Interactive Case-based Online Network (ICON) in a problem based learning environment. *Advances in Health Sciences Education, 10*(3), 215–230.

NCIHE. (1997). *Higher education in the learning society* (No. NCIHE/97/850). London: HMSO.

Neumann, S., & Oberhuemer, P. (2009). User evaluation of a graphical modeling tool for IMS learning design. In *Advances in web based learning–ICWL 2009*. Berlin/ Heidelberg: Springer.

Nicol, D. J., & Boyle, J. T. (2003). Peer Instruction versus class-wide discussion in large classes: A comparison of two interaction methods in the wired classroom. *Studies in Higher Education 28*(4), 457–473.

Noss, R., Hoyles, C., Mavrikis, M., Geraniou, E., Gutierrez-Santos, S., & Pearce, D. (2009). Broadening the sense of 'dynamic': A microworld to support students' mathematical generalisation. *ZDM, 41*(4), 493–503.

Novak, J. D. (2002). Meaningful learning: The essential factor for conceptual change in limited or inappropriate propositional hierarchies leading to empowerment of learners. *Science Education, 86*(4), 548–571.

Nussbaum, M., Alvarez, C., McFarlane, A., Gomez, F., Claro, S., & Radovic, D. (2009). Technology as small group face-to-face collaborative scaffolding. *Computers & Education, 52*, 147–153.

OECD-CERI (2003). PISA 2003 Country Profiles. from www.pisa.oecd.org

Oliver, M., & Conole, G. (2002). Supporting structured change: toolkits for design and evaluation. In R. Macdonald (Ed.), *Academic and educational development: Research, evaluation and changing practice in higher education* (pp. 62–75). London: Kogan Page.

Oliver, R. (2007). Exploring an inquiry-based learning approach with first-year students in a large undergraduate class. *Innovations in Education and Teaching International, 44*(1), 3–15.

Oliver, R., Harper, B., Hedberg, J., Wills, S., & Agostinho, S. (2002). Formalising the description of learning designs. In A. Goody, J. Herrington & M. Northcote (Eds.), *Quality conversations: Research and development in higher education* (Vol. 25, pp. 496–504). Jamison, ACT: HERDSA.

Osborne, M. (2003). Increasing or Widening Participation in Higher Education?—a European overview. *European Journal of Education, 38*(1), 5–24.

Otten, M. (2003). Intercultural learning and diversity in higher education. *Journal of Studies in International Education 7*(1), 12–26.

Palmer, B., & Marra, R. (2004). College student epistemological perspectives across knowledge domains: A proposed grounded theory. *Higher Education, 47*, 311–335.

Papert, S. (1980). *Mindstorms: Children, computers, and powerful ideas*. Brighton, Sussex: The Harvester Press.

Papert, S. (1996). *The connected family: Bridging the digital generation gap*. Marietta, GA: Longstreet Press.

Papert, S., & Harel, I. (1991). Situating constructionism. In I. Harel & S. Papert (Eds.), *Constructionism: Research reports and essays, 1985–1990*. Norwood, N.J.: Ablex Pub. Corp.

Paquette, G., Marino, O., Teja, I. D. l., Lundgren-Cayrol, K., Léonard, M., & Contamines, J. (2005). Implementation and deployment of the IMS learning design specification. *Canadian Journal of Learning and Technology, 31*(2).

Pask, G. (1976). *Conversation theory: Applications in education and epistemology*. Amsterdam: Elsevier.

Pea, R. D. (2004). The social and technological dimensions of scaffolding and related theoretical concepts for learning, education, and human activity. *The Journal of the Learning Sciences, 13*(3), 423–451.

Perkins, D. (1991). Educating for insight. *Educational Leadership, 49*, 4–8.

Perry, W. G. (1988). Different worlds in the same classroom. In P. Ramsden (Ed.) *Improving learning: New perspectives* (pp. 145–161). London: Kogan Page.

Perry, W. G. (1970). *Forms of intellectual and ethical development in the college years*. New York: Holt Rhinehart and Winston.

Pfister, H., & Oehl, M. (2009). The impact of goal focus, task type and group size on synchronous net-based collaborative learning discourses. *Journal of Computer Assisted Learning, 25*, 161–176.

Pilkington, R. M., & Walker, S. A. (2003). Facilitating debate in networked learning: Reflecting on online synchronous discussion in higher education. *Instructional Science, 31*, 41–63.

Poole, D. (2000). Student participation in a discussion-oriented online course: A case study. *Journal of Research on Computing in Education, 33*, 162–177.

Porayska-Pomsta, K., Mavrikis, M., & Pain, H. (2008). Student affect from tutor perspective. In S. Carberry & F. de Rosis (Eds.), *The international journal of personalization research* (Special Issue on "Affective modeling and adaptation" user modeling and user-adapted interaction).

Postman, N., & Weingartner, C. (1969). *Teaching as a subversive activity*. Penguin Education.

Prensky, M. (2003). Digital game based learning. *Computers in Entertainment (CIE), 1*(1), 21–24.

Prosser, M., & Trigwell, K. (1999). *Understanding learning and teaching*. Buckingham, UK: SRHE Open University Press.

Puntambekar, S. (2006). Analyzing collaborative interactions: Divergence, shared understanding and construction of knowledge. *Computers & Education, 47*, 332–351.

Puntambekar, S., & Hübscher, R. (2005). Tools for scaffolding students in a complex learning environment: What have we gained and what have we missed? *Educational Psychologist, 40*(1), 1–12.

QAA (2007). *Subject benchmark for history*. Gloucester, UK: The Quality Assurance Agency for Higher Education.

Quintana, C., Zhang, M., & Krajcik, J. (2005). A framework for supporting meta-cognitive aspects of online inquiry through software-based scaffolding. *Educational Psychologist, 40*(4), 235–344.

Ramasundaram, V., Grunwald, S., Mangeot, A., Comerford, B. N., & Bliss, M. C. (2005). Development of an environmental virtual field laboratory. *Computers & Education, 45*(1), 21–34.

Ramsden, P. (2003). *Learning to teach in higher education*. London: Routledge.

Ravenscroft, A. (2007). Promoting thinking and conceptual change with digital dialogue games. *Journal of Computer Assisted Learning, 23*(6), 453–465.

Reeve, H., & Gallacher, J. (2005). Employer-university 'partnerships': A key problem for work-based learning programmes? *Journal of Education and Work, 18*(2), 219–233.

Reigeluth, C. M. (Ed.). (1999a). *Instructional-design theories and models: A new paradigm of instructional theory, Vol. II.* Mahwah, NJ: Lawrence Erlbaum Associates.

Reigeluth, C. M. (1999b). What is instructional-design theory and how is it changing? In C. M. Reigeluth (Ed.), *Instructional-design theories and models: A new paradigm of instructional theory, Vol. II.* (pp. 6–29). Mahwah, NJ: Lawrence Erlbaum Associates.

Reigeluth, C. M. (2003). Knowledge building for use of the internet in education. *Instructional Science, 31,* 341–346.

Reznitskaya, A., Kuo, L., Clark, A., Miller, B., Jadallah, M., Anderson, R., Nguyen-Jahiel, K. (2009). Collaborative reasoning: A dialogic approach to group discussions. *Cambridge Journal of Education, 39*(1), 29–48.

Robertson, S. N., M., Dale, R., Tikly, L., Dachi, H., & Alphonce, N. (2007). *Globalisation, education and development: Ideas actors and dynamics*: Department for International Development.

Romiszowski, A. (1999). The development of physical skills. In C. M. Reigeluth (Ed.), *Instructional-design theories and models: A new paradigm of instructional theory, Vol. II* (pp. 457–481). Mahwah, NJ: Lawrence Erlbaum Associates.

Roschelle, J., & Teasley, S. D. (1995). The construction of shared knowledge in collaborative problem solving. In C. O'Malley (Ed.), *Computer supported collaborative learning.* (Vol. 128, pp. 69–97). Berlin: Springer.

Roussou, M. (2004). Learning by doing and learning through play: An exploration of interactivity in virtual environments for children. *Computers in Entertainment (CIE), 2*(1), 10–10.

Rummel, N. & Spada, H. (2007). Can people learn computer-mediated collaboration by following a script? *Scripting Computer-Supported Collaborative Learning, 6*(1): 39–55.

Säljö, R. (2004). Learning and technologies, people and tools in co-ordinated activities. *International Journal of Educational Research, 41,* 489–494.

Salmon, G. (2002). *E-tivities: The key to active online learning.* London: Kogan Page.

Salmon, G. (2003). *E-Moderating: The key to teaching and learning online,* 2nd Edition. London: Taylor and Francis.

San Diego, J. P., Cox, M. J., Quinn, B., Newton, T., Banerjee, A., & Woolford, M. (in press). Research haptics in Higher Education: The complexity of developing haptics virtual learning systems and evaluating their impact on students. *Computers and Education.*

San Diego, J. P., Laurillard, D., Boyle, T., Bradley, C., Ljubojevic, D., Neumann, T., Pearce, D. (2008). Towards a user-oriented analytical approach to learning design. *ALT-J, 16*(1), 15–29.

Scanlon, E., Blake, C., Joiner, R., & O'Shea, T. (2005). Technologically mediated complex problem-solving on a statistics task. *Learning, Media and Technology, 30*(2), 165–183.

Scanlon, E., Littleton, K., Gaved, M., Kerawalla, L., Mulholland, P., Collins, T., Conole, G., Jones, A., Clough, G., Blake, C., & Twiner, A. (2009). Support for evidence-based inquiry learning: Teachers, tools and phases of inquiry. Paper presented at the 13th

Biennial Conference of the European Association for Research on Learning and Instruction (EARLI), Amsterdam.

Scardamalia, M. (2004). CSILE/Knowledge Forum®. In *Education and technology: An encyclopedia* (pp. 183–192). Santa Barbara: ABC-CLIO.

Scardamalia, M., & Bereiter, C. (2006). Knowledge building: Theory, pedagogy and technology. In K. Sawyer (Ed.), *Cambridge handbook of the learning sciences* (pp. 97–118). Cambridge, UK: Cambridge University Press.

Schank, R. C., Berman, T. R., & Macpherson, K. A. (1999). Learning by doing. In C. M. Reigeluth (Ed.), *Instructional-design theories and models: A new paradigm of instructional theory, Vol. II.* (pp. 161–181). Mahwah, NJ: Lawrence Erlbaum Associates.

Schellens, T., & Valcke, M. (2006). Fostering knowledge construction in university students through asynchronous discussion groups. *Computers & Education, 46,* 349–370.

Schellens, T., Van Keer, H., De Wever, B., & Valcke, M. (2009). Tagging thinking types in asynchronous discussion groups: Effects on critical thinking. *Interactive Learning Environments, 17*(1), 77–94.

Schön, D. A. (1987). *Educating the reflective practitioner.* San Francisco: Jossey-Bass.

Schwartz, D. (1999). The productive agency that drives collaborative learning. In P. Dillenbourg (Ed.), *Collaborative learning: Cognitive and computational approaches* (pp. 197–218). New York: Elsevier Science/Permagon.

Schwartz, D. L., & Bransford, J. D. (1998). A time for telling. *Cognition and Instruction, 16*(4), 475–522.

Schwartz, D., Brophy, S., Lin, X., & Bransford, J. (1999). Software for managing complex learning: Examples from an educational psychology course. *Educational Technology, Research and Development, 47*(2), 39–59.

Senge, P. (2006). *The fifth discipline: The art and practice of the learning organization.* New York, NY: Doubleday.

Seo, K. K. (2007). Utilizing peer moderating in online discussions: Addressing the controversy between teacher moderation and nonmoderation. *The American Journal of Distance Education, 21*(1), 21–36.

Sfard, A. (1988). On two metaphors for learning and the dangers of choosing just one. *Educational Researcher, 27*(2), 4–13.

Sharp, H., Manns, M. L., & Eckstein, J. (2003). Evolving pedagogical patterns: The work of the pedagogical patterns project. *Computer Science Education, 13*(4), 315–330.

Sharples, M., Taylor, J., & Vavoula, G. (2007). A theory of learning for the mobile age. In R. Andrews & C. Haythornthwaite (Eds.), *The sage handbook of e-learning research.* (pp. 221–247). London: Sage Publications Ltd.

Shuell, T. (1986). Cognitive conceptions of learning. *Review of Educational Research, 56*(4), 411–436.

Shulman, L. S. (2005). Signature pedagogies in the professions. *Daedalus, 134*(3), 52–59.

Simon, H. A. (1996). *The sciences of the artificial,* 2nd Edition. Cambridge, Mass: The MIT Press.

Slavin, R. E. (1991). Synthesis of research of cooperative learning. *Educational Leadership, 48*(5), 71–82.

Slavin, R. E. (2004). When and why does cooperative learning increase achievement. In H. Daniels & A. Edwards (Eds.), *The RoutledgeFalmer reader in psychology of education* (pp. 268–293). London: RoutledgeFalmer.

Slotta, J. D. (2004). Web-based inquiry science environment (WISE): Scaffolding teachers to adopt inquiry and technology. In M. C. Linn, E. A. Davis & P. Bell

Internet environments for science education. Hillsdale, NJ: Lawrence Erlbaum Associates.

Solomon, N., & McIntyre, J. (2000). Deschooling vocational knowledge: Work-based learning and the politics of the curriculum. In C. Symes & J. McIntyre (Eds.), *Working knowledge: The new vocationalism and higher education.* Buckingham: Open University Press/SRHE.

Spellings, M. (2006). *A test of leadership: Charting the future of U.S. higher education.* Jessup, MD: Education Publications Center, U.S. Department of Education.

Squire, K. (2006). From content to context: Videogames as designed experience. *Educational Researcher, 35*(8), 19–29.

Stahl, G., Koschmann, T., & Suthers, D. (2006). Computer-supported collaborative learning: An historical perspective. In R. K. Sawyer (Ed.), *Cambridge handbook of the learning sciences* (pp. 409–426.). Cambridge, UK: Cambridge University Press.

Steeples, C., Goodyear, P., and Mellar, H. (1994). Flexible learning in higher education: The use of computer-mediated communications. *Computers & Education 22,* 83–90.

Stein, J. S., Isaacs, G., & Andrews, T. (2004). Incorporating authentic learning experiences within a university course. *Studies in Higher Education, 29*(2), 239–258.

Steinkuehler, A. C. (2006). Why game (culture) studies now? *Games and Culture, 1*(1), 97–102.

Strijbos, J. W., Martens, R. L., & Jochems, W. M. G. (2004). Designing for interaction: Six steps to designing computer supported group-based learning. *Computers & Education, 42,* 403–424.

Susskind, J. E. (2005). PowerPoint's power in the classroom: Enhancing students' self-efficacy and attitudes. *Computers & Education, 45,* 203–215.

Sutherland, P., Badger, R., & Goodith, W. (2002). How new students take notes at lectures. *Journal of Further and Higher Education, 26*(4), 377–388.

Swann, J. (2007). Designing 'educationally effective' discussion. *Language and Education, 21*(4), 342–358.

Teichler, U. (2004). The changing debate on internationalisation of higher education. *Higher Education, 48*(1), 5–26.

Topping, K. J. (2005). Trends in peer learning. *Educational Psychology Review, 25*(6), 631–645.

Trigwell, K., Martin, E., Benjamin, J., & Prosser, M. (2000). Scholarship of teaching: A model. *Higher Education Research and Development, 19*(2), 155–168.

UKCES. (2009). Ambition 2020: World class skills and jobs for the UK.

Umbach, P. D., & Wawrzynsk, M. R. (2005). Faculty do matter: The role of college faculty in student learning and engagement. *Research in Higher Education, 46*(2), 153–184.

UNESCO (2005). Towards knowledge societies. *UNESCO World Report.* Paris.

Urhahne, D., Schanze, S., Bell, T., Mansfield, A., & Holmes, J. (2010). Role of the teacher in computer-supported collaborative inquiry learning. *International Journal of Science Education, 32*(2), 221–243.

USDoE. (2010). Transforming American education: Learning powered by technology. Washington D.C: U.S. Department of Education, Office of Educational Technology.

Valaitis, R., Sword, W. A., Jones, B., & Hodges, A. (2005). Problem-based learning online: Perceptions of health science students. *Advances in Health Sciences Education, 10*(3), 231–252.

Van Eck, R. (2006). Digital game-based learning: It's not just the digital natives who are restless. *EDUCAUSE Review 41*(2), 1–16.

van Joolingen, W. R., de Jong, T., Lazonder, A. W., Savelsbergh, E. R., & Manlove, S. (2005). Co-Lab: research and development of an online learning environment for collaborative scientific discovery learning. *Computers in Human Behavior, 21*(4), 671–688.

van Merriënboer, J. J. G., Schuurman, J. G., de Croock, M., & Paas, F. (2002). Redirecting learners' attention during training: Effects on cognitive load, transfer test performance and training efficiency. *Learning and Instruction, 12*, 11–37.

VanLehn, K. (2006). The behavior of tutoring systems. *International Journal of Artificial Intelligence in Education, 16*(3), 227–265.

Vermetten, Y. J., Vermunt, J. D., & Lodewijks, H. G. (2002). Powerful learning environments? How university students differ in their response to instructional measures. *Learning and Instruction, 12*(3), 263–3284.

Vygotsky, L. (1962). *Thought and language.* Cambridge MA: MIT Press.

Vygotsky, L. S. (1978). *Mind in society: The development of higher psychological processes.* Cambridge, MA: Harvard University Press.

Wegerif, R. (2007). *Dialogic education and technology: Expanding the space of learning.* New York: Springer Science+Business Media, LLC.

Weinberger, A., Ertl, B., Fischer, F., & Mandl, H. (2005). Epistemic and social scripts in computer-supported collaborative learning. *Instructional Science, 33*(1), 1–30.

Weinberger, A., Ingo Kollar, I., Dimitriadis, Y., Mäkitalo-Siegl, K., & Fischer, F. (2009). Computer supported collaboration scripts. In N. Balacheff, S. Ludvigsen, T. de Jong, A. Lazonder & L. Montandon (Eds.), *Technology-enhanced learning. Principles and products.* Springer.

Weiss, G. & Dillenbourg P. (1999). What Is 'multi' in multi-agent learning? In P. Dillenbourg (Ed.) *Collaborative learning: Cognitive and computational approaches.* New York: Elsevier Science.

Weller, M., Pegler, C., & Mason, R. (2004). Use of innovative technologies on an e-learning course. *The Internet and Higher Education, 8*(1), 61–71.

Wertheimer, M. (1959). *Productive thinking.* London: Harper and Row.

Wheeler, S., Yeomans, P., & Wheeler, D. (2008). The good, the bad and the wiki: Evaluating student-generated content for collaborative learning. *British Journal of Educational Technology, 39*(6), 987–995.

Wiliam, D. (2010). The role of formative assessment in effective learning environments. In H. Dumont, D. Istance & F. Benavides (Eds.), The nature of learning: Using research to inspire practice (pp. 135–159). OECD Publishing.

Wilke, R. R., & Straits, W. J. (2001). *Taking the mystery out of inquiry: Strategies for college educators.* Paper presented at the Lilly Conference, San Marcos, TX.

Wilson, T., & Whitelock, D. (1998). Monitoring the on-line behaviour of distance learning students. *Journal of Computer Assisted Learning 14*, 91–99.

Winer, L., & Cooperstock, J. (2002). The "intelligent classroom": Changing teaching and learning with an evolving technological environment. *Computers & Education, 38*(1–3), 253–266.

Winne, P. H. (1997). Experimenting to bootstrap self-regulated learning. *Journal of Educational Psychology, 89*, 397–410.

Wise, J. C., Lee, S. H., Litzinger, T., Marra, R., & Palmer, B. (2004). A report on a four-year longitudinal study of intellectual development of engineering undergraduates. *Journal of Adult Development, 11*(2), 103–110.

Wolpert, L. (2003). Causal belief and the origins of technology. *Philosophical Transactions of the Royal Society of London, Series A, 361*(1809), 1709–1719.

Wu, D., & Hiltz, S. R. (2004). Predicting learning from asynchronous online discussions. *Journal of asynchronous learning networks, 8*(2), 139–152.

Young, M. F. D. (2008). *Bringing knowledge back in: From social constructivism to social realism in the sociology of education.* Abingdon, UK: Routledge.

Zimmerman, B. J. (2002). Becoming a self-regulated learner: An overview. *Theory Into Practice 41*, 64–70.

Zurita, G., & Nussbaum, M. (2007). A conceptual framework based on Activity Theory for mobile CSCL. *British Journal of Educational Technology, 38*(2), 211–235.

Index